SAVED BY
A SERIES OF MIRACLES

by Rodman Dickie

Cover Art by Kendra Clark
12 Miracles Art by Adam Spencer

∞INFINITY
PUBLISHING

Copyright © 2012 by Rodman L. Dickie

ISBN 978-0-7414-8342-3 Black and White Paperback
ISBN 978-0-7414-7850-4 Color Paperback
ISBN 978-0-7414-7851-1 Color Hardcover
ISBN 978-0-7414-7852-8 eBook

Printed in the United States of America

Published February 2013

INFINITY PUBLISHING
1094 New DeHaven Street, Suite 100
West Conshohocken, PA 19428-2713
Toll-free (877) BUY BOOK
Local Phone (610) 941-9999
Fax (610) 941-9959
Info@buybooksontheweb.com
www.buybooksontheweb.com

TABLE OF CONTENTS

Foreword

Some write books with great candor, declaring their many victories accomplished and glories achieved. Few, write to give glory to God; the Giver of those glories and accomplishments achieved. To this end Rodman has penned an accurate, heartfelt and memorable story of family, tradition, challenge, war and life on the open seas. This, coupled with many life-threatening close calls during WWII, blend to make an exciting, yet down to earth story of one man's life, his career, and a great and mighty God, who was actively involved in both. Seldom is a book written that so truly reflects the heart of the author. This is one of those books!

The only thing better than reading the story is knowing the man! The only thing better than knowing the man is knowing the God who cared for the man. This is Rodman's desire, for that is the heart of the story.

Reverend Doctor Thom Christian, D. Min.
Pastor, First Christian Church
83 North Main Street
Wolfeboro, NH 03894

Author's Foreword

A PROFESSION OF FAITH

My baptism by immersion took place at the First Baptist Church of Arlington, Massachusetts on Palm Sunday in the year 1933. The pastor was Dr. Grady Feagan. I was twelve years old.

Before the baptism I attended a class on the meaning of the ceremony of baptism. Next, after I attended Sunday school on a February morning, the committee of deacons interviewed me. Three men approached me. I knew two of them as deacons. And the third man, younger than the other two, was introduced to me as a member of the baptismal committee. They all were happy when I agreed without hesitation to the baptism. The baptismal committee member spoke up. "The waters will cleanse you and purify you of all your sins." The deacons reacted immediately. "No," they said, "The baptism is symbolic of the death and resurrection of Jesus Christ. It's the act of receiving Jesus Christ as personal Savior that cleanses. The result is that when God looks into your heart, He sees Jesus, the perfection of Christ. All your sins – past, present, and future – are covered."

That incident, during the interview, impressed me. I never doubted the eternal value of receiving Christ as Savior the rest of my life. It was to me, not only a matter of belief, but also as a matter of fact.

During the four years of WWII, not only were there many miracles that God performed to save the ships I was on, but also there were at least three remarkable, even strange coincidences. First, was the loss of #1 lifeboat on the SS *Pennsylvanian* during a North Atlantic storm. I was Second Mate on this vessel when a huge sea came on board and plucked away the #1 lifeboat and damaged the #3 lifeboat at the same time. Many months later, I was Chief Mate on the SS *William J. Worth* when a rogue sea came aboard and lifted away #1 lifeboat without further damage. The *Worth*, A Liberty ship, obtained a replacement lifeboat in England, but the *Pennsylvanian*, a much older ship, had to wait and find a replacement at home.

The second remarkable coincidence was the loss of two starboard anchors on the same two ships. One anchor was lost in the Firth of Forth, off Edinburgh, Scotland and the other anchor was lost in the harbor of Le Havre, France. The anchor became trapped in the bombing debris lying on the bottom of the harbor.

The third remarkable coincidence of a different sort happened again on the *William J. Worth*. Looking back many years, the timing seems to me to be a miracle. Returning from a long voyage to the Philippines, the *Worth* was docked in Long Beach, CA, when the next day, everyone celebrated the surrender of Nazi Germany. Later, the *Worth* steamed through the Panama Canal to New York, where we arrived before the Japanese surrendered. The ship's whistle sputtered and squirted water but finally joined in the harbor cacophony of many ships' whistles.

Dedication

I am happy to dedicate this book to my loving and very patient wife, Barbara. She is a dedicated land person, yet I found her reading pages of this manuscript with great interest. I had tried hard not to bore her with sea stories, but at maritime luncheons and at other times she inevitably heard a variety of salt water tales. In addition I found that I had to submit to her commentaries of things I had typed poorly. I retyped her penciled corrections, so she is a part of this book.

Acknowledgements

My principal advisor was a talented lady, Carla Zwahlen, musician, artist and author of two books and many articles. Carla read through the evolving book several times, asked pertinent questions that needed written answers, recreated sentences and suggested corrections to my grammar. Her suggestions greatly improved my original writing; however, I didn't always take her advice, and so to the extent that the language is still deficient, the fault is mine. She reorganized her busy schedule to help me so that God would get the glory for all these timely miracles. Without her advice and encouragement this book may never have come to pass.

While the story is mine, the effort of transcribing and organizing it into a book has been a group effort. Claire Gibbons, my sister-in-law, did most of the initial typing of my handwritten manuscripts and untold revisions upon revisions of what were originally in the form of a series of short stories. My son-in-law, John Buttrick took Claire's individual articles and combined them into one document with consistent formatting. His spouse, my daughter Sara, read through the book with Carla's edits several times and sat down with me to review changes and corrections as my eyesight began to fail from macular degeneration. My daughter Pam created the index, did research on publication options and shepherded the book through the publication process.

In July 2009, I was contacted by an Epping, New Hampshire man named Eric Stone. Mr. Stone explained he was married to the grandniece of Bernard Connors, Chief Mate on the SS *Arkansan*. He added that Mr. Connors was one of the four men lost when the *Arkansan* was torpedoed and sunk on June 15, 1942. Mr. Stone was looking for men who had sailed on the ship and might have some knowledge of Mr. Connors and the ship itself.

Subsequently, I met Mr. Stone and his wife when we attended an alumni dinner of the Massachusetts Maritime Academy at The Old Salt Restaurant in Hampton, New Hampshire. It turned out that he helped me more than I helped him. His research on the ship was quite thorough and he had obtained several pictures of the ship when it was new, showing the name changes through the years: *Celestial, Margaret Dollar, Arkansan*. Mr. Stone had also obtained a complete listing of all American-Hawaiian ships and the final disposition or fate of each vessel. I greatly appreciate his knowledge and information.

The primary goal of this book is to serve as a witness to the miracles. It is not intended to be a work of historical reference. The primary source of information is my recollections. When possible, I attempted to verify dates, places and names from other sources; however, no representation is made as to the historical accuracy of the information presented.

The log entries were transcribed from information obtained from the National Archives and is believed to be public record. Other sources of information were:

Irving, David. *The Destruction of Convoy PQ-17*. Richardson & Steirman, 1968. Permission granted by the author.

Moore, Arthur, R. *A Careless Word – A Needless Sinking*. American Merchant Marine Museum, 1988. Permission granted by Dennis A. Roland Chapter of the American Merchant Marine Veterans of WWII.

Project Liberty Ship – S.S. *JOHN W. BROWN*, Baltimore, MD.

Steamship Historical Society of America, Cranston, RI.

Part 1: 1920 to 1940 - The Early Years

As a senior in Arlington High School in Massachusetts, I had no idea what I would do with my life. What I did know was that I had to find out - like soon. The guidance counselor and aptitude tests given to me didn't help much. It was frustrating.

One winter evening, when my dad came home from his job as a bank teller at The Old Colony Trust Company, he brought some pamphlets that a customer gave to him. As I dutifully began to read them, a sense of conviction grew within me.

Mr. Queen, one of Dad's customers, and a member of the Board of Directors of a nautical school in Boston, had pamphlets stating that the Commonwealth of Massachusetts and the Federal Government helped support the school. It was the Massachusetts Nautical School or MNS. Could the information I read about ships lead me to what I wanted to do with my life? As I read about the ship, a sailing ship, with an iron hull and a steam engine, I was hooked. Wow! THIS WAS IT.

I read about the entrance exam, the physical exam, date, place, time, and that no special preparation was needed except that a high school education was an advantage. It all looked good to me.

Nervous, uptight, but ready, I took the written exam on the tenth floor of the main U.S. Post Office in Boston in the early spring of the year 1938. The exam was not difficult, but waiting for the result was difficult.

Meanwhile, it occurred to me that I could be carrying on a family tradition. My dad's parents came from Nova Scotia. My grandfather sailed on coastwise schooners as a cook perhaps around 1880.

Grampa told stories about the food he cooked. A lot of the food on the menu was preserved and dried, plum duff and bread pudding. One of the stories he told was why he quit going to sea. His schooner, docked in the Bay of Fundy, sat on the bottom of the harbor at low tide. Because the vessel sat high and dry, he walked around the hull on the hard bottom of the bay. When he saw a piece of scrap metal cargo sticking through the hull planking, he reboarded the vessel, packed his gear, and departed, never to return.

Grampa's oldest son Thomas, 24 years old, went to sea on sailing ships and became a ship's carpenter. In a storm off the Grand Banks of Newfoundland in the year 1913, Thomas was washed overboard and lost when his ship was dismasted.

My dad carried on the tradition in the Navy during the last year of WWI.

At last, my letter came, accepting me into the April class of MNS. It was the surprise of my life. I reasoned that my small boat experience on Lake Wentworth in Wolfeboro, NH helped my qualifying, along with my ease with mental arithmetic, which had been part of the written exam.

My family was pleased, perhaps mindful of the family tradition. Now I had direction in my life.

Achieving acceptance brought up a problem – the expense. We did not have the $275 for the first year's tuition. My Aunt Lydia Gore, teacher of history and science at the Norcross Girls School in South Boston, and my mother's older sister, came to the rescue and gave me the money.

In late April 1938, Mr. Morrill, Assistant Principal at Arlington High, handed me my diploma and some kind words. It was the first of countless good byes in my life.

The school ship *Nantucket* was docked at Pier #1 Boston Navy Yard. I was impressed. It was bigger and cleaner than Admiral Byrd's ship, the *Bear,* which I visited, and smaller than the USS *Constitution*, docked on the other side of the same dock as the school ship. When I was a child my aunt took me to visit both historic ships. Now, here I stood alone in a crowd of young men, ready to begin my nautical education.

Thirty-two young men, 17 to 20 years old, winners of an entrance exam taken by more than 100 candidates. Winners? We were greenhorns, some greener than others. We lined up on the quarter deck, our toes on a tarred seam of the wooden deck. We were told what was going to happen and just what we would do. We were issued uniforms, underwear, dungarees, hammocks, mattresses and covers, and instructions on how to stencil our names on everything, and "do what you are told."

When everything was stowed in our too small lockers, we mustered on deck.

"See that mast there? That's the foremast. It's over a hundred feet tall and all of you will climb to the very top and come down the other side. Do not go through the lubbers hole. Go out over the futtocks shrouds. Who will go first? You – go, and you and you." We went. I was not the first. I was glad to watch. I had no idea what the lubbers hole was or what the futtock shrouds were. I soon found out the hard way – by doing it. I made it OK.

1938: USS *NANTUCKET*
LEARNING THE HARD WAY

I learned how sailing ship masts were made. The foremast was really three masts in one. Three pieces doubled side by side where they met and strapped together with iron bands. At the top of the lower mast there was a large platform, called a crosstree, to which were secured the stays that held the middle piece of the mast, as well as the uppermost piece of mast. The crosstree was secured by chains called futtock shrouds. These chains lead from the lower mast to the bottom of the platform at approximately a 45° angle. The chains gave stability to the crosstrees and a good anchor for the stays, the top mast, and the t'gant mast.

More daunting was the command to memorize all one hundred "lines" needed to set sails and take in sails. Each line had a name and a purpose which we had to know. There are only two ropes on a sailing ship, a bell rope and a hand rope on the gangway. All the others are lines.

Being new, green, and a fourth classman, meant that on the ship, each member of our class was a fourth class citizen. Nowhere was our status more evident than when choosing swinging hammocks for sleeping. Preferred places went to first and second classmen. On the gun deck the overhead beams had strong hooks and the upper classmen took places clear of obstacles and near their lockers. The third and fourth class strung their hammocks in the eyes of the ship, which is the forward most part of the bow, or front of the ship. Hammocks were strung over the laundry trough, in the shower outside the head, next to the galley, and near the refrigerator – anywhere there was a large enough space.

Upper classmen were allowed to use hammock stretchers, which widen the nettings and spread the mattress. Lower classmen slept in an almost round contrivance, which had a tendency to capsize. When this happened, the falling victim would reach out in blind desperation and take someone down with him six feet to the deck below. I fell out one time only. I landed on my hands, elbows and knees, more angry than hurt.

Cadets were hard working, still growing, and always hungry. As a fringe benefit of the inexpensive meals, we named some of the foods, like tapioca which we called fisheyes, creamed beef on toast was s--- on a shingle or SOS. Our generic cornflakes had a notice: "Fit for human consumption." Fowl was seagull. Pancakes, we called bunker plates, which were a covering for coal chutes. We named syrup bug juice, and on and on it went.

Usually fourth classmen or rookies were the victims of hazing. Third classmen were hazed less often. A small group of upper classmen were malicious and mean (the M&Ms). A favorite punishment was to take the unlucky man to the engine cadet's shower room that was built in the top of the engine room. The temperature in the shower room reached one hundred degrees or more. Cadets were ordered to do push-ups and deep knee bends. One day, I became the victim at the hands of one of them, who chose me for some trivial reason.

"Put your head against that steel bulkhead," he said to me, "And bend over. I'm going to kick you so hard your head is going to dent that bulkhead." His icy stare quelled any thought of my resisting. Just at the critical moment, somebody loudly whispered, "Beat it. An officer's coming." I was saved, or was it a faked conspiracy?

On May 14, 1938, the *Nantucket* sailed 40 miles on its summer cruise to Rockport, where we anchored.

In preparation for the cruise, all the cadets coaled the ship and carried out a Field Day to clean the whole ship. We scrubbed decks with salt water and polished the brass that tarnished quickly in salt air. We participated in sail drills, rifle exercises, and other exhausting and irritating drills. To us cadets, maybe this exercise just seemed like an irritant.

MAY 1938 - TO BALTIMORE

When we left Boston, relatives, family and friends crowded the dock to say their goodbyes. The next day, visitors were brought out in ships' boats to the anchored ship in Rockport. One visitor asked why those round brass plates were in the middle of that beautiful clean wooden deck. "They cover the chutes to the coal bunkers." The next question was about mechanical loaders. He shouldn't have asked, because it reminded us of that dirty, repetitive labor of loading coal by hand that tested our physical limits.

Teams of two cadets picked up canvas bags full of coal filled from the huge pile that trucks had dumped on the dock. Each bag weighed 70 pounds and had two rope handles, one cadet to a handle. Cadets ran the bag up the gangway, dumped the contents down the chute as directed, ran back with the empty bag through the exit gangway to the dock pile, and picked up another bag of coal. The upper classmen filled the bags using scoop shovels. The lower classmen ran while carrying the full bags of coal.

While anchored in Rockport, windy weather pitched the ship, a precursor of a storm brewing. When we weighed anchor and proceeded to Baltimore, the wind turned into a storm that helped push us down the coast.

As we sailed down the coast, I did not feel well, but I decided it was not seasickness. Maybe I was homesick? One classmate urged me to report to sick bay. The professional pharmacist stuck a thermometer in my mouth, read it, told me to lie down, and then disappeared. Soon our new young doctor appeared, had me strip down and thumped me fore and aft. He told me to climb into the sick bay bunk, and then he disappeared. Maybe I slept. The next thing I knew when I woke surprised me. I lay on a wire net stretcher. Hands carefully lifted my stretcher up steep ladders to the main deck two decks above. To my further surprise, we were docked in Baltimore. The dock was level with the main deck, and my stretcher was handed over to the people on the dock. One cadet looked into my face and announced, "We'll never see him again!"

The *Nantucket* departed without me. I remained in the Baltimore Marine Hospital suffering from pneumonia. Sulfanilamide was given to me. It cured the pneumonia infection; however, an apparent overdose of the medication made me sicker than the pneumonia. A few days later I was up and around. I was told my aunt was coming to take me home to Boston. I would be discharged at that time. Meanwhile, if I wanted to go to town, I could. So I went to two movies in a row. At the second movie, I bought a ticket and walked up a concourse to the theatre, where I saw Robert Taylor walking toward me. I recognized him, so he pulled his felt hat to hide his face and did not stop.

My aunt arrived at the hospital. She was very upset that her very sick nephew had been allowed out to two movies in a row. Heavens!! Don't "they" know any better? When my aunt realized I was OK to travel, we took the next train Boston-bound. My parents met us at South Station.

At home, I put my ship gear aside and packed a suitcase to take to Lake Wentworth, New Hampshire. The next morning, my aunt and I rode the train to Sanbornville, New Hampshire. Doris Stockbridge met us at the train station. I began a summer at Camp Ellis on Triggs Shore.

What a summer it was. Both my aunt Lydia Gore and her teacher friend Edna Henderson planned and cooked hearty meals to build me up for what lay ahead. And what lay ahead?

For me, a new beginning lay ahead. I rejoined the school ship the first of October, happy to join a new class whose outlook was different from the attitude of the spring class.

A heated structure made of portable sections had been bolted in place over the weather deck of the *Nantucket*. It looked weird, but kept us warm in cold weather. It also gave us more sleeping space to swing hammocks. And so it was that I went aboard in early October 1938 and was ushered into the wardroom to see Commander Robert Gray, the Executive Officer.

THE WARDROOM INTERVIEW

I was uncomfortable and should have been appreciative that I had been accepted to start my training again with the new class, but I didn't know how to say thank you to the Executive Officer who wore three stripes on his sleeves. There was another thing. A cadet was required to salute a superior officer. However, in the wardroom, I could not wear a hat. I had to hold it in my hands. The Executive Officer was gracious and eased my tenseness. Very soon, I was back into the new version of the old routine. New, because all my classmates were new. Old, because my former classmates had six months experience behind them. All my former shipmates greeted me with enthusiasm even though they did not forget to remind me that I was still a rookie. Life was somewhat better than I had expected. Yes, the hazing lessened, but the food was the same — bland "bunker plates" with the cheapest "bug juice," "fit for human consumption" generic cornflakes, etc.

Why did I return to the rigid life of the school ship? Because it was the only thing I had. The only way I had open before me. I embraced it with a singleness of purpose, because I knew it was for me.

Because of my family's seafaring history, I followed this tradition. I felt certain the Lord had led me to the sea. It was helpful to discover that the Massachusetts Nautical School had an excellent reputation among mariners.

LIFE ABOARD THE SCHOOL SHIP USS *NANTUCKET*

Morning classes filled the winter of 1938-1939, and in the afternoons we learned canvas sewing, knot tying, sienna weaving, rope splicing, and practical seamanship. Evenings were for study, reading, and entertaining. Once or twice a week the movies at Ingram Hall in the Navy Yard were a welcome escape. I believe I escaped a lot of hazing because this was my second beginning aboard ship. My new friends in this class were Lee Van Gemert from North Quincy, Reg Curtice from Belmont, Donald Dee from Taunton, and 26 others, all from Massachusetts. Classmate Joe LaBranche was under the regulation height, but his guitar expertise and his outgoing personality increased his stature on the application. He contributed to the cohesion and friendliness of this class. I was not an outstanding student.

When finally spring arrived, I was glad when the shed structure was removed from the main deck. At least two sets of sails were produced from storage and one set was secured on the appropriate yard arms. The other set was stored below in case of need. The running rigging (100 lines) was bent on and secured in place by three professionals, a bosun, and two able bodied seamen with some of the more experienced cadets helping.

The new fourth class appeared. "Rookies," they were called. Automatically, my class became the third class; "Boots," we were called. The preparations for the cruise began – coaling ship, taking truckloads of stores, food and supplies. We carried it all into the depths of the ship.

MAY 1939 - TO EUROPE

This year, our destination was Europe. None of us had been to Europe. Our first port was London, and then Antwerp, but it was Paris we were excited about. When we arrived in France, liberty was arranged so that half of each class would have two days off. Each cadet was allowed to have a maximum of $50 to spend for the entire cruise. We were told to use $25 for the train trip from the port of Le Havre to Paris (and return) plus overnight in Paris. The train rates were so reasonable that we still had spending money left over for food, hotel rooms, and a visit to the Eiffel Tower. I had only $20, but it proved to be sufficient.

Our small group stayed one night at a hotel that had been recommended by our ship's agent. The cost was reasonable and the rooms large, partly because the wash basin and toilet were part of the room. In fact, there were two toilets, or so we thought. The French landlady appeared and tried to explain the other toilet. I was the interpreter, having had three years of French in high school. Conversational French was not practiced in school, so a meeting of minds was elusive. Finally, we understood; one of the toilets was for women only, and we were not to use it. We learned the French word *bidet* but did not need to use the word often.

During the cruise, most cadets were assigned to specific jobs, or details, and the jobs changed every two weeks. Early on, I was assigned to a coal passer's detail. The job was hot and dirty. However, coal passers were never hazed. In addition, they had the privilege of more fresh water for showers and laundry and were treated with a certain deference. Maybe I became a coal passer because the assigning officers were mindful of my past illness of pneumonia, and they felt I should not participate in deck wash downs and other weather deck assignments. When I requested a second or repeat assignment as coal passer, it was so ordered. I liked the job and its fringe benefits.

Although I did not intend to become an engineer, I found the unique horizontal steam engine interesting. I would have liked to tend the fires under the Scotch boilers; however, I could not. The first and second class engineering cadets tended the fires. So it was not to be for me. That horizontal steam engine now resides in the Maritime Museum in San Francisco.

I wanted to be a navigator, to know the ship's position, where it was going and the course required to get there.

On the way home from Europe, we stopped at the Azores' Ponta Delgada, where liberty was granted. The island was mountainous. The only level ground was located near the harbor. Two memories stand out: Reg Curtice and I led a double column of classmates, perhaps 12 or 14, on a march around the city. We received a few snappy salutes from police and military personnel. With little money left, we bought fresh pineapples and retreated to a park to eat the fruit. We used our cadet knives to open the pineapples. I usually hated pineapples, but I found the fresh pineapples delicious.

USS *NANTUCKET* HOMEWARD BOUND

The last time we coaled the ship before we left Europe, we took on extra coal. We filled burlap bags and stacked them on deck just in case we did not find the trade winds to keep us moving. For several months of every year the trade winds, a moderate to fresh breeze, blow from east to west in the southern part of the North Atlantic. Countless sailing vessels made their way from Europe to North and South America beginning in 1492, or even before that. Today sailing yachts and the few tall ships still use the trade winds. When we did find the trade winds on this trip they were so light that we used the extra coal. We made it back to the east coast and anchored in Gardiners Bay at the east end of Long Island. There we took our final exams – no shore leave. After the exams we looked forward to leaving for home and two weeks of vacation.

My class looked forward to becoming upper classmen along with the privileges that tradition built in. Right now, before vacation, we had to make a critical decision. We had to decide between working deck, engine, navigation and seamanship, steam, or electricity. That decision was not a problem for me; I decided that since I was interested in the ship's position and course, I would study navigation and seamanship.

1939: USS *NANTUCKET*
THE SECOND YEAR OF TRAINING

The second year of training was a piece of cake in some respects. We knew the routine. We knew our way around on the ship, both aloft and down below. We knew everyone on board, except the new class. Best of all, we did not have to worry about upper classmen hazing and their whims, especially the M&M's (mean and malicious). They had graduated.

We still had to work hard, study hard, and toe the line, yet we enjoyed more freedom. We had fun climbing up to the foremast crosstrees to see the graceful shape of the ship's hull. We climbed out on the bowsprit to watch the bow cleave the water. If we were lucky we saw some dolphins playing around the bow.

We had excellent officers. Louis (Dapper) Woodland; Lt. Commander John (the Apple) Rounds; Jack Thompson, Navigator; Commander Robert Gray, Executive Officer; Captain Abele, U.S.N. (Retired).

After the grind of the winter came to an end, the preparations for the cruise got underway. There was much speculation on where the training cruise would take us. We guessed South America. Not so. It was the Caribbean. The European war was on – we were to stay close to home.

MAY - SEPTEMBER 1940: THE CARIBBEAN

SECOND CRUISE OF THE *NANTUCKET* SCHOOL SHIP
OF THE MASSACHUSETTS NAUTICAL SCHOOL

Sailing day arrived in the middle of May. Families crowded on the dock. My family was kind enough to bring my girl friend, Doris Hellman. I kissed her goodbye. That was the extent of our romance. We had met during vacation, at a party.

As was customary, the *Nantucket* steamed to the nearby port of Gloucester and anchored. Some cadets had their girlfriends meet them there for last goodbyes. The short overnight trip from Boston to Gloucester was a break-in time for the ship and the crew on board. Then we departed for the Caribbean. The year before, a storm blew us south. The fore topsail blew out and ripped from top to bottom. This time the trip was quieter. We sailed through an amazing display of dolphins, swimming and leaping out of water. We were the only audience.

Then we came upon another phenomenon, the Sargasso Sea. What appeared to be a solid field of grass-like growth on closer inspection revealed a gentle undulation, caused by the slight swell of the sea. As with the dolphins, I never saw such a mass display. Only this time, it was a huge expanse of gulf weed.

The *Nantucket* steamed through the gulf weed, but we had to take in the speed indicating device we towed when it became fouled in the weeds.

Into the Caribbean we sailed, bound for several different ports. The Virgin Islands' Charlotte Amalie was quiet and undeveloped. There did not seem to be entertainment or anything to do, but the scenery was beautiful. As we walked outside the town, we found a commercial stable and hired horses to ride. Horses? They were small, skinny nags. They walked reluctantly away from their stables. After we had our fill of riding and admiring the scenery, we turned the horses back towards home. The horses suddenly galloped for home with instant energy. We held on for dear life. One cadet lost a stirrup and held onto the pommel as he leaned far to the right. We survived the experience, but sacrificed our uniforms which were undress whites, now boasting large brown leather stains. We decided the next port had to be better – but it was worse and too hot.

Guantanamo was a naval base with a large anchorage. Not long after we anchored, a fever epidemic started among the cadets. Healthy crew rigged an awning over the quarter deck and sick cadets lay on the deck on the mattresses from their hammocks. This arrangement was more comfortable and cooler for the sick cadets than lying slung on hooks between two beams in the gun deck. The doctor and the pharmacist ministered to the sick in the makeshift hospital. It took six days for this affliction to run its course, almost the entire time we were in Guantanamo between July 2 and July 8, 1940.

I was one of the healthy cadets. My memory tells me that, as a first class cadet, I carried out assigned or voluntary assignments. The care of the large majority of the sick was done by the healthy regardless of which class they were in. They also manned an oar in the Captain's gig or polished brass or carried water.

Finally, we left Guantanamo. The procedure of raising or heaving the anchor had been redesigned by marine architects of the 1870s. They devised a steam windlass that raised the old fashioned anchor until it could be seen at the water's surface. Then the crew secured a large tackle to the anchor and it was hauled up by hand. A dozen or more cadets pulled it up to the edge of the deck. This was called "catting the anchor." It was secured on a special bed or cradle.

Our life on that old ship was certainly better than that of the sailors in the 1880s and 90s. The guns had been removed from the gun deck, so we had more space. We had better food and more of it, more fresh water, better communications, and better medical care than those sailors.

Nevertheless, our living conditions left much to be desired. This was indicated by the six days in Guantanamo. One hundred and forty men crowded into a small ship designed and built 60 years earlier.

One incident put all these advantages in the background. Near the end of our cruise, we anchored in Gardiners Bay, Long Island, New York. Greenport Village, located on the bay, was used as a quiet place to take final exams.

Near the end of this special time, a message came aboard for Cadet Richard Keane. His mother had been hospitalized and his family wanted him home. Captain Abele said we would be in Boston within two days and Cadet Richard Keane could leave then. Keane had other ideas.

As we hove anchor, Keane decided to jump overboard and swim ashore because land was close. After he collected some money from friends, he jumped. Once ashore, he planned to buy some clothes, and travel by train from the eastern end of Long Island to New York City and then on to Boston. However, he was sighted immediately. The ship was stopped. Mr. Gray, the Executive Officer, ordered a boat put in the water. They caught up with the desperate cadet and brought him back to the ship. Captain Abele was said to have stated, "If he wants to go that bad, we'll take him ashore now." This time in uniform.

Later, Cadet Keane rejoined the *Nantucket* and graduated with his class.

In the year 2007, I compared notes on past events (called sea stories) with one time school shipmate George Duffy of Seabrook, New Hampshire. George remembered the incident. George said when he stood on a special platform to heave the sounding lead and call out the water depth, he saw Cadet Keane dive overboard.

George passed the word for Mr. Gray to come quickly. When Mr. Gray arrived, George pointed to the swimmer splashing in the water. Mr. Gray, the Executive Officer, called away the lifeboat and its assigned crew. George realized that his assignment as a rower in a "man overboard" lifeboat took precedence. He passed the sounding job to someone else and ran to the lifeboat to row out and rescue Cadet Keane.

In the year 1944, I bumped into Richard Keane when I was ashore in an English port. He was a Chief Engineer on a U.S. merchant vessel, and I was a Chief Mate on another vessel. We were both trying to obtain a taxi at a small store front taxi headquarters. As we turned to leave, Keane bumped a man behind him and apologized, saying, "I thought you were one of the drivers." The man in military uniform was offended. He took a punch at Keane and said, "You've insulted the King's own." Keane, big and strong, grabbed the British Sergeant in a bear hug and held him until their emotions settled.

Back on the school ship in 1940, in keeping with the apparent policy of having the school ship call at ports near home yet giving cadets experience measured in sea miles, we visited Norfolk to coal ship. We visited Portland, Greenport, and Cataumet to wait out a hurricane, then to Boston where we again coaled ship and sailed on to Boothbay Harbor, New Bedford, and East Lamoille, a small inlet near Mt. Desert Island.

I suspected the only reason we stopped near Mt. Desert Island was because someone gave an invitation to all hands to attend a lobster and clam bake. However, in most ports, a post office address was established and an upper class cadet was assigned to be mail messenger.

In East Lamoille, my assignment was Cox'n of the ten oar cutter. Several times a day, we made ship to shore trips for mail and visitors. The distance was short, perhaps a quarter of a mile, but when we made the trip in dense fog, which way was the dock?

I was an upper classman about to graduate and knowing the location of the dock was like a final exam question. If I knew how the ship was headed, I could set a course for the dock using the small boat compass in a wooden box. I ran to the bridge and checked the steering compass. The ship headed east. The dock was on the north shore and if I set a northeast course, we should find the dock.

We shoved off from the ship, headed in the right direction, and with a few strokes of the oars the ship disappeared from sight in the dense fog. A few dozen more strokes – we must be getting near land, we thought. I looked up from the compass and stared ahead and saw nothing – then something. A rift in the fog revealed a telephone pole. It couldn't be. The rift widened. There was another telephone pole – oh it was a piling and another piling standing out of water because of low tide. When we saw the wharf, I shouted, "OARS!" The crew stopped rowing. The momentum carried our boat towards the floating dock at the foot of the wharf pilings. With my hand on the tiller, we safely glided alongside the wharf.

At the end of August, our ship headed south to Glen Cove, where some of us visited the World's Fair, then we sailed to Fall River where many people visited us. On September 22, after we waited for a hurricane to pass off shore, we sailed to Boston.

After that cruise, graduation was almost anticlimactic. Mayor Fitzgerald honored us with his presence to deliver the main message. We said many more goodbyes. Now we faced the hard part – taking a four-day exam to win a Third Mates' license.

AFTER GRADUATION - MY FIRST JOB
OCTOBER 1940

Everyone in our class passed the examination for Third Mate. As Third Mate, finding a job became the next important step. Classmate Donald Dee and I decided to go to New York to make the rounds of the various steamship companies. There were several American firms that were called intercoastals. A few other companies made foreign runs to Africa, Australia, and Europe.

Our limited resources mandated that we stay at the YMCA on 34th Street. Donald and I rode the subway downtown, and then we separated. I visited one company whose ships ran to West Africa. They did not have any jobs available. I approached American Hawaiian Steamship Co., and after a brief interview Captain Bain hired me as a Cadet Officer. With a pay of only $75 a month, I realized I was still in training.

1940: INTERCOASTAL FREIGHTERS ON THE EAST COAST LOOP

After I checked out of the YMCA, I went to the SS *Nebraskan* and reported to Chief Mate Mr. George Wilson, who took me under his wing. Mr. Wilson, an outgoing enthusiastic man, knew his job. He showed me around the ship. Far from new, the ship was unremarkable, yet efficient and clean. The crew's head, a facility exactly like the one on the training ship, surprised me. Shaped seat boards sat on top of a galvanized metal trough. Salt water ran through the trough 24/7. Mr. Wilson laughed at my familiarity. He said the company had agreed with the labor union to replace the trough with flush toilets. I, thankfully, never saw a trough toilet again.

Much of my time was spent watching special cargo being loaded or discharged from special compartments kept lock and key secure. Mr. Wilson had all the keys. At 8:00 A.M., he would hand me one or more keys and order me to unlock the locker in #3 upper 'tween deck and stay there until the locker was full or until lunch. Sometimes I was relieved by a ship's mate or watchman in order for me to have a coffee or restroom break. Watching the loading of special cargo was drudge work; nevertheless, I enjoyed learning about the ship and the different cargo compartments and running up and down the straight steel ladders in the holds.

Later, I realized that Mr. Wilson must have given me a good recommendation. When the *Nebraskan* left the east coast, I was promoted to Fourth Mate, SS *Texan*. Terrific! My pay more than quadrupled.

Yet, it was disastrous. The personalities on the *Texan* were drastically different. The Chief Mate was an opinionated loudmouth. I became clumsy and defensive, but I was tolerated – only just. Then, the disaster.

A company official came aboard with a bottle of expensive whiskey. He gave it to the Chief Mate to deliver to a mutual friend, an official on the West Coast. The Chief Mate handed the bottle to me. That was bad.

A CAREER-THREATENING DISASTER

Although I had no respect for hard liquor, I took the whiskey to the Chief Mate's office. When I set the bottle on the place he had directed, the bottle cracked! The office filled with the pervasive odor of high grade whiskey. To me it smelled like doom. I moved the leaking bottle into a nearby wash basin. There was no way to fix this problem. This brand new Fourth Mate was crestfallen. I made my way back to the Chief Mate, expecting to be the object of his aggressive personality. He was angry and swore, but not at me so much. He swore at the situation which he had to remedy. I'm sure he wanted to fire me. He must have written a negative report to the office, because at the end of the loop I was transferred to the SS *Alabamian*, as Cadet Officer again – a demotion, if there ever was one.

A voyage around the East Coast Loop took about two weeks. My next transfer was again Cadet Officer on the SS *Ohioan*. I spent only three days on the *Ohioan*, and then I was transferred to the SS *Kentuckian*, and finally to the SS *Arkansan*. After Captain Paul Jones promoted me to Fourth Mate, we sailed for the West Coast. It was to be the last intercoastal voyage of the *Arkansan*.

Part 2: 1941 - SS *Arkansan*

1941: TO SEATTLE

AT SEA FINALLY - FEBRUARY 1941

A voyage from New York to the Panama Canal takes one week. For the first 1,000 miles, the ship headed due south on the open sea. Landfall came at San Salvador Island, very likely the same landfall Christopher Columbus made in 1492. Between then and now, a substantial lighthouse was constructed. The lighthouse now has a bright light of nearly one million candlepower. On a clear night, ships can sight this light many miles away.

It was my bridge watch, 0800 – 1200. The Captain appeared on the bridge about 0930. We expected to make our landfall at about 1000 in reduced visibility. We had had no position fix in the past 24 hours. Our anxiety was palpable – and gave us dry mouths. Every few minutes we looked through the binoculars. We changed our position from wheelhouse to bridge wing, and kept scanning. Captain Jones and I sighted the lighthouse almost at the same time. The sunlight pierced the overcast sky in a kind of reversal and lit up the lighthouse. The Captain's dead reckoning was right on and we breathed deeply again. I tried not to imagine how it would feel to be on a ship that ran aground. It would be many years before I found out.

Our voyage continued through the Bahamas, around the eastern end of Cuba, past Nassau, and across the Caribbean to the Panama Canal.

I noticed we used the same charts trip after trip. The Second Mate's job was to keep them corrected and up to date from *Notice to Mariners* published by the U.S. Hydrographic Office. The course lines on the charts were drawn in ink and the course in degrees was written on that line. It was routine and efficient. Our company's motto was "Be sure you are right, then go ahead." We did not joke about mistakes.

THROUGH THE PANAMA CANAL

My first time through the Panama Canal left me agog with interest.

When we anchored at the Atlantic end, a huge bunch of ripe and delicious bananas was the first delivery we received aboard ship. Someone paid a dollar for the bunch of about 100 bananas. They hung them in the alley way near the galley for everyone to eat. I ate three. The pilot, who was American, came aboard next, followed by the gang of line handlers, who were native Panamanians. Everything was new and novel to my 20 year old eyes. The marvelous line handlers never missed with their heaving lines. The work to pass through the lock progressed slow and smooth. The pilot who stood on the bridge never became flustered. We watched the ship rise as the water flowed into the locks. Fascinating. The canal had been operating only a little more than a quarter of a century.

Someone pointed out the place where the French had attempted to build a canal. The canal area was small and almost covered by lush vegetation.

When we came to Culebra Cut, we saw high-pressure hoses and dredges move a mountain. The wakes of passing ships undercut the steep bank of the canal and caused avalanches of dirt to fall into the canal from the side of the mountain. The pilot slowed the ship to prevent our wake from disturbing the moored barges and tugs that hauled the dirt to a dumping area.

The canal runs in a north-south line. In fact, the south end at the Pacific was slightly east of the north end in the Atlantic, because of a major twist in the isthmus and the choice of site that the planning engineers made.

PANAMA CANAL AND NORTHWARD TO LOS ANGELES

It took a mental adjustment to get used to the fact that the exit course to steer is due south, 180° at the Pacific end; yet Los Angeles is a far distance to the north.

As soon as we cleared the bay, the compass course turned more northwesterly from lighthouse to lighthouse situated on points of mountainous land; then we turned more northwesterly. Much of the time, I felt like a sightseeing tourist. Seeing every lighthouse was a new experience. I kept the ship's position on the chart's inked course line, reckoned the distance off when passing lighthouses, wrote the name and time in the log book, and always informed the Captain whether he was on the bridge or not.

All this implies I saw everything as if I were a tourist on a fair weather trip. The Third Mate, senior citizen Harold Adams, who stood the 12:00-4:00 watch, often informed me as the Fourth Mate what to expect on my watch. His outgoing personality was a plus. Captain Jones took an interest in me. He pointed out and commented on coastal features like Acapulco. He identified the two sharp peaks of the Paps of Coyuca. I thought, for this pleasure I get paid!

There was a lot of ship traffic from other companies. These companies – Luckenbach, Calmar, Waterman, Ithstmian – used the same routes and were our competition.

I was surprised to find it necessary to do some celestial navigation while crossing the Gulf of Tehuantepec when we were a day or more out of sight of land. It was prudent to confirm the ship's position whenever possible in the morning and noon by taking sun sights, and before dawn and after sunset by taking star sights.

Even though I was still in training, I purchased a Plathe sextant – used, but of excellent quality. I put it and my school ship training in practice and quickly learned to pick out navigational stars. I learned to bring one – like Rigel – down to the horizon, click my new stop watch; then walk into the chartroom to the chronometer, click the stopwatch, and take the time off the chronometer. I then wrote down the time and the altitude of the star. Sighting a total of five stars was ideal. Working out the sights using the nautical almanac and Ageton tables took about 20 minutes. I found plotting on the charts fun. A pinpoint cross? Not often, but the position was reliable, even if it was not a pinpoint cross. The transfer to the navigational chart was the final step.

Cape San Lucas, at the south end of the Baja California peninsula and a part of Mexico, came into view. The rugged coastline betrays the desert located behind it. The mountainous area was not part of the Rockies. The Californians on board were getting close to home.

We felt disappointed because several miles of haze over the port hid the city of San Pedro. Nearby and connected was Long Beach. Neither port was attractive, except for an occasional palm tree and patch of grass behind acres of sheds and terminals. The harbor and waterfront were crowded and space-deprived.

After docking, I went ashore and rode on an oversize Pacific Electric street car to Long Beach. That city was interesting, but the ride more so. Now I was a tourist on land.

My grandmother had given me the address of her relatives in Los Angeles, but I did not have time to see them.

When I returned to the ship, I worked in the holds to watch the discharge of special cargo. Shoes, whiskey, and many other items were pilferage prone and had to be kept under lock and key.

The longshoremen were militant but effective. Our old ship was an old story to them. They knew its holds and compartments better than I did.

We were on a schedule with many other ships of our company. We left port right after the last draft of cargo was landed.

The trip to San Francisco was for me a tourist's dream trip of picturesque islands, coastal mountains, a visible highway with spectacular bridges across deep ravines, and picture perfect lighthouses on high points of land. The lavish homes high above the surf enjoyed neverending views.

SAN FRANCISCO - 1941

California had many faces: the praying mantises of Signal Hill, the smog, the affluence of Santa Barbara, scenery without parallel and, oh yes – the Golden Gate. The wonder of it all. Our ship became part of the spectacular scene as we passed under the bridge into the harbor.

Inside the harbor, on the seaward end of the docks, we passed a pier shed topped with a glass structure. The Captain used a megaphone to hail the man in the shed. The man in the shed shouted back. In a brief formalized report from Captain Jones, we became part of the "shipping news" when he gave our ship's name, cargo and pier of destination.

Our ship landed gently at the end of Pier 26 which adjoined our loading pier of destination, Pier 28. The helmsman needed to turn the ship left 90° into the slip between Piers 26 and 28 against the visibly moving flood tide. With the Bay Bridge directly overhead, the noise of many vehicles was distracting.

The bow was more than halfway across the end of the slip pointing toward the end of Pier 28. A crew member must throw a heaving line onto the apron of Pier 28. The crew member needed to be an experienced seaman to accurately throw the weighted end of the heaving line onto the other dock apron. Linemen on the dock, who were ordered to meet the ship, helped moor the ship. They picked up the heaving line and pulled it hand over hand, until they came to the end tied to the eye of the hawser. The ship's crew payed out the hawser through the bow chocks until the hawser floated on the surface of the water, while the linemen pulled the floating hawser about one ship length up the slip. Next, they pulled the eye up on to the surface of the dock and placed the eye over a bollard. On the ship, the crew took the hawser to the windlass drumhead and hove up the slack, until there was a heavy strain on the hawser. The Captain ordered the rudder hard left and the engine slow ahead. The vessel pivoted slowly on the corner of Pier 26. The windlass heaved on the hawser and pulled the ship ahead, while the propeller pushed the ship, and the rudder turned the ship. As the ship moved into the slip, the linemen took a stern line to the dock, and the ship was hove starboard side to Pier 28. I entered the time in the bell book, "First line ashore." A slow ahead command and a command to put the rudder hard over followed, and our ship turned slowly into the slip, but only for about two minutes, when we realized we were stationary. The ship became hung up on the corner of the pier by the force of the tide. Captain Jones risked a half ahead bell and progress resumed. Timing was critical. Stop engines too soon, and the tide wins. If we waited too long, the ship would gather momentum, resulting in inadequate stopping distance. But we did not commit those errors and passed the test to dock successfully. As soon as the vessel was safely moored, the engine room telegraph was placed on F.W.E., Finished With Engines.

On the ship, we maintained the same routine and emptied the holds that had San Francisco cargo. Big deal, I thought – but it was necessary, and it was different. It was home port, so we had a Relief Mate at night and could go ashore.

SAN FRANCISCO WATERFRONT

Cobblestones covered the streets of the Embarcadero and old buildings lined the streets. The Ferry Building was a curiosity because it was no longer used. Bridges replaced all the ferries. I walked up Market Street, even though I didn't know what to do or where to go. I was a mesmerized tourist again until I saw a cable car, rode it, and enjoyed the scenery. I would have enjoyed a guide, like Chief Mate Wilson on the *Nebraskan*, who took me to Times Square on New Year's Eve when we were on shore leave in New York just a few weeks ago.

After riding the cable car I stopped by the window of a restaurant and watched the chef grill steaks. I lingered at the window, finally succumbed, and stepped into the restaurant because the thought of tasting a steak was too enticing to resist.

When I returned to the ship I knew I needed to put down the tendency to be a tourist and focus on tending to business with a new Captain on board.

Captain Jones left the ship to take a vacation. Captain Greenlaw was the Master for our trip to Seattle-Tacoma.

When it was time to leave San Francisco, we undocked without incident, until we steamed under the Golden Gate Bridge. We were hit with a surprise. The ocean rollers pitched the ship high and plunged it low. The pitching made me realize why the Chief Mate had insisted on the strong braces and shoring for unsupported blocks of cargo. We sailed northbound into new territory for me.

SAN FRANCISCO TO SEATTLE

Captain E.E. Greenlaw of Boothbay Harbor, Maine was the relief master when Captain Paul Jones went on vacation, while the SS *Arkansan* called at West Coast ports known as the Loop.

We left San Francisco and sailed under a light fog that became dense as we headed north toward Puget Sound. The bright sun shining through the dense fog and the fresh breeze blowing from ahead set up a potentially dangerous situation. We could not hear another ship's foghorn, until it was close. The noise of the wind and the fog muffled the sound.

We faced another potential danger. If we suddenly stopped to avoid colliding with another ship as required by the rules, our ship might broach if the ship turned sideways into the waves because we carried little cargo, which allowed the ship to ride high on the water. We sounded our ship's whistle every two minutes in this high traffic density route. We expected to meet other ships. Sure enough, we heard a ship's whistle on the port bow. Captain Greenlaw did not want to stop the ship, as it would soon lose steerage way. We waited for the next whistle. It sounded closer and slightly on the port bow.

The Captain gripped the wooden windscreen with white knuckles.

Then again we heard the other ship sound its whistle, close on the port bow – five or six points. Even though we strained our eyes to see the ship pass less than 200 yards away, we failed to see it. Captain Greenlaw relaxed and said, "Keep sounding the fog signal – I'm going to lie down. Call me if you need me."

The whistle handle, manually operated, required a strong pull. A wire ran from the handle through pulleys to the flying bridge and the forward side of the smoke stack, where a steam pipe was mounted. The whistle's steam valve was screwed into the end of the steam line. The wire opened the valve and released steam into the whistle. Sometimes the steam condensed into water in the pipe. If this happened when someone pulled the handle, hisses, gurgles, and other strange noises emitted from the pipe. Pulling the handle on the whistle was an important part of the test of all bridge equipment before we sailed.

IN SEATTLE

On my first trip into Puget Sound, I enjoyed the clear weather and the beauty of the scenery.

Docking in Seattle was routine. I stood the 4:00 P.M. to 12:00 A.M. evening watch; at the same time the longshoremen boarded to work cargo. The longshoremen opened every hatch. It was my duty to see that the cargo booms and gear were properly rigged. The Mate's job, rigging the portable cargo lights in five hatches, required intense labor. Other crew members were knocked off sea watches and allowed to go ashore. I spent most of my time watching all cargo operations, in order to record a cargo plan to use for the new loading we would receive when we arrived at several ports of discharge located on the East Coast.

In the midst of all this activity, a messenger from the pier office came aboard and found me. He said with some bemusement, "There's a chauffeured limousine on the dock near the gangway. There is a girl in it who wants to talk with you."

Then I remembered the story Reg Curtice, a school ship classmate, told me. Reg, a Third Mate on another American Hawaiian vessel, visited Seattle two weeks before my ship docked. He said that he met a girl who took him to her big beautiful home in suburban Seattle, and entertained him in a way sailors dream about.

After he finished telling me his detailed story, he said, "I told her you would be coming here, and she said she might visit your ship."

And here she was.

I looked a mess, trapped in my greasy khakis, with dirty work gloves covering my hands, and a flashlight bulged out of my pocket. But I walked off the ship to meet this girl who rode in a limousine.

The limo's rear side windows were tinted as black as the car's paint. I had never seen privacy glass before. As I stared, the car door opened and out stepped a cute girl.

My situation to meet with her for longer than a moment or two was hopeless. Not only was the ship sailing the next day, but I faced three hours more of hard work. While the girl and I talked, the longshoremen and company employees stopped their work on board ship in order to watch us. Getting to know this girl, I knew, was hopeless, so I just said goodbye to her and watched the limo maneuver its way around the moving forklifts and pallets of canned goods stacked high.

As I watched, I thought someday, someday, I will have a wife who meets my ship. It was to be many years away.

SAN FRANCISCO, SOUTHBOUND - SPRING 1941
WRONG DECISIONS

Mr. Plant, the C.E.O. of American Hawaiian S.S. Company, worked from his home port of San Francisco. Ship captains disliked this port because they were expected to dock their ships in strong tidal currents, preferably without tow boats. The Captain might have to turn his ship around in the bay and land gently on the end of the pier headed into the current; then run a new hawser the length of the dock and heave on it to help turn the ship into the slip. Sometimes dropping an anchor became necessary in order to use it as a turning point and a brake. Docking in this port possessed the potential to turn into a fiasco if the current was too strong, if the hawser broke, if the ship gained too much speed turning into the slip, or if longshore gangs on pay were waiting to work cargo.

Personally, I would rather ride out a gale at sea than to try without help to dock a ship on a strong tidal currant. Hiring a towboat to assist in docking was a last resort and a career negative for ship captains.

When we were inbound from Seattle, we docked successfully, thanks to our capable Captain E.E. Greenlaw. Longshore gangs were waiting in spite of the heavy rains and strong winds. Those of us on board ship thought the hatches should not be opened, but it was not our decision. All the hatches were opened, tents were rigged and cargo operations began. From 8:00 A.M. until noon the wind blew, tents billowed, and the rain poured into the holds, soaking the men, cargo, and the tents. Decision: Knock off at noon and send the gangs home.

At 1:00 the sun came out, and nature defeated the best minds of the experienced decision makers.

The remainder of our trip was on schedule and routine, except for one incident that happened in San Pedro. The fully loaded ship sat deep in the water. The gangway to the dock was level, when suddenly the gangway shook and vibrated. I stood nearby and became alarmed, until a nearby longshore boss said, "Oh, that's only a minor tremor," as he explained the earthquake we just experienced.

SAN PEDRO TO NEW YORK

We experienced one more surprise on the trip to New York. As the ship sailed far out to sea and somewhere between the two ports, the captain received the message informing him the *Arkansan* had been chartered to the U.S. government. When we arrived in New York, and after all the cargo on board was off-loaded, we were to load "lend-lease" cargo. Next, we received orders to buy charts for all of Africa, the Red Sea, and all of India – a big job for Geoffrey Blackett, our Second Mate.

Our cargo, ordered by the British for their army in Egypt, was strange to us, except for a few vehicles. A barge crane lifted four two engine bombers and placed them on top of our hatches. The bomber's wheels chocked and firmly tied down. We were told that, except for fuel, these planes were ready to fly.

Quite a sight – these four graceful yet menacing aircraft, tied down on our deck and ready to fly upon our arrival in Egypt!!!

1941: TO INDIA VIA EGYPT

On July 2, 1941, our ship was loaded and ready for sea. With a new crew we sailed for Cape Town, South Africa, and thence to the Red Sea, because the Mediterranean was closed to Allied shipping by the German enemy.

NEW YORK TO CAPE TOWN
THE DIABETIC WHO "FORGOT" HIS INSULIN

On a voyage from New York to Cape Town in the summer of 1941, the old freighter *Arkansan's* up and down main engine pounded along at 11 knots, making about 1,000 miles every four days. Thus the steaming time for this voyage of 8,000 miles was about one month.

When we were well into the first week of the voyage and sailing along in the middle of the southern North Atlantic, a crew member came to the Captain and told him, "I don't have much insulin left, and I'm a diabetic. What shall I do?" The question of why seemed to be beside the point, so the Captain decided to radio for advice. After some discussion by wireless and telegraph with medical authorities in New York, the Captain was told to confiscate whatever supply of insulin remained and ration it. The medical authorities also made some suggestions as to his diet. It worked! Although sick but still alive, he had to be taken off the vessel on a stretcher when he arrived in port at Cape Town. Because our stop in Cape Town lasted only a few hours for fuel, we sailed without our diabetic crew member. Presumably, he was shipped home on a northbound vessel.

THE SPUD LOCKER

Our lend lease cargo was war goods and supplies of all kinds, including the four Mitchell bombers that sat on deck. This aging ship had only sailed on the inter-coastal run for many years, and was not designed to carry six months stores, food, and supplies for the ship and its crew. To add more storage, one adjustment was made. On the after end of the boat deck, a shore gang built a large bin to store potatoes. They thought that louvers facing aft would provide plenty of ventilation for the potatoes.

However, the builders of the locker didn't understand that the locker's exposure to the sea salt might compromise the potatoes. When the ship moved through salt water, an invisible yet constant flow of salt moisture covered everything. Added to that was the stack exhaust's greasy dirt and soot that swirled around and entered the spud locker.

Our Chief Steward, a German-American, spoke with a strong accent laced with profanities. Our potato supply was his responsibility. Cursing in German and English seemed to help him cope when he pulled out sack after sack of wet potatoes. He opened the sacks, took out the spuds and spread them out on the deck to dry. Early in the voyage, he cut off the rotten spots and large sprouts, but later on, he found enjoyment by throwing overboard those spuds that did not pass his test. As the potato supply dwindled, more and more pastries helped fill the void.

A LONG TRIP ON A SLOW SHIP - SPEED 11 KNOTS
SUMMER 1941

On a clear night on the open sea, a ship's white range light could be seen from a long distance, perhaps 15 miles. If the range light was more than that distance, the curvature of the earth's surface would interfere with its visibility. Come daylight, that same range light 15 miles away would become a topmast, seen only with binoculars. No other part of that ship was visible as it was below the horizon. I thought this was striking evidence that the world was a huge ball suspended in space. It is referred to in the Bible as "the circle of the earth." It is a somewhat vague reference. A more exact phrase would be "the curvature of the earth's surface." The "circle of the earth" could refer to the circle of the horizon around you.

A four hour watch on the ship's navigation bridge on a dark night seemed like either time stretched or the clock moving slower. One way I broke the sometimes long and boring night watch from midnight to 4:00 A.M. was to anticipate receiving a mug of hot coffee from the relief helmsman when he came to the bridge at 1:20 and again at 2:40. Usually the fresh perked coffee tasted good. The coffee came from a percolator and was carried to me by the standby seaman. Occasionally it tasted overly strong from sitting too long. I would say, "A spoon won't stand up in this solution because it would dissolve." The rejoinder would be, "The other guy made it. I drank some and I'm still living."

Pre-World War II, the helmsman would repeat the bells sounded by the wheelhouse clock every half hour. He sounded the bell mounted outside the wheelhouse by pulling on a long rope run through large screw-eyes from the bell to the helmsman. The lookout on the bow, hearing the wheelhouse bell, repeated the time on the ship's large bell. He called every half hour, "Lights are bright, sir," meaning that the ship's running lights shone brightly.

The four-hour watch was also broken up by the three seamen on the watch. They shared duties. First, one became the helmsman, then lookout, and then standby. Every 80 minutes they relieved each other's position in sequence.

Again prewar, the lookout used the ships bell on the bow to report a light or object – sounding one bell for the starboard side, two bells for the port side, and three bells for ahead.

During the war, telephones came into general use, and then direct voice P.A. systems to various stations were used. The Mate on the bridge could tell the lookout that the light he had reported was the tip of the moon rising.

While at sea, Jocko Carlson, Fourth Mate, stood the 8:00 to 12:00 watch on the bridge both A.M. and P.M.

I was the Third Mate, and while at sea I stood the 12:00 to 4:00 watch A.M. and P.M. When I met Jocko on the bridge just before noon and just before midnight, he told me the course being steered, along with any other necessary information. Once I relieved him of this watch, he left the bridge to eat lunch at noon or turn in at midnight. Once more, we met at supper, as he relieved the Second Mate from 5:00 to 5:20 P.M. So, we might talk after 5:20 for a few minutes while we ate supper.

This all goes to show how life at sea could be lonely, almost monastic at times, at least before World War II.

TO THE RED SEA FROM CAPE TOWN - SEPTEMBER 1941
CLEAR WATER (SEA BOTTOM AT NINE FATHOMS)

After we refueled, hospitalized our diabetic crew member, gazed like tourists at the cloud tablecloth on Table Mountain, and looked at the Lions Head on top of the island mountain west of Cape Town Harbor, we left Cape Town far astern.

Steaming south, we rounded the Cape of Good Hope and we gave thanks for lack of a heavy swell for which the Cape of Good Hope is noted. Heading east, we passed Port Elizabeth, Durban, and the large island of Madagascar. Everything was wonderful – the weather, the trip, the ship, and my auburn beard (a surprising ego trip, for my sister had beautiful auburn hair); wonderful, except for one thing – my conscience. I had failed to write home.

Captain Jones called me on it. He said, "Did you write home from Cape Town?" I said "No sir, but they knew I'd be gone a long time." Weak excuse. In Boston last January at Raphael's on Bromfield Street, I had bought a portable typewriter and learned to type – letters were no longer a chore. It became enjoyable to type letters home and I set to it so as to be ready for our next port of call.

CAPE TOWN TO PORT SUDAN – SEPTEMBER 5, 1941

We steamed northeastward along the coast of East Africa. As we neared the Equator, heat, haze, and a poor horizon bore down on us. Sun sights and star sights for navigation were not practical. We had to rely on dead reckoning for our locations. Our pilot chart, which showed information not available on navigational charts, indicated a favorable current of up to 5 knots.

Captain Jones studied the charts with great concern, because it was possible to go past the Gulf of Aden and run up on the beach of Yemen, driven by the favorable current. He said, "It's time to break out our deep sea sounding lead." If we were far ahead of our dead reckoning, we would have been within the 100-fathom curve, off the horn of Africa.

Other than a radio shack, radio operator, telegraph key, transmitter and receiver, our aging freighter possessed few navigational aids. No direct voice communication was possible. In the chartroom, we had a radio direction finder, but there were no shore transmitters in this part of the world.

SOUNDINGS – THE OLD FASHION WAY
OR
WHAT IS AN ELECTRIC MOTOR

Under the watchful eye of Captain Jones, I rigged out the seven foot boom that kept the sounding apparatus away from the side of the ship. First, I connected the deep sea lead. It's an attached brass tube that contained an open ended glass tube with a telltale chemical. At depth and under pressure, water entered the glass tube. When I hauled up the deep sea lead, I removed the glass tube and compared it to the wooden scale. With remarkable accuracy, the scale showed the depth in fathoms; one fathom equals six feet.

All of this apparatus was attached to a long wire on the drum of a hand winch, outfitted with a brake lever. I remembered to fill the hollowed end of the sounding lead with bar soap in order to pick up a sample of the ocean bottom. When all was ready to let go, I held a tool on the wire, called a finger, that looked like a screwdriver with a bent end. After I released the brake, it seemed to take a long time, but I could feel the lead hit bottom. The winch had handles to wind in the wire. It was part of the job and it was not fun. When the wire was all wound in, I took out the glass tube and applied it to the wooden scale. It showed 92 fathoms. The soap on the bottom of the lead showed broken shells and white sand. I ran to the chartroom and looked for the place on the chart that showed the depth and bottom characteristics. Panic time – we were not anywhere near our dead reckoning position. We looked 50 miles ahead, then 70 miles ahead and finally 80 miles ahead where we found the place on the chart showing 92 fathoms and broken shells. It was almost time to turn west into the Gulf of Aden.

Much later, I learned that Captain Jones taught Purser Bob Trost the same lesson on the deep sea lead, much to my surprise.

Perhaps Chief Mate Thomas should have done the deep sea lead sounding. He was a veteran tobacco chewing sailor, rough and gruff. He delighted in slapping his big ham hand palm down on the chart covering hundreds of square miles, and saying, "Here we are, right here." Then he laughed and pointed his finger, an inch in diameter, to a guesstimated position.

I suspected Captain Jones liked Mr. Thomas' management of the main deck maintenance, but did not appreciate his bridge presence.

When the time came to turn west into the Gulf of Aden, the Captain smiled with satisfaction because he had established the correct position of his ship. It proved he was master of the situation. The hazy atmosphere cleared as we neared the entrance to the Red Sea.

The high barren rocks on both sides of the southern entrance to the Red Sea seemed to pass quickly even as the ship passed the entrance at 11 knots. We looked forward to our first port of discharge at Port Sudan, not far away. An ancient steam tug met and helped us to dock. Once docked, a floating steam crane said to be over 50 years old was soon moored to our offshore side. I wondered, was that ancient monstrosity going to offload our beautiful ready to run flying machines? I did not see any other facility in sight that might do the job.

AT PORT SUDAN – SEPTEMBER 6, 1941
A SLING BREAKS – A BOMBER DESTROYED

We goggled at our "longshoremen" for a reason. They were referred to as "fuzzy wuzzies" because of their beautifully coiffured black frizzy dressed hair. They wore one garment around their middle, sometimes over one shoulder of their skinny brown bodies. Barefoot, they worked hard and knew what to do.

We watched with concern as the slings were hooked on to the airplane on #3 Hatch and the ancient steam crane slowly took the weight of the plane. The steam engine puffed and labored to lift higher the graceful aircraft from its chocks.

Then it happened! The sling broke. That beautiful aircraft pancaked on to the deck and broke into a tragic mess, its gracefulness destroyed.

A British Army Sergeant sighed in despair but said, "Nobody is hurt and now we have spare parts." The sergeant, there to receive the four bombers, instead received three bombers and spare parts. A new wire sling safely off loaded the other three aircraft.

Our fuzzy wuzzy longshoremen went to work clearing the decks of chocks and lashings, in preparation for our departure to Port Tawfik, Cairo, Egypt.

When we departed the next morning, we received a thrilling surprise. We looked up to see the three bombers that we had carried on deck for over six weeks fly low overhead in formation. They dipped their wings in salute. We speculated on how air crews could prepare those planes for flight so fast.

Answer: The planes were towed right to the airport. There was no infrastructure, no utility poles, no wires, bridges, buildings nor trees. Just a dirt road in the desert. The crews inspected, familiarized and filled the fuel tank and then were ready to take off immediately. It was goodbye, too. We would not see them again. Little did we know that within three days we would see more planes – German bombers!!!

SEPTEMBER 7 - 11, 1941
PORT SUDAN TO PORT TAWFIK, CAIRO, EGYPT

Captain Jones showed me a note printed on the chart. The note called attention to the very clear water in the Red Sea near the mouth of the Gulf of Aqaba. Since the sea bottom was white sand and shell, it was visible to passing ships. Because of this, it could be assumed that the ship was in shallow water and about to go aground. The depth of water was near 50 feet, and our ship drew 27 feet.

Nevertheless, a few hours later we looked over the side into the water and saw that the bottom was not only visible, but looked too close for comfort. It was an eerie feeling. I tensed up, because what I saw did not seem to agree with the charted depths, which were the true depths in a heavy traffic sea lane to the south end of the Suez Canal.

It reminded me of the summers I spent on Lake Wentworth in Wolfeboro, New Hampshire. The lake presented numerous rocks and ledges known for good fishing, and most marked with buoys. While boating on that lake, I learned the hard way to keep our motorboat away from those hazards. I recoiled from the thought of hitting the submerged rocks on Lake Wentworth, just as I recoiled from the apparent shallow water in that spot on the Red Sea.

PORT SUDAN TO PORT TAWFIK, CAIRO, EGYPT
SEPTEMBER 11, 1941

We found the Red Sea to be a beautiful body of water – unpolluted, clear, and clean. As we approached the north end of the Red Sea, Port Tawfik was near the southern end of the Suez Canal. However, our attention was drawn to a burned out rusted shipwreck in the middle of the bay. It had been a large modern passenger ship of particular graceful appearance, judging from the cruiser stern above the water and the nearly submerged flared bow.

AT PORT TAWFIK, CAIRO, EGYPT

We docked without incident – except that boarding officials warned us of a probable air raid this very night, saying, "They like to raid us on certain nights, and this is one of those nights." One added, "It's a great show with all the searchlights, flares and ack-ack." He didn't mention the word bombs.

In September of 1941 in Port Tawfik, Cairo, Egypt, the main topic of conversation among English speaking personnel was the sinking of American flag freighters in the Red Sea by the Germans.

SEPTEMBER 12, 1941

The sirens sounded long after nightfall. At 2:45 A.M. I stood on the navigation bridge with Captain Jones and Joe Martin, a seaman our Captain tutored to sit for a Third Mate's license. We moved out to the unprotected wing of the bridge hoping to see the searchlights catch an aircraft in its beam. We did see an aircraft, but the sound of anti-aircraft guns, exploding shells, bombs, and rain of shrapnel became overwhelming. Something exploded in the water close to the ship.

About this time, Joe Martin exclaimed, "Something hit my hand, it's bleeding!" Then the show ended. We went below to take care of Joe Martin's hand. We met Second Mate Jeff Blackett and the Chief Steward emerging from under the big pile of dirty laundry bags They had more sense than we did. They found protection and used it. We found an exposed place and Joe Martin paid a price.

CAIRO, EGYPT - SEPTEMBER 14, 1941

The first morning after the air raid, I was able to send a cable home, "All is well." I was sure the air raid would make the Boston newspapers because of the damage to our ship. As I learned later, it was not only the damage to the ship that made the news, but also the fact that two of the officers on board were suburban Bostonians. I, the Third Mate, came from Arlington, and Fourth Mate John Carlson came from the adjoining town of Winchester. My cablegram was given to the press and served as a follow up story to the air raid.

When I went ashore to send the cablegram, father and son professional tour guides accosted me, offering to drive me to the pyramids. I thought, yes, good idea. I'm much too close not to visit one of the wonders of the world. I arranged to meet the father and son the next morning at 9:30.

When I left the tour guides, I decided to walk around the port area. Even though it was very hot, I wanted to see the sights and check out what souvenirs were available. The locality was densely populated and I did not like what I saw. Mothers carried babies whose little faces were covered with a plague of flies. The mothers did not seem to care, which surprised me. As I walked among plenty of small stalls and shops, I was also surprised to see no damage from the prior night's air raid. Apparently, the German aircraft pilots concentrated their bombs on the port's docked ships. One shop sign read, "American Bar." I should have known better, but thirst overcame my judgment. I stopped and ordered an ice cold soft drink, much to my later regret. I returned to the ship and turned in. It was necessary for me to stand an alert watch on the midnight to 8:00 A.M. duty. My country was not officially at war, but our ship was part of the war in Cairo.

IN PORT TAWFIK, CAIRO EGYPT
GOODBYE EGYPT, HELLO, INDIA

At breakfast, I was sick. I went ashore anyway and met my guide and his son. I felt so terrible, I asked them to take me to a hotel where I checked in for a two hour rest. After I rested, they drove me to the camel station near the Sphinx. They helped me mount a large camel to have my picture taken and then they drove me back to the ship, where I paid them off. My routine became a blur. Somehow I stood my deck watch, getting better though not back to normal.

PAINT AND PATCH

The next morning, Captain Jones met with his department heads and our ship's Egyptian Agent. Six weeks of dirty laundry went ashore as did the wounded seaman. Earlier, arrangements had been made to hire 100 painters. They were to come aboard to paint any white paint on the ship with grey paint. We were told that our white paint made our ship show up as a bright centerpiece during the raid. The Captain was told that a "stick" of three bombs had straddled our ship. Two bombs exploded on the solid quay to which our ship was tied, and the third bomb exploded in the water very close to the offshore side of our ship. Several fragments pierced the ship's side just above the water line. A repair gang patched the holes. Best of all, five gangs of longshoremen came aboard to discharge cargo.

SNUG AND SMUG

Part of my duties on the midnight to 8:00 A.M. watch was to see that the ship was snug alongside the quay. Dawn usually brought a breeze that pushed the ship four or five feet off the dock if the mooring lines were slack. This hindered cargo work that started at 8:00 A.M. So routinely at 6:00 A.M. or after, I went to the wheelhouse, blew into the engine room speaking tube, and requested steam on deck. Once I had the steam, I warmed the anchor windlass and carried the slack mooring line to the drumhead. I manned the throttle with one hand and the hawser on the drum with the other hand. After the ship slowly came alongside, I tied off the hawser with a rope stopper and secured the hawser to the bollards. Once I completed that task, I walked to the other end of the ship and repeated the operation using the docking winch.

One morning after successfully completing this process at both ends of the ship, I felt a smug confidence in my growing abilities as a young (20 year old) Third Officer. I was accosted by the Chief Mate who raised his voice in anger "Do you know what you just did? You crushed the gangway ladder between the ship and the quay." Then he relented just a little – "It was only the bottom step and we can fix that."

Months later when I joined the Masters, Mates and Pilots union, I was informed, "You oversee and supervise; you do not do the work."

Cargo discharged and cargo holds cleaned, we departed for India. Our voyage south in the Red Sea held some interest for us.

FROM CAIRO, EGYPT TO VIZATAPATAM, INDIA
SEPTEMBER, 1941
MECCA AND SUDAN CONTRAST

Inbound, we steamed north on the west side of the Red Sea. On the outbound route, we steamed south on the east side where we saw Mecca. We were glad to see Port Tawfik recede over the stern, glad to be free of German air raids, and glad to get rid of that sad sight of the beautiful cruise ship, partly submerged in the harbor, wrecked and rusted. Again we steamed over the area where the clear water allowed us to see the sea bottom. We saw passenger ships of all sizes crowded with people, all headed for the port of Mecca. For an hour or so we had the white buildings of Mecca in sight. We looked through binoculars and saw great crowds of people at their pilgrimage destination, Mecca. What a sight to behold. A sea of Muslims dressed head to foot in white. I thought what a difference between the white robed Muslims and the naked, poverty stricken fuzzy wuzzy Sudanese natives, surviving in the desert on the west side of the Red Sea.

We steamed out of the Red Sea into the Gulf of Aden and then into the Port of Aden to refuel. The heat in Egypt was unpleasant, but here in the Port of Aden the heat was intense. There was nothing attractive about the Port of Aden. There was no shore leave and no other contact with anyone except for the fuel barge personnel and a required formal visit by the ship's agent. Everyone was glad to leave that hot place. Nevertheless, Aden was strategically located and serviced many nations' vessels.

ADEN TO VIZAGAPATAM, INDIA
HEAT IN PORT AND AT SEA

In Aden, there was no time to go ashore. We departed without regret, set course for the passage between Ceylon and the tip of the India peninsula, and then we steamed north to the port of Vizagapatam, where we were to load about 3,000 tons of chromite ore. It was heavy grey black rocks of all sizes. The rocks gave us stability and didn't take up much space. We were to fill the ship with jute (bales of burlap) at Calcutta.

On our passage from Egypt, we sighted many dhows. They provided cheap and slow transportation for people in Yemen, Persian Gulf, India and Africa. Few dhows had engines. Most were under sail and we had to avoid them.

From Vizagapatam, we steamed northeast to the Hooghly River. There we picked up a pilot who notified us we would be mooring to a large mooring buoy using our anchor chain, as the bore tide was due and there was no berth available.

In a hurry, we had to turn the crew to, tie off an anchor, and disconnect the anchor chain.

CALCUTTA, INDIA
MOVING ANCHOR CHAIN BY HAND

It was good news that the patent link that connected the chain to the anchor disassembled with relative ease. The bad news was that anchor chain had to be used to tie the stern to another large mooring buoy.

It was a struggle for the deck crew of 11 men to move 90 feet of anchor chain by hand from stem to stern, because each link weighed nearly 50 pounds.

There was a time constraint because the bore tide was due soon. There were built in helps: The main deck was free of obstructions from deck cargo, and the deck was slightly downhill from bow to stern.

The crew moved the chain and attached the ship to the mooring with the chain just in time before the bore tide appeared. The approaching bore tide disappointed me. I watched a tame wave about two feet high roll in, stretching the width of the river. No big deal. The wave reached our bow without noticeable effect, until the anchor chain became taut and the big mooring buoy tipped enough to become perpendicular to the bow. But it held. It was a big deal.

The next day, when we were ordered to a loading dock, we faced another struggle. We had to get the anchor chain from the stern forward to the chain locker before the deck was cluttered with hatch boards and beams. We tied lines to various links and led them to winch drums. The winch drums helped move the chain up the deck from stern to the bow.

THE PERSONAL INJURY ACCIDENT IN CALCUTTA, INDIA
ABOUT OCTOBER 10, 1941

The hard working 11 man crew struggled to move the 90 foot length of anchor chain from the stern to the bow just in time before docking. After docking, we needed to attach one end of the chain to the anchor, and then the other end to the rest of the anchor chain in the chain locker. The accident happened while moving the chain. Two of the links were dragged over the Chief Mate's foot. The Chief Mate, who was in charge of the procedure, was in extreme pain and needed immediate hospital treatment.

Captain Jones had gone ashore on ship's business and then to a dinner invitation. Somehow I was included in the dinner invitation. My arrival at dinner was delayed by the accident. I felt it was necessary to explain my late arrival by saying there was an accident on the ship. The Captain insisted on knowing the details. I was forced to relate the unpleasant facts while the others were eating, which made me quite uncomfortable. After I told my story, Captain Jones realized he had to see the ship's agent about Chief Mate Lewis' hospitalization and a possible replacement.

Before we departed from Calcutta, a new Chief Mate came on board. His name was Bernard Connors. I was disappointed to have a young Chief Mate replace the father figure I respected. I was not informed that he was a fellow nautical school graduate, about 10 years prior to my graduation.

My illness, acquired in Egypt, was not severe enough to prevent my standing my watch on the bridge, although I spent most of my watch below (i.e. off duty time) in my bunk. That meant that I did not have much contact with Mr. Connors.

OCTOBER 1941
CALCUTTA - A DIFFERENT WORLD (IN 1941)

Even though the Hooghly River was brown, it served as the bathtub and wash tub for the people. People slept, worked, ate, gathered, sold, confronted, and walked on the sidewalks. Traffic consisted of the greatest variety of wheeled vehicular craft that human ingenuity could devise. For safety, swivel necks would have helped. Because of the aggressive traffic, one had to keep a good lookout all around in order to prolong life.

When I went ashore, I found the best thing was to hire a motorized rickshaw with a loud horn because walking was an adventure. If one had a purpose, it became an expedition. From a large shop with a sidewalk production factory, I purchased an ivory and wood hinged chest decorated with inlaid scenes on the sides and front. I had it delivered to the ship. I asked the ship's carpenter to make a crate so that I could ship it home from New York. If we ever got there.

I had not fully recovered from Egyptian stomach. In Calcutta, the war was a distant non-happening. Although I possessed a radio, broadcasts were few and the reception terrible. Once in awhile, I found a BBC broadcast.

CALCUTTA TO NEW YORK

Finally we were fully loaded, ready to sail, and glad of it!

The only heat relief was the breeze as the ship moved through the water. For ventilation, we had wind scoops that fit in the open portholes. However, in a loaded ship, the wind scoops were close to the water. Sometimes they captured spray or even the top of a wave. When this happened, it meant a wet bunk, a wet man, or water in the room. It provided a source for kidding and teasing – a diversion.

Looking back, Calcutta was an experience, or rather a series of them.

On the voyage home, Captain Jones was concerned about my health. Although I managed to stand all my watches, he asked me several questions. Was I eating well – no. Was I keeping my food down? No. Bowels OK? No.

My illness did not incapacitate me; nevertheless, the trip home was an ordeal. At least I was never bored.

As we steered northeast of the Caribbean Sea, the radio operator heard the news that the Japanese had attacked Pearl Harbor. We were at war. It was one week to New York. Would we make it? We arrived safely in New York on December 15, 1941.

DECEMBER 15, 1941

Much to my surprise, on the morning we docked in New York, my dad met the ship. I invited him on board to have breakfast with me. He ordered fried eggs, but couldn't eat them. He said they tasted old. I assured him the Chief Steward had faithfully turned the egg crates over every week. Then I tasted my eggs. They tasted awful. I was used to the gradual deterioration as the voyage progressed. After all, the eggs were only six months old.

My dad helped me pack and get my gear off the ship, including the crated chest, which he arranged to have shipped home to Arlington, Massachusetts. We rode home on the New York to Boston train. Mother greeted me and took me right to Dr. Foye because I weighed only 114 pounds. My treatment lasted two months.

Goodbye, SS *Arkansan*. I never saw that ship again! Because she was a peacetime ship, she had to be outfitted for war. Later I heard that during the month of June 1942 while sailing the Caribbean, she was torpedoed and sunk.

AT SEA - 1941
RITUAL AT NOON

Everyone knows that the sun is at its highest point in the sky at noon. Well, yes, but not exactly. It depends where you are on the earth, or where your ship is at sea. Therefore, knowing your approximate position and the exact time the sun reaches its highest point can be calculated using information from a nautical almanac. At that instant, an observation of the sun's altitude by a sextant quickly reveals latitude. Hence the ritual: The mate on watch calculated the time of local apparent noon, known as LAN. In land lubbers' language, the mate figured the time the sun reached its apex, and he posted the time on a little blackboard.

The Master and all his Mates came to the bridge, got out their sextants and lined up on the wing of the bridge nearest the sun. Everyone compared altitude from their sextants until all were the same or nearly so and the sun stopped rising. Latitude was reckoned, the morning longitude was run up on the course line and voila – a noon position.

The Second Mate was the navigator. He made up a noon position slip, worked out the miles run from yesterday's noon position, and took the slip to the Chief Engineer. The Chief Engineer worked out his own noon slip, showing fuel consumption, fuel left and propeller revolutions and other information.

That was then; however, now it is different and much better. Now the same information required to know how the vessel performed and the ship's position is always available from space satellites on bridge receivers. It is quicker and more accurate. No more concerns about overcast skies, hazy horizons and questionable positions. The perfect position fix is always available.

From then to now was a period of transition. From post World War I to 1980 – about 60 years. From Bowditch trigonometric tables through speedier Ageton or other columns of number tables, to pocket navigational calculators, to special navigational computers, which reckoned several star sights and gave a position fix in a few minutes – are all now obsolete.

One hundred years ago, a ship's wheelhouse was a cubicle big enough for a large wheel, a small helmsman and a pilot. Today, all ships have a spacious navigation bridge. Instead of a large megaphone to shout orders to the bow and stern, today's ships have an extensive telephone system throughout the ship, plus a public address system. Ships most likely have a console for electric controls for engines and thrusters. Today, ships carry two radar sets and myriad instruments with telltale and warning lights, toilet facilities, and a coffee maker cabinet. Now the windows are mechanized with spinning disks, which are better than wipers. Ships have TV sets and TV cameras for sighting channels and harbors.

Today's navigator must be current on electronics, somewhere between a working knowledge and a repair genius, because the large wooden wheel with many spokes has been replaced by a joystick. Engine controls, computers with electronic charts prove the maritime industry can use advances of other industries.

Part 3: 1942 to 1943 - SS *Samuel Chase*

MARCH 22, 1942

My assignment to the *Samuel Chase* was not only gratifying, but also a relief. I had been home for nearly three months, recovering from an illness I contracted in Egypt during the time I served on the SS *Arkansan*. In February, I took a refresher course to sit for a Second Mates' license. On March 9, 1942, I completed the exam in one day. Now I was ready to ship out. I packed my gear and journeyed by train to New York, and the company offices of American Hawaiian Steamship Company at 90 Broad Street.

"No jobs," Captain Bain said. Incredible, I thought. This was war. There was a tremendous effort to mobilize all our resources. There had to be jobs and lots of them.

I was galvanized by President Roosevelt's messages. Maybe my timing was off, I thought. I never factored in the many American ships sunk on the east coast. Loosing those ships created the likely effect of a temporary excess of third mates, other ship personnel, and survivors.

Ten days later, I received the call for my assignment. "Assigned where?" I said, "What? The Southern Hotel in Baltimore? My orders were to go to the Southern Hotel and report to George Wilson, Chief Mate. When I reported, Mr. Wilson said to be ready for work at 8:00 A.M. The next morning Mr. Wilson, Second Mate Fred Raley, and I boarded a nearby new streamline streetcar that sped us directly to Fairfield shipyard.

What a revelation we saw at the shipyard. We gawked at a long train of flatcars. A different piece of a ship, ready to assemble, sat on each car. We saw kingposts with mast tables, crosstrees, steel blocks, and booms – or derricks – ready for people to set on deck and weld in place. They seemed to me like a huge three dimensional puzzle.

Even though our ship, the SS *Samuel Chase*, had already been launched, it was far from finished. Machinists, riggers, pipe fitters, plumbers, electricians and welders showed up at the shipyard and worked furiously around the clock to assemble all those ship pieces sitting on the train flat beds.

Our jobs were to order supplies and charts and to get to know the ship. Some activities we coordinated involved designating who marked the shots of anchor chain, who hung the clocks, and who made the station bills for fire and boat drills. We also notified supervisors about mistakes.

Chief Engineer Seel discovered a mistake. Someone installed a steam pipeline over the cylinders of the main engine in such a way as to inhibit any future repairs to the cylinders. Big mistake. It took two days to reach the proper decision, design an alternative, remove the offending pipeline, and replace it with the new design. The correction was a quick and a satisfactory fix.

31

With almost breathtaking speed, as far as shipbuilding was concerned, the finish work on the *Samuel Chase* came to completion. Workers finished the cargo holds with roseboxes (bilge water strainers), battens, and beams, and then they installed the hatch boards. Once the engine room became functional with boilers, pumps, generators, and controls, they were tested and working. Communication was a rudimentary telephone system to the engine room, bow, stern docking stations, Captain's office, Chief Engineer's office, and the crow's nest.

On the crow's nest, the telephone systems became useful on two occasions during the voyage after we left Halifax to cross the North Atlantic. First, Second Mate Fred Raley climbed into the crow's nest to sight other ships in our convoy obscured by a low layer of fog. Second, later in the voyage, I climbed up to the crow's nest to verify whether a strange cloud mass ahead, partially over the horizon, was a mountain or not. It was a mountain on Novaya Zemlya, an archipelago marking the eastern boundary of the Barents Sea. There was no P.A. system, no megaphones. If the telephones failed, as they sometimes did from salt water causing short circuits, we used hand signals and screaming as the last resorts. In and near the wheelhouse, licenses, certificates, warnings and legal requirements were signed, framed and posted. It seemed like the war must wait while we witnessed on board examinations and made reports. All the work had to come to an end sometime.

Finally on April 17, 1942, the officers and crew signed on. The vessel, now fueled and stored, was ready to depart. There was no time to put out extra mooring lines. Whatever for? There was no time except to conduct tests on the main engine's ahead and astern capabilities on the propeller and other engine room equipment. The bridge and navigation equipment was tested as well. All was well, when we departed on a trial run, and to "swing ship" in order to determine the error on our magnetic compass on all headings. A specialist adjusted the vertical magnets and the two iron spheres, one on each side of the compass binnacle. He made a graph so that we could pick out the magnetic compass error, called deviation, on any given heading. This procedure seemed to be almost superfluous because we had a gyro compass, a marvelous modern advantage on our basic ship. However, it was smaller than the standard Sperry issue and not quite as reliable.

Our ship was handed over to the American-Hawaiian Steamship Co. to operate under the orders of the United States Maritime Commission. There was one more essential procedure, called degaussing. This procedure protected the ship from magnetic mines. Degaussing made the ship as safe as modern science allowed.

Now we were ready for the loading dock. Our cargo consisted of everything that an army needed in wartime. All five holds were filled with trucks, battle tanks, equipment in crates, boxes on pallets, pipes in bundles, wires on giant spools, food, and supplies. The main deck was crowded with lashed down Sherman battle tanks ready to run. What a sight – heartening, one might say.

Disquieting were the three empty gun tubs on the bow of our new ship. The largest one was for a three inch anti-aircraft gun. The other two were supposed to hold .50 caliber machine guns. There were not enough guns on hand to complete the armament of every ship; therefore, it was some to all rather than all to some. It was, to us, sad. We had four .50 caliber machine guns, two .30 caliber machine guns – called pop guns by some – and the four inch deck gun on the stern. Every gun proved to be ineffective in battle. The one time the four inch deck gun was fired, it needed a range finder. Our guessing at the range was way off. There was a vague promise of 20 mm guns to replace the .50 calibers.

32

MAY 1942

The *Samuel Chase* was ordered to complete loading at a different dock – a special cargo. The last compartment to be loaded was the 'tween deck in the #1 hold. It was designated for special cargo, explosives.

On the morning we were to load this special cargo, I was the mate on watch under the direction of Chief Mate George Wilson. It was almost 8:00. I stood on deck near the gangway to wait for one gang of longshoremen to come aboard. As I contemplated the cargo of explosives soon to be loaded on board, suddenly a voice from within me spoke 11 clear and strong words: "*You shall never be on a ship sunk by enemy action.*" Being a Christian by profession of faith, I knew the voice came from the indwelling Holy Spirit of God, who spoke this special message to me.

After I heard God's message, the longshoremen came on board followed by a tall man in a strange uniform of coarse wool. He wore a visored cap with a wide red band around it. He came to me and introduced himself. "I'm Captain Petrofsky," (not his real name) "and I'm here to oversee the loading of 50 tons of dynamite consigned to the Soviet Army." This was the first confirmation that the *Samuel Chase* was bound for Russia.

Every man on board received a fur collared deep blue corduroy jacket lined with sheep wool, a full-length rubber suit complete with attached boots, and a hood that fitted tightly around the face.

The appearance of the Russian Army officer quieted all the rumors and dispelled all doubts. Not Alaska or Greenland, but Russia was our destination. No one mentioned that summer, soon to come, did not quite fit in with the heavy fur collared mackinaw. Everyone appreciated the rubber suit, because the Arctic waters were always cold, too cold, located near the polar ice cap.

The Russian Army captain and I watched the experienced longshoremen crew carefully hoist the first pallet of dynamite on board. One tier high wooden boxes covered with a tied down net secured the boxes in place in order to minimize the danger. The longshoremen were experienced and careful to minimize the danger.

1942: TO RUSSIA WITH PQ-17

I was reminded of my duty on the SS *Arkansan* a year earlier, when we sailed from New York Harbor with four two-engine bombers on deck, in plain sight for all to see. That was peacetime. Now we were sailing with a dozen battle tanks on deck for all to see. This was war, and we were steaming into it.

A MAIDEN VOYAGE – TIME TO SAIL

It was time to sail. Yet before taking departure, the official moment of time between port time and sea time, there remained some essential tasks to accomplish. Each task seemed more important than the other, yet there had to be an orderly progression.

As soon as all the longshoremen loaded the cargo, the hatches covered securely for sea, the booms lowered and locked in their cradles, the gangway taken up and stowed in its place, and all the crew members checked as present, the ship was ready for sea.

The number one task immediately after undocking was accomplished by a towboat that began to turn the ship in a circle. A technician called a compass adjuster, assisted by the ship's deck officers, positioned magnets in the two magnetic compass binnacles in the wheelhouse and on the flying bridge.

The compass adjustment seemed complicated and took about two hours. Even though we had a gyro compass, in case of a power failure, the backup magnetic compass had to be ready and reasonably accurate. After the compass adjuster technician made a graph of errors on different compass headings, he left the ship and returned to shore on another boat.

The number two task involved the large copper cable built into the inside of the hull and circling the ship which was used to counteract the attraction of magnetic mines to the steel hull. No work was required by our crew, but authorities had to know it was in working order.

HURRY UP – AND WAIT

In the number three task, we met a U.S. Navy barge in Hampton Roads, Norfolk. While we were anchored, the barge carrying the ammunition came alongside the SS *Samuel Chase* and loaded the ammo on board. The gun crews stowed the ammunition for the ship's guns. The ammunition included large canisters of belts of .50 caliber cartridges for the machine guns and smaller drum canisters for the .30 calibers. Loading the four-inch shells for the deck gun mounted on the stern platform proved to be the hard work. The gun crew carried these shells aft, lowered them into the magazine, and stowed the shells into the racks. Although the crew started task number three and completed it on April 24, it was too late to make Delaware Bay before nightfall. This was significant, as ships in transit went to a sheltered anchorage for the night if possible. Daylight steaming was safer.

And so it was early on April 25, 1942 that the *Chase* hove up the anchor and proceeded at full speed to Delaware Bay anchorage, where we anchored and waited for daylight. On the morning of April 26 we heaved anchor and hurried to New York. When we neared New York early on April 27, a pilot came aboard to pass the ship through Hell Gate into Long Island Sound. We steamed on and arrived at the Cape Cod Canal in Buzzards Bay, where we anchored.

The pilot for Cape Cod Canal came aboard on the morning of April 28, 1942. As soon as the tide was suitable to him, we transited the canal. After we transited the canal, we dropped the pilot off into the pilot boat and put the engine room telegraph on full speed for Halifax, Nova Scotia.

The ship arrived late in the day, and the Halifax pilot promptly took us into harbor. We were glad to be taken into Bedford Basin's shelter.

We had neither seen nor heard any warnings of enemy subs and assumed they must have been doing their dirty work off the East Coast of the United States.

The *Chase* steamed into a crowded Bedford Basin. Before we nosed carefully into that body of water, I couldn't help think about the horrific World War I explosion that occurred at this very place which caused massive destruction and many deaths.

After we anchored and the ship swung around too close to another ship, we had to heave anchor and move.

Halifax anchorage was peaceful, even with the anxiety caused by too many ocean-going ships crowded into a "lake" of modest size.

We had a shore liberty of sorts. The water taxi's schedules were not always convenient because most crewmembers had watches to stand, and there was not much entertainment ashore. Each man aboard had to see for himself. The seamen's club was a huge room filled with dozens of round tables. Beer and cigarettes were available but this was not entertaining to me. When I was a 17-year-old cadet, I tried to learn to like beer. I visited the saloons with other young cadets in Charlestown located outside the Navy Yard. The more I drank, the worse the beer tasted, like bitter medicine.

While our ship was anchored in Halifax, a man arrived in a water taxi and delivered a message to the gunnery officer. The message said that the Canadian Navy was going to hold a fly-by target practice. A pilot flew his aircraft towing a target for our machine gunners to practice hitting, using real bullets. There were 15 naval seaman on our ship: four gunners, four loaders on the .50 caliber machine guns, and seven men to man the four-inch stern gun. The two .30 caliber machine guns on the flying bridge were not manned. The gunnery officer and the chief mate decided that I, a young third officer, could be volunteered to man a .30 caliber machine gun. Even though I was not thrilled, I attended the practice session.

Four U.S. Navy gunners, the petty officer, and I took the water taxi ashore where a bus took us to a target range. The target range had a shelter. Gunners from other ships also arrived for target practice. A Canadian naval officer, a young lieutenant (J.G.) instructed us. The bi-plane flew by towing a sleeve target. One gunner tried to hit the target. I saw no tracers in the ammunition he used, so I could not tell if the gunner hit the target. My turn came, and the lieutenant said, "Be sure and lead the target." I fired. The aircraft pilot dropped his target and flew away. The lieutenant said to me, "You fired too close to the plane. The practice is terminated."

We returned to the ship and the humdrum life on board a ship at anchor. Day after day we waited for orders. Our wait ended on May 6 when the Captain, Purser and Gunnery Officer were taxied ashore to a convoy conference. On May 7, a pilot came aboard. At a certain time and in a particular order some ships hove up anchor and proceeded to sea.

Another small convoy formed up. We were informed our destination was the U.K. Because of the patchy and sometimes layered fog, every ship except the last ship in the column towed a fog buoy.

35

These buoys were equipped with scoops that forced up a column of water. This was the only way that ships in columns could keep station on the unseen ship ahead in a dense fog.

One morning not long after we departed, the fog showed a curious characteristic. The fog was dense from the surface of the water to a height of about 80 feet. Those of us who stood on the bridge could see the fog buoy towed by the ship ahead and sometimes the tip of a mast of another nearby ship. Usually around noontime the Captain and all three mates stood on the bridge. Second Mate Fred Raley said, "I'd like to go up to the crow's nest and see what I can see, if the convoy is keeping its formation." This was our first convoy experience.

With the Captain's permission, Fred Raley, an overweight six-footer, clambered up the foremast ladder and squeezed into the crow's nest. In a few minutes, the bridge telephone rang and Fred reported, "I can see the topmasts of every ship. They're in a good tight formation."

THE LONGEST ROUTE
HALIFAX TO GLASGOW TO REYKJAVIK

There had to be a reason for this seeming madness of taking the long way to Reykjavik. This convoy was bound for U.K., not Iceland. When the weather cleared, we saw that the convoy was no longer small, for many ships now sailed with our convoy. We reasoned that Bedford Basin had no space for more vessels. The long arms of the sea near Glasgow had many miles of sheltered waters, where the ships gathered, anchored, and waited for orders.

Later, we realized that the allied navies had to scrape up a large number of scarce warships for escorts. The task required a lot of planning and time. The escorts were necessary because it was clear that the Germans had the upper hand in the North Atlantic, and that bases in Norway and France presented a continuous threat.

Meanwhile, my crew members and I had time to become acquainted with our new ship. Most of the ship was typical of the freighters of the last twenty years. The engine room, cargo holds, hatches and cargo gear were much the same as on the older vessels. New to the ship's construction were the welded seams throughout the ship, less rope, and more wire on cargo gear to hold booms – or derricks – in place. The flush toilets and wash water discharged over the side via pipelines cut through the hull plating wherever convenient. This was an awkward and embarrassing arrangement. Years later after the war, remedial measures became law.

IN CONVOY

Ships ready to sail from a port were usually gathered at one or more anchorages. Naval authorities chose the time for the Commodore to send a message to every ship's captain ordering them to attend a convoy conference. At the conference, the Commodore introduced himself and assigned each captain a number for his ship which indicated the ship's position in the convoy. A sequence of sailing times was announced so that all the ships exited the harbor or anchorage in an orderly procession. No time or place for a jam up here. Once each ship received a number and sailing time, it proceeded to the area and took its assigned position relative to the Commodore's ship.

There was a noteworthy circumstance regarding the position of the *Samuel Chase* in the convoy. Our ship was assigned to be the lead ship in the outside column nearest the Norway coast as the convoy steamed north from Iceland. It was the most vulnerable position in the convoy.

It was essential to know the International Code Flags and their letters and numbers, because the Commodore's orders to all ships for course and speed used these hoisted flags. Each captain received a secret signal book contained in a perforated steel box. The signal book contained the written meanings of the Commodore's flag signals. The perforated steel box also contained the secret documents that gave rendezvous positions for stragglers. The box was perforated so that it would sink if a ship was sinking or captured. The Captain would toss the box with its contents overboard.

These procedures were new to us on the *Samuel Chase*. Keeping a ship's position in the convoy was nerve wracking, hard work. Many ships sailing in close proximity to each other demanded that we pay strict attention to careful lookouts. When the convoy was in position and the weather remained clear and calm, our tensions eased. When the Commodore hoisted a flag signal, all watch standers on the bridge were alerted, as all ships hoisted the same signal. Once the flags were hoisted, the Captain got out his secret book, called Mersigs, and read the meaning of the signal flags. Radio signals were never used except in disasters, but in dense fog whistle signals were used.

The two-week voyage from Halifax to Glasgow gave the Captain, deck officers, helmsmen and engineers valuable experience keeping station in convoy so that when in battle and under attack, keeping station became routine.

The Second Mate kept a daily record on a spreadsheet to track the ship's movements. Our passage from Halifax to Clyde Pilot Station near Glasgow, Scotland took 14 days, 20 hours and 24 minutes. The average speed of the convoy, time divided into 2,507 miles, gave an average speed of 7 knots. A moderate storm lasting three days forced the convoy to reduce speed to under 6 knots. Fine weather produced speeds over 8 knots for four days. It was a good passage. A huge plus: We lost no ships.

The *Chase* arrived on May 22, 1942 and anchored in a long narrow bay called Loch Long where we waited three days for orders. On May 26 at 0200, we left the bay and steamed 270 miles to another anchorage, called Loch Ewe.

Ours was not to reason why, just do it. It soon became obvious while we remained at this new anchorage, that another convoy would be formed at the destination of Reykjavik, Iceland. We enjoyed another successful voyage at a convoy speed of 7 knots and traveled 734 miles in four days arriving on June 1, 1942. Little did we know we were to wait four weeks at anchor, for other ships to join us. We watched the extraordinarily large escort, said to be 75 ships, gather.

Our convoy's arrival at Reykjavik, Iceland, contributed to the makeup of Convoy PQ-17. The convoy conference for Masters, Gunnery Officers and Pursers took place on June 27, 1942. I learned from the Captain through the Purser and Chief Mate that the convoy would have a strong escort. The convoy would have the protection of the Allied battle fleet waiting just over the horizon. This was heartening and welcome news to us. Nevertheless, our mood was somber because we knew that attacks would come.

JUNE 28 TO JULY

The 36 ships of Convoy PQ-17 departed Reykjavik Harbor at the end of June 1942. Even though the harbor was open to the sea, pilots were required to escort ships out of the harbor, because of hazardous shoals. One ship ran onto the rocks and missed the sailing. Thirty-five convoy ships headed north off the west coast of Iceland. We discovered that the arctic night was short and the visibility less than ideal. When the visibility cleared, we sighted a field of ice ahead.

Second Mate Fred Raley, on watch, reported the ice to Captain Martin. Once he studied the ice field through his binoculars, he decided to hold the ship in its convoy position, because he said the ice looked soft.

Whatever part of the ice field the ship hit did not feel soft. The ship shook violently and threw me out of my bunk. I woke up on my hands and knees on deck beside my bunk. I dressed as quickly as possible and climbed up one deck to the bridge, only to find that the Captain had gone back to bed. The ship, still in convoy, steamed along in open water. The Second Mate gave me a rundown on the brief happening and suggested I go back to bed.

My morning four-hour watch began at 8:00. The weather was clearing, and that was welcome. Unwelcome was a large German float plane I saw circling the convoy at a distance out of firing range. The German observation aircraft circling Convoy PQ-17 was identified as a Blohm and Voss float plane. Many hours later, the German observation aircraft was replaced by the largest German plane we had ever seen, a four engine Dornier transport. It looked much more menacing than the float plane. Day after day a succession of enemy aircraft kept up 24 hour a day observation.

Meanwhile, life on board the *Samuel Chase* became quite routine. Watch after watch, four hours each, went by without interruption until the Commodore's one signal came requesting all ships to suppress black smoke. The request came too late. The Germans already knew where we were and where we were going. Besides, there were two coal burning freighters in our convoy. On a calm day, their smoke rose high and drifted in layers, visible to the enemy.

While we sailed, we got to know each crew member better. The Chief Steward, one of four communist sympathizers, revealed his unrestrained enthusiasm for Communism, even at age 60.

Shawn Maloney was not a communist sympathizer. He had never been to sea before and had signed on as an ordinary seaman. Tall and handsome, he had been blessed by God with extraordinary distance vision. When on watch, Shawn sighted the new relief German observation plane. He was, in fact, the unofficial convoy lookout. None of the convoy had radar, but we had Shawn Maloney. He sighted everything first, even – uh-oh – the squadron of German attack planes. He identified the German attack planes that carried torpedoes!! Time for us to man the battle stations!

JULY 4, 1942

It was July 4, 1942, and it was as if Adolf Hitler sneered, "I'll give you a July 4 celebration you won't soon forget. Independence Day! HA!" The single engine enemy aircrafts, each supplied with a torpedo under its belly, broke formation and spread out to attack. Suddenly, one two-engine airplane, a decoy without a torpedo, flew right at us. It flew low about 50 feet above the water. Every gunner on our ship aimed his gun at the enemy plane. The German pilot banked sharply around our stern and flew between the first and second columns of ships to the front of the convoy. I manned the .30 caliber machine gun on the starboard side of the flying bridge and pointed the gun at the fast approaching airplane. The gun, mounted on a tripod, could swing through an arc of 360°. I realized my bullets could hit another ship. With my finger on the trigger, I tried to follow the fast moving plane. As he flew around our stern, I swung my gun around to keep the plane in my sights. Instead of seeing the enemy plane, I saw our ship's life raft secured to the mizzenmast stays; then I saw the mast itself, and then the raft on the other side, and then something white. White hair. The Captain's head!!! He had walked in front of my swinging machine gun while I had my finger on the trigger. I stood up straight, in shock. In the meantime, the enemy launched their torpedoes. Someone shouted. I turned to see a torpedo and its wake streaming straight toward the middle of our ship. While I stared at this coming disaster, the torpedo made a drastic change of direction, as if guided by a giant hand.

I caught sight of the Second Mate Fred Raley who stood at the stern frantically signaling that the torpedo passed astern and streamed into the convoy. I waited. Who, what ship would the torpedo hit? There was little chance of the torpedo propelling itself through the entire width of the convoy without hitting something. After a minute, maybe longer – it seemed longer – I heard a muffled explosion. Another wait, and then I saw the Liberty ship *Christopher Newport* slowly fall back from its convoy position. It stayed on an even keel and did not appear to be sinking, but it was. As soon as the *Christopher Newport* lost momentum and came to a stop, the crew abandoned ship. One of the two rescue ships accompanying the convoy took the crew on board. We intercepted a signal ordering the ship to be sunk if it was not already in sinking condition. An escort ship was ordered to shell the *Christopher Newport's* hull to sink it, because it could not be towed in the convoy and must not be left behind afloat. The convoy steamed on to the sound of gunfire, a shocking requiem.

The sinking of the *Christopher Newport* prevented us from seeing another dramatic incident. The decoy plane that had so effectively distracted gunners also distracted gunfire shot from the torpedo planes that were attacking us. Without firing any guns, the decoy plane passed over the escort ships that were sailing out ahead of the convoy. The escorts concentrated their gunfire on that plane and brought it down into the sea. The pilot survived and climbed onto the still floating wreckage.

WARRIORS OF COMPASSION

With perfect timing, a German float plane landed at the floating wreckage, pulled the downed pilot into the rescue plane, and took off. The decoy and the rescue airplane did their jobs.

Our rescue ships supplied rescue facilities for seamen whose ships were sunk. Human forethought successfully carried out these rescues; however, I believe that the Lord our God intervened in the rescues. I also believe that Lord saved the *Samuel Chase* from destruction. I base that belief on the promise God gave to me, *"You shall never be on a ship sunk by enemy action."* According to Titus 1:2, God cannot lie. It was the first miracle while I was on the *Samuel Chase*. I was about to witness more of God's promise while I served aboard the *Samuel Chase*.

Later that day at 4:00 P.M. Chief Mate George Wilson came on the bridge to stand his regular watch and relieve Second Mate Fred Raley. Chief Mate Wilson's watch required his constant attention to the ship's speed and course in order to maintain the ship's station in the convoy. Maintaining station requires constant attention. Often small changes in course and speed were needed. When Mr. Wilson stepped from the wheelhouse on to the port wing of the bridge to check the ship's position, he looked down into the water and saw a frightening sight. Just below the water's surface, an active torpedo ran about 25 feet from the ship's side and along the same course as the ship.

The actual course of the torpedo appeared to be closing in on the ship. When it struck, it seemed likely the torpedo would strike well forward of the ship's bridge. Mr. Wilson shouted to the helmsman, "Hard right!"

The helmsman failed to obey. He was an ordinary seaman with modest experience and on edge from the recent attacks, and he was probably scared. Instead of turning hard right, the young seaman responded in alarm, "What's wrong, what's wrong?"

The Chief Mate ran back to the wheel, pushed aside the sailor, grabbed the wheel and turned it. Silence: The torpedo did not explode. The Chief Mate returned the ship to station and sounded the alarm on the ship's whistle. Twice he gave the whistle five short blasts, and then he sounded on the whistle in Morse code in order to give the other ships the bearing from which the torpedo originated.

The Naval signal man who was stationed on our flying bridge at the flag locker and flag hoists read the signal by blinker light coming from the Commodore vessel to an escort vessel. The signal read, "Go astern of the convoy and keep that sub down."

At 5:00 P.M. I relieved the Chief Mate on the bridge. The Chief Mate and our naval signalman went to supper. That left a relief helmsman and me, the Third Mate, alone on the bridge. The Commodore ship called us on the blinker. I answered the Commodore on our large port wing blinker. The message from the Commodore was long, complicated, and complimentary. We had averted tragedy because of the Chief Mate's quick actions. I had no recorder and no one else was around to record the message.

When the Chief Mate returned to the bridge after supper, he was quite annoyed that the message from the Commodore had not been recorded. He waited until the signalman returned before he called the Commodore vessel and asked to have the message repeated in full, only to find that he was the subject of all the compliments.

Later on, during the Second Mate's watch, the convoy steamed through the wide passage between Bear Island and Spitsbergen. The passage through was uneventful, although Fred extolled the beauty of the huge icebergs. Most of the icebergs were grounded in water too shallow for them but deep enough for ships.

Convoy PQ-17 headed east in the Barents Sea with North Cape, Norway, far to the south. If German surface ships were to attack, this was the time and place. None of the German ships appeared. The weather was clear and cold, and the visibility unlimited. To the north, the horizon presented a strange glitter. The glow indicated ice just over the horizon, perhaps 10 miles at a guess. We enjoyed a quiet time until signal flags rudely interrupted the peace. The codebook interpreted the signal. "Convoy is to scatter, and proceed independently to port of destination." We could not believe it, so we read the signal flags again. No question. The signal still meant scatter and proceed independently.

JULY 4, 1942
CONVOY PQ-17

The convoy held together through the July 4 torpedo plane attack. Chief Mate George Wilson foiled an attack by one or more submarines when he sighted a torpedo headed toward our bow. At the last minute he changed course, preventing the torpedo on its direct hit course from smashing into the *Samuel Chase* and exploding. It was the second miracle of the voyage.

The convoy sailed as far north as practical before the ships came in contact with the ice barrier just over the horizon, maybe six or eight miles at the most. If we sailed any closer, maneuvering the ship to avoid small bergs or growlers faced us. We progressed eastward at a slow 8 knots, when we entered a potentially critical area.

Although the crew on the *Samuel Chase* was not fully aware of the dangers, the crew on the bridge knew this was as close as we would get to North Cape, Norway. We were unaware that the German High Command had ordered their surface warships to gather at a particular anchorage near

North Cape, where they awaited Hitler's orders to attack our convoy. That order never came because Hitler had been informed that an aircraft carrier protected our convoy, and he was reluctant to risk his capital ships to a bombing attack.

The British Admiral knew the convoy was at its most vulnerable position. The observation planes told the Admiral that all the fighting ships of the German fleet left their respective berths in the Norwegian fjords. The admiral thought that surely the Germans would attack, and quickly. Because of this threat, the convoy needed to scatter just as quickly to frustrate the German attack. The German surface vessels never attacked.

JULY 5, 1942

We received a message informing us that the *Tirpitz* and *Prinz Eugen* were on their way to attack the convoy. We believed this was why we were told to scatter.

The Captain, Chief Mate Wilson, and Second Mate Raley held a conference and decided to try and make Matochkin Strait, the middle of the Novaya Zemlya archipelago. The archipelago, 600 miles north to south, is the eastern boundary of the Barents Sea. The Matochkin Strait that separates Severny and Yuzhny islands has a large bay without a city or defenses, just a scientific outpost of some sort, possibly meteorological.

It seemed unlikely that we could sail to that outpost without incident. My thoughts tumbled over each other, part memories, part anticipations. I remembered the torpedoed ship *Bellingham* as a vignette. Someone on board the *Bellingham* panicked and lowered an empty lifeboat down onto the sea before the stricken ship came to a stop. The boat falls unhooked. The sea painter, a long length of rope secured to a forward part of the ship, towed the boat. Unfortunately, the long painter towed the boat at least 50 feet away from the ship. Because the crew could not reach the boat, two rescue ships moved in and rescued the crew.

MORE PERILOUS TIMES

Our Chief Engineer followed the prescribed instructions to make all possible speed at maximum revolutions. We made 12.3 knots. That afternoon when I woke from a nap, I decided to visit the bridge. Because the weather was ideal, I used an outdoor ladder to reach the bridge deck. I looked around at the blue skies and sharp horizon and felt a light breeze. When I started up the ladder, the skies were clear. A moment later, dense fog enveloped the ship. I could not see the four-inch deck gun located on the stern. The mizzenmast, perhaps 80 feet away was a blur. Where? What? I heard the chilling sound of many aircraft engines. I knew by the sound that they flew very low overhead. Even though the enemy planes passed directly over us, they did not see us. As soon as the planes disappeared, the fog bank began to disburse and the blue sky returned. Amazed, I looked around me. I saw no clouds, no sign of fog. Nothing was in sight as far as the horizon.

I believe that the dense fog created the miracle of protection. The fog covered us for three or four minutes while the German squadron of planes flew low overhead. We kept a strict lookout and expected the worst.

This was the third miracle of the PQ-17 voyage. God was attentive to His promise to me.

The low flying planes proved that the German Air Force was on the hunt for our convoy, as the aircraft came from the direction of northern Norway. We did not have Allied air defenses. German submarines had been harassing the convoy. No doubt they would return to hunt individual ships.

We sighted a vessel astern overtaking us. At first, we watched with concern, until we identified it as the *Palomares*, one of the anti-aircraft vessels that accompanied the convoy. The vessel took about three hours to overtake us and was on the same course as ours. We signaled by blinker light to the *Palomares* and asked permission to accompany it. We received a not-so-polite brush off. "My speed is 14.3 knots. Suggest you make for Matochkin Strait." We were not to enjoy its protection. In three hours, it was hull down – well ahead of us.

We had been aware that all escorts making 15 knots or more were ordered to return to the U.K. Escorts making under 15 knots were ordered to independently continue on to port of destination. The converted heavily armed trawlers, corvettes, and two large anti-aircraft vessels could not make 15 knots.

The anti-aircraft ship did not brush us off because it disdained our plight. It ran under orders to proceed independently. The *Palomares* appeared to head towards Matochkin Strait, also our destination. However, we never saw the ship again.

We knew there were no Allied aircraft within many hundreds of miles because the airwaves were filled with distress calls from scattered ships once part of our convoy. The ships under attack were sinking. When would our turn come? We didn't have long to wait.

Our gunnery officer ran to the Captain and said, "One of my men has spotted something on the horizon. He thinks it is the conning tower of a German sub."

All eyes turned to that spot, about two points aft the starboard beam. Soon we verified that a German submarine had locked onto our sailing course. The submarine moved faster than our ship. We knew its strategy was to move ahead of us and then dive for the attack. In a few minutes, the sub came abeam of us. The gunnery officer asked permission from the Captain to take a shot at it with the four-inch deck gun. Because no one knew the range a discussion followed. The distance to the sub was only a guess of eight miles. The shot followed the guess. We tried to see the splash as the shell struck the water. Nothing happened. The submarine continued to gain on us until it was broad on the bow. Then it disappeared.

What could we do?

Even though I was not on watch, I wandered around the bridge deck and watched with my crew mates. The Chief Mate called me into the chart room as I walked by and said, "The Captain has decided to abandon ship." I stared at him, mute. He continued. "The Captain says he has seen too many ships lose lifeboats on the side, where the torpedo hits, and there is not room for all of us on the two remaining boats." I couldn't think. Chief Mate Wilson continued. "The gunnery officer has refused to leave the ship, but the gun crew will go with us."

Turmoil ruled my thoughts. I did not want to go. However, I was in charge of one of the lifeboats. There seemed no purpose in not obeying. In fact, I had to obey. The gunnery officer who refused to leave the ship must answer to the U.S. Navy. Perhaps he felt he had to stay.

I had to obey the Captain. I could not stay.

Captain Martin stopped the ship with an astern bell. When the ship was dead in the water, he put the bridge to engine room telegraph on Stop. He ordered the engine room crew to kill the boiler fires and come up on deck to the lifeboats.

All four lifeboats were lashed in a swing-out position to facilitate a quick lowering as soon as the turn buckles were released. A kick at the pelican hooks released the lashings, and the boats swung free. Chief Mate George Wilson, who was in charge of the process, received a gesture from the Captain, and Mr. Wilson ordered us into the lifeboats. Everyone mustered at their boat wearing their life preservers. One seaman manned the winch brake on each boat. As the boats lowered, we remembered to screw on the plug to the drain. It was like a drill. The fact is that this part of the event turned out to be just that, a drill. No one brought anything extra such as food, cigarettes, blankets, or extra cloth. No one panicked.

We did what we had to do – abandon ship – and we accomplished it in an orderly fashion.

As soon as the boats touched the water, the remaining crew still on deck clambered down rope ladders into their respective boats. The boat crew unhooked the boat falls, setting us adrift. The men sitting on the thwarts took up the oars and rowed the boat away from the ship.

The weather was ideal – calm and clear. All the life boats went astern of the ship. We sat in the boats, rested, and waited. Waiting for what?

Later, the Chief Mate and Second Mate Raley said they saw the periscope of the submarine. I did not see it, and no one pointed to the periscope when it broke the surface of the sea nor mentioned it or confirmed it. After we sat in the life boats for about two hours, the Captain ordered us back to the ship.

We rowed back to the ship. I've never seen an entire crew so eager to work fast and efficiently with few words and orders to get us back aboard the ship. Once we arrived at the ship's side, everyone on board the life boats knew what to do next. After the boats were hoisted and secured, the engine room crew lit the fires, the deck watch resumed, and the gun crew went on lookout in the gun tubs. The crew returned to normal duties, almost as if the incident never happened. Later, I wondered if this was a miracle. I remembered the promise God made to me, "*You shall never be on a ship sunk by enemy action.*" (April 29, 1942.)

I asked myself, why wasn't the *Samuel Chase* sunk? My answer: Because our Lord said so, and He cannot lie (Hebrew 6:19). That was good enough for me. However, the submarine commander had to report a logical reason to his superiors in Germany. Why didn't you attack a ship when it sat dead in the water? I consider this to be the fourth miracle of the PQ-17 voyage.

I remembered a story I heard during World War I, purported to be true.

A resourceful captain of a well-armed merchant ship was under attack, much as the *Samuel Chase* was attacked. That Captain stopped his ship and ordered the boats away. A small number of crew members manned the boats. When the sub surfaced to attack, the dead-in-the-water ship opened fire and sank the sub.

In our situation, we were at the German sub's mercy. My guess was that the sub commander was suspicious of our intent, possibly sensing a trap; therefore, he broke off the attack.

In both cases, the ships stopped and launched four lifeboats. In one case, it was a deadly trap. In our case we were under special protection.

I thought that it was as if the Lord spoke these words: "See? My promises hold true. First, a German aircraft squadron flew low over your ship and I turned the torpedo from the aircraft to miss the ship. Then the torpedo shot from the submarine headed for the 50 tons of dynamite stored in your #1 hold and failed to explode. I protected your ship from attack by hiding you in a fog bank, and just now I caused the enemy sub commander to abort his close in attack." The Lord did not speak these words, but I thought His actions fulfilled them. Four miracles were covered in this mystical statement.

JULY 6, 1942

Our mindset was cautious as the *Samuel Chase* crept into the large bay of Matochkin Strait. We had no detailed chart for this place. There was no port or city and no reason for a commercial ship to enter, except for the exigencies of war. Our general chart showed no outstanding hazards. We were glad to see a half a dozen ships from our Convoy PQ-17 already anchored in the bay. Their presence built our confidence and showed us that this was a safe anchorage. We anchored and wondered what would happen next. We did not have long to wait. If we had hoped for a respite, there was no rest for the weary. A power boat came alongside and ordered us to form a convoy, move out as soon as possible, and head for the White Sea.

A nearby ship heaved up her anchor. Her anchor windlass strained noisily. Each link of the chain fit into its socket on the shaft of the windlass with a distinctive plunk. That ship led us out into the Barents Sea and turned south, bound for the White Sea. That same ship was our defacto commodore.

At first we all started off together with no problems, until our visibility decreased as a light fog increased; at the same time, we saw the ice field. We were stuck in the fog with zero visibility to escape the ice. Our ships were not ice breakers and our unprotected propellers were at risk. There was no practical solution except to wait. So we did, safe for the moment.

JULY 7, 1942
MATOCHKIN STRAIT TO MOLOTOVSK

As the fog began to lift, some cracks appeared in the ice that provided a way out of the ice field. As soon the fog lifted we proceeded through the open places in the ice field. We were not far from open water where our little convoy reformed.

Because of the excellent visibility, we were concerned that the German enemy would find us. Our radio operator reported that distress calls from sinking ships and ships under attack filled the airwaves. These calls came from the Barents Sea. We were in the eastern part. It was too much to expect that the Germans wouldn't hunt down all ships still afloat, especially if they knew that all surviving vessels had to make for the White Sea entrance.

Sure enough, the Germans found us.

We had not experienced attacks by dive bombers yet, but here they were. The first attack plane dropped bombs from a height of perhaps 1,000 - 1,200 feet. They dropped three bombs in a cluster. The trajectory of the bombs appeared that they would hit us directly amidships, right down our smokestack.

When the attack came, Chief Mate George Wilson and I were on the starboard wing of the bridge. Because I felt certain the bombs would hit us, I stepped into the wheelhouse for shelter. I thought the four inch thick panels of a concrete composition might protect me, but the panels were designed to stop bullets and shrapnel, not bombs.

The horrific noise filled the air as all three bombs exploded in the water at the same time.

JULY 8, 1942
APPROACHING THE ENTRANCE TO THE WHITE SEA

When the bombs exploded, the *Samuel Chase* shuddered violently. The ship's steel plates rippled and bent. Loose objects flew into the air and crashed back down to the deck. The magnetic compasses jolted out of their gimbals. They came to rest, still on the frame of the gimbals but out of their sockets. We steamed ahead and waited for the next attack to come from more enemy planes circling overhead.

During these attacks, the gun crew manned and fired the four .50 caliber machine guns without apparent effect. The gunnery officer said these planes flew too high for .30 caliber machine guns, which I would man, to hit. So I stayed on the bridge instead of manning the guns.

The second plane dropped its cluster of three bombs on us. Again, the three bombs headed directly for our stack. This time I stayed on the bridge and watched the bombs fall all the way down. The bombs separated. One bomb fell in the water on one side of the ship. The other two bombs fell in the water on the other side of the ship. I believed I watched a miracle. How or why the bombs separated, I could not comprehend. We were attacked again. Three more times, the planes flying over our ship dropped bombs. All the bombs hit the water and narrowly missed our ship.

Suddenly, all was quiet and calm. The planes disappeared as quickly as they appeared.

Between attacks on our ship, we saw a column of dark smoke rise from a ship ahead. We were not the only ship under attack. Unfortunately, at least one ship had been hit.

The gun crew's Petty Officer suggested we try to utilize the guns of the Sherman battle tanks we had on deck. With the Captain's permission, and the Gunnery Officer's supervision, we tried to use the tanks until we discovered we had to start the tank's engine, and the tanks had no fuel. We had only a few gallons for our one motorized lifeboat. Without fuel for the tanks, the question was moot regarding the location of the ammunition for the tanks' guns.

All the bomb clusters straddled our ship. That was the fifth PQ-17 miracle.

JULY 8-9, 1942
ELEVEN SHIPS SURVIVE AND ENTER THE WHITE SEA

In the midst of the dive bombers' attacks, the bridge telephone rang. The engineer on watch called with dismaying news. One of the steam lines broke and could not be bypassed. Much to our consternation and peril, the ship slowed, leaving us more vulnerable. We sat on the water, a crippled ship and a perfect target.

However, the engineers were equal to this emergency. After a time that seemed like an eternity, the engineers were able to repair the problem and resume the ship's full speed.

When the attack was over – no planes in sight – we were exhausted. Those that could turn in did. Even though I was exhausted, I had to stand watch. So once again, the helmsman and I stood alone on the bridge.

This was normal. The gun crew and navy signalman were on the flying bridge, which was the deck above. I was so tired that I hung onto the wind dodger on the bridge wing. Then I tried sitting on the end of the bridge wing where a horizontal steel plate housed the starboard running light. Too fatigued and fighting sleep, I had to keep moving.

Suddenly, I saw an aircraft approaching from the south. The adrenalin rush shocked me and I was alert and wide awake. I looked through my binoculars and could not believe what I saw. Were we maybe expecting a fighter escort? No way. It was an old biplane with large wings. It was so slow it seemed to float along. What possible reason could it have to be here? It did not stay long.

My guess was it counted the ships to alert the port authorities who had to plan berthing and cargo operations.

JULY 10, 1942
THE NEW SECRET PORT OF MOLOTOVSK

We steamed inside the entrance to the White Sea and anticipated arrival at the big city of Archangel.

But it was not to be for us. Our ship received orders that a pilot would board us at a certain time. Captain Martin appeared on the bridge. I had not seen him since our ship was stuck in the ice field. He had not been well for some days. Indeed, before the convoy had been ordered to scatter by the British Admiralty, a boat from one of the two rescue ships came alongside our ship at sea and took our Captain to see a doctor on the rescue ship. Our Chief Mate and the rescue ship's doctor were unable to diagnose Captain Martin's problem. Captain Martin continued to monitor the Russian pilot's anchoring of our ship in an alcove surrounded by a marshy area. The pilot declared this was a secret port named after the communist Foreign Minister Molotov. Our ship swung on its anchor and grounded on a mud bank. The tide soon floated us off.

During our run to the White Sea, some of the escort vessels that were unable to make 15 knots and did not return to England found us in the ice field and helped some of the ships to get out of the ice. Other escorts rescued crews in lifeboats after their ships had been sunk by the dive bombers. While at our anchorage, a Russian tug came alongside us with the crew who survived the sinking of the American freighter *Hoosier* and had been picked up by a rescue ship. The crew came aboard to live with us.

JULY 12-31
THIS IS RUSSIA?

For a few days, the crew of the SS *Hoosier* stayed with us while the authorities sorted out the survivor problem. When I was on watch, the Chief Mate of the *Hoosier* camped out on my long leather settee and slept on my bunk. Two crews on one ship was at least a potential problem. But no! The *Hoosier* gang was grateful. And they knew that they were on their way home. Also, they were on a brand new ship – the *Hoosier* being, I think, a relic of World War I.

While our ship was at anchor in Molotovsk, I had a quick sentimental reunion with a school ship cadet. When I was on the school ship USS *Nantucket*, two upper classmen were identical twins, A.T. Wilder and A.L. Wilder. A.T. had a tiny scar near his left eye so I could tell them apart if I could get close enough. Few could I.D. them.

A tug came alongside our ship. I was the mate on watch and went to the rail to see who was coming aboard. There was a man standing on the tug's foredeck. He looked familiar. We looked into each other's eyes. Happy surprise! It was one of the Wilder brothers. He wasn't close enough for me to tell which one. He said he was OK and then the tug pulled away. The Wilders were well liked. I was glad to know this one was safe.

We were glad to dock our ship. The dock was new. One large traveling crane would augment our ship's gear. We saw a few nondescript buildings. This was it?

It wasn't much but it had to do. We had delivered a cargo of war supplies. If it had been peacetime, Molotovsk would have been a huge disappointment. But we had accomplished our goal. The voyage had succeeded in spite of many attacks and the constant threat of attacks.

As soon as we docked, and the main engine was secured, the Chief Engineer took a detailed survey of his engine room. His findings impelled him to rush to the officers' mess, where the Captain was eating lunch. I witnessed the Chief's report because I had just come off watch and was eating lunch with the Captain. The Chief was in the depths of despair. "We'll never make it home, never," he said to Captain Martin. "Every shaft bearing is cracked except one. It will never hold together." The Chief was sweaty and dirty, which served to raise his report to the crisis level. The concussion of repeated near misses of 18 or more bombs was to blame for the damage.

After the Chief calmed down a little, he and the Captain launched into an intense discussion about repairs. The Captain said he would speak to the agent and the commissars. The Chief agreed. But it was to no avail. There were no repair facilities. Except for the nearby village, it was a wilderness area. Repairs were up to the Chief. I have no idea what he did, if anything. Yet we made it home in extreme conditions of weather. I considered this the sixth miracle of the voyage. We made it to a New York shipyard, where new pedestal bearings were installed.

The Lord's promise was fulfilled. Our ship was spared. The bearings holding was the last of seven miracles carried out on the *Samuel Chase* during the voyage of convoy PQ-17.

JULY-AUGUST, 1942
THE SECRET PORT OF MOLOTOVSK, RUSSIA

The secret port of Molotovsk had been dug out of the modest delta system of a small river. The new dock was well built.

The port officials (commissars) warned us to black out the ship at night, and they told us there would be no night cargo work. It was like a prediction. As soon as the darkness of the short night fell, a flight of enemy bombers flew overhead in the direction of Archangel. It was a scary reminder that the war was going on. The 10 ships that arrived at this port had just received a "greeting."

The Commissars also informed us that we would have interpreters on board during cargo operations and that they would not be allowed into the crews' living spaces.

When the cargo operation started, the first interpreter came aboard. Wow! We had not seen a pretty girl since Philadelphia, maybe six weeks ago. There were four young ladies assigned to our ship. Usually only one was on duty at any given time. They were smart, always in control, spoke excellent English, and were well dressed. They wore dresses and apparently were chosen for their good looks! They could have been models! OK, so we had been at sea for a long time. They were out of bounds for us, and they let us know it. During the 50+ days we were in Molotovsk, I saw an interpreter only come into the crew quarters once. And she came into my room! I was the mate on watch and had gone into my room to write the logbook. I heard her run along the alleyway (corridor) and stop. She read the sign *3rd Officer* over my doorway, and walked through the open door and into my room. She spoke quickly. "There's been an accident – oh!" she said, staring into my open clothes locker, "The government gives you many clothes." Then she caught herself and said, "A sling broke in #3 hatch, if you want to make a report."

I answered, "The government gave us all a mackinaw, the blue one. All the other clothes I bought with my own money." I could tell from the expression on her face she didn't believe me. It was outside her lifestyle. Then we hurried outside.

Other than these pretty women interpreters, there wasn't much to endear us to Russia or to Communism. There was a period of time when swarms of mosquitoes made our lives miserable. Our only defense was to cover all exposed skin. We made Foreign Legionnaire hats out of face towels. Now only part of our bare faces hung out as enticement to the swarms of mosquitoes that responded quickly to any exposed flesh. Our vigorous arm swatting helped part a way through the swarms. Fortunately, the mosquito season lasted only about two weeks. When it was over, our working conditions improved drastically and allowed us free movement without swatting.

Despite the misery of mosquito swarms and the lack of essential helps for handling the cargo, such as forklifts, conveyors, trucks, pallets and the like, cargo operations continued –slowly.

Much to our surprise, the large heavy lift crane was used to load trucks with our cargo after it had been discharged onto the dock. One power conveyor loaded small items onto trucks. Our five hatches discharging cargo overwhelmed limited facilities for moving cargo to its ultimate destination.

The big dock crane was a problem. Its huge counterweight swung over our boat deck and came close to hitting our lifeboats and their davits. Even though we protested many times, the crane operator continued his reckless operation. Our captain went to the .30 caliber machine gun mounted on the flying bridge, stripped off the cover and pointed the gun at the crane operator. This got his attention and he modified his operation so that our lifeboats were safe. No one mentioned the lack of a magazine loaded on the gun.

The village near us had only a few hundred people, not counting political prisoners who were our longshoremen. There was no infrastructure, no paved road, no repair facilities, and limited utilities. The government operated the new wharf and appeared to have little to do with the local population. The commissars, the interpreters, and maybe the hatch bosses were all imported to service this port.

Our new Liberty ship intrigued the Russian hierarchy Commissars. They sent marine architects to examine it and ask questions. They seemed to concentrate on the all welded seams without rivets; they were also interested that major components were constructed at some distant factory, that the shipyard was an assembly yard, and that it only took a few weeks to turn out a ship. How could these ships be appearing by the dozens soon after we got into the war?

We answered their questions as best we could. Later we wondered why they didn't take pictures or draw diagrams. The possible answer was that plans were obtained through inter-government channels.

At long last the end of cargo discharge was near. Part of my job was to examine every compartment in all five holds to be sure every piece of cargo was gone.

SEPTEMBER 1942
GOODBYE MOLOTOVSK

In an escape hatch, I found a bag of flour weighing over 100 pounds. Instead of reporting it to the Chief Mate, I found the interpreter, who had a longshoreman carry it ashore.

I made a wrong decision that backfired my initiative. The Chief Mate went to find the bag of flour he had pulled out of the cargo early that morning. It wasn't there. He found me and listened to my story. Then he told me the rest of the story. The Chief Steward informed the Captain we were low on flour. The Captain went to the Commissars and requested flour. Denied. So our Chief Mate appropriated one bag. So far, so good. Except they forgot to inform me, the searcher. The irony was that in November 1940 on the SS *Nebraskan*, Chief Mate George Wilson trained me as a cadet to search holds in every port for carry-over. As a result, the Chief Mate, the Chief Steward, and the Captain were disgusted and angry with me.

Our orders were to join the 10 ship convoy as it passed our port northbound out to the Barents Sea.

We loaded 1,500 tons of an unidentified ore for ballast. We closed hatches and secured for sea. Even the four Communist sympathizers were glad to be homeward bound.

SEPTEMBER 1942
HOMEWARD BOUND

REFLECTIONS OF MOLOTOVSK AND THE "SOCIABILITY" OF SOCIALIST COMMUNISM

We expected German submarines to be waiting for us near the entrance of the White Sea. They were not there. Perhaps an attack there was too obvious, making the subs vulnerable.

Somewhere soon – they would pick the time and place to attack.

Meanwhile, we had time to compare notes on events in Molotovsk. It had become evident early on that all Russians had been given strict instructions not to talk with those capitalistic Americans unless it was connected with work.

I struck up a friendship with the hatch boss at #2 hatch. He spoke fluent English and mentioned relatives in one of the Scandinavian countries.

He said, after we had been talking about five minutes, "I cannot talk with you for very long. I will be reported." In our brief conversations, he never spoke against Communism.

During a snow squall at sea, Chief Mate George Wilson told of one of the seamen on his watch to walk up the fore deck and stand lookout. The seaman was dressed in shirt sleeves. The Chief Mate called him on the bow telephone where the lookout stands and asked him where his heavy mackinaw was that had been issued to him. The seaman said, "I gave it away to someone who needed it a lot more than I did."

The Chief Mate then instructed him to borrow one from a shipmate. That worked.

The pretty college girls who were our interpreters were a case in point. They never came into the crew quarters or mess rooms. When cargo work was finished for the day, they went ashore. The girl who rushed into my room to report an accident was so shocked at the sight of all my wardrobe in the open closet that it became more important to her than reporting the accident, but only for a few seconds. It wasn't a chink in the iron curtain; it was more like a peek through a knothole. Every item of clothing that I could hang on hangers was there – shirts, trousers, jackets, oilskins, and shore going clothes. Drawer space was limited. It was easier to hang than to fold.

The one obvious thing we did not talk much about with the Russians was the lack of infrastructure. The one road into the village was a two rut lane. We did talk about that. There was a steel bridge that spanned the river a mile upstream, but I never saw any traffic on it. The river under the bridge never had traffic either.

The port officials often asked our advice about how to improve their operation, but they never gave us information that might help us to help them, like tonnage reports or man-hours per compartment.

Our convoy of 11 freighters with its escort vessels progressed northward then westward, expecting attack at any time.

Captain Martin had not been feeling well for many weeks and stayed in his quarters nearly all the time. After the convoy cleared the White Sea entrance, he appeared on the bridge one morning during my watch. I was trying to take a sun sight with my sextant amid fast moving clouds called scud.

Captain Martin watched for patches of blue sky and said, "Here comes one. Take it now." He wasn't helping. He was too much of an annoyance. Finally, he took to watching three goony birds on the surface of the sea that were fishing in front of our bow wave. When the bow wave got close, they flew ahead and settled down again. The Captain and I stood on the port wing of the bridge. I had my sextant in hand. Both of us watched the goony birds. Just then, a bow wave approached. The first goony dove to the sound of "plop," then the second bird dove – another "plop," also the third. I looked at the Captain. He had performed the sound effects.

What do professional seamen do at sea for amusement? Don't ask.

One never knows what a new morning will bring – something routine? Two eggs, bacon, toast, coffee, a cigarette; then up the ladders to the wheel house, two steps at a time, to see a glum Chief Mate. "Take a look around," he said. I counted but could not get to 11. "We lost two ships last night to sub attacks," he grieved.

Maybe the ships lagged. Hopefully, the escorts rescued survivors.

The German attackers had picked their time and place successfully. Our exit route from the Barents Sea had no escape choices.

SEPTEMBER 1942
THE GREAT STORM THAT PROTECTED US

Worsening weather gave us some protection. As we turned south near Bear Island, the winds grew stronger. The waves built higher, coming from the north and driving us south. Our ships rode high in the water, allowing our propeller to turn partly out of the water. A large sea lifted the stern high and the propeller came out of the water, spun faster, and shook the ship with a fierce vibration. An engineer dampened the worst of the shaking most of the time. The ship's vibrations tested Chief Engineer Seel's repairs on the cracked bearings.

The bright moonlight filtered down through the fast moving clouds and spotlighted the 440 foot ships on huge seas that were 1,300 feet long.

I intently watched a series of tableaux. The moonlight spotlighted a ship as a huge sea lifted the ship's stern out of the water, its great propeller spinning in the air. The huge sea progressed the length of the vessel, from stern to bow, almost lifting the stem, almost submerging the stern. Then the ship wallowed in the trough, awaiting the next wave.

The wind, clouds, ship and seas all moved south together; the wind maybe 60 mph and the clouds nearly as fast, the seas maybe 25 to 30 mph. The nine ship convoy presented a dramatic spectacle that lasted all night and the next day, 24 hours or more.

The uneven foaming sea between crests caused the ships to roll 5-10° or more at times. The safety factor was gratifying because no subs could be effective in this. The closer we got to home, the safer we felt – a comforting delusion. Yet north of Iceland and into the Barents Sea, the Germans were in control. South of Iceland, the Germans were having an increasingly difficult time.

Our nine ships made it to Northern Ireland safely. The *Samuel Chase* was assigned to a North Atlantic homeward bound convoy.

I found it incredible that the *Samuel Chase* survived her harrowing maiden voyage to Russia. Our 36 ship convoy not only attempted to steam through seas controlled by the Germans, but under skies that had no allied air defenses. As a consequence, the Germans sank 22 merchant ships loaded with war cargo. Eleven ships delivered their cargo, and two ships were unaccounted for. Homeward bound, three more ships were lost. The *Chase* was one of eight survivors.

Now it was October 1942 in New York harbor. The ship was so damaged by near misses that several weeks were needed in the shipyard to repair cracked shaft bearings, replace hastily repaired steam lines, and a host of other needs – including better armament.

Captain Martin was diagnosed too late with appendicitis and died on the operating table. Chief Mate George Wilson was promoted to Master. I, the Third Mate, was promoted to Second Mate.

AN ITINERARY

THE MAIDEN VOYAGE OF THE NEW LIBERTY SHIP SS *SAMUEL CHASE*, BUILT AT FAIRFIELD SHIPYARD, BALTIMORE, MD ON APRIL 11, 1942. COMPLETED VESSEL TURNED OVER TO AMERICAN-HAWAIIAN S.S. CO. TO OPERATE.

Apr 14	Began loading cargo.
Apr 17	Crew signed on.
Apr 22	Completed loading.
Apr 22	In harbor, swing ship with aid of tug to adjust magnetic compasses.
Apr 22	Degaussing range procedure.
Apr 23	Hampton Roads, load ammo for ships' guns.
Apr 24	Anchored awaiting daylight.
Apr 25	Depart Cape Henry, Arrive Delaware River.
Apr 26	Depart Delaware River anchorage. Arrive New York.
Apr 27	Depart NY through Hell Gate Long Island Sound.
Apr 27	Arrive Buzzards Bay, Await tide.
Apr 28	Transit Cape Code Canal and depart.
Apr 29	Arrive Halifax. Anchor in Bedford Basin.
May 7	Depart Halifax in convoy for U.K.
May 22	Arrive Clyde Pilot Station (Glasgow).
May 26	Depart Clyde Pilot Station for Reykjavik, Iceland.
Jun 1	Arrive Reykjavik, Iceland anchorage.
Jun 27	Depart Reykjavik in convoy bound north.
Jul 4	German torpedo planes attack convoy.
Jul 4	FIRST MIRACLE – aircraft torpedo aimed at us, swerves and misses.
Jul 4	SECOND MIRACLE -Submarine torpedo converges on our bow and fails to explode.
Jul 5	Convoy scattered - British Admiralty – Enemy surface vessels threaten.
Jul 5	THIRD MIRACLE - Fog bank hides ship in ideal weather as German planes fly over.
Jul 5	FOURTH MIRACLE – German submarine aborts close in attack.
Jul 6	Anchor in shelter of Matochkin Strait.
Jul 7	Depart Matochkin Strait in convoy.
Jul 9	Detention eight hours, caught in field ice.

Jul 10	FIFTH MIRACLE – Dive bombers attack. Many (at least 18) near misses. Concussion damage to engine room. Repairs require two and one half hours.
Jul 11	Arrive MOLOTOVSK, White Sea, Russia. Anchor mouth of Durvina River.
Jul 12	Dock at Berth #1. Commence off load cargo.
Jul 28	Complete offloading, await loading berth.
Aug 6	Commence loading cargo.
Aug21	Complete loading, anchor, await convoy.
Sep 13	Depart MOLOTOVSK, in convoy.
Sep 19	SIXTH MIRACLE – Sub attacks at night, two ships sunk. We are spared again.
Sep 25	SEVENTH MIRACLE – HIGH SEAS. Ship hogs and sags through huge seas. Cracked bearings hold.
Sep 26	Arrive Loch Ewe, Glasgow, Scotland.
Oct 2	Depart Loch Ewe, North Atlantic crossing eight days rough, ten days moderate.
Oct 20	Arrival New York, anchor Bay Ridge.

ARMED GUARD ABOARD SS *SAMUEL CHASE*

NAME			RATE
SEXTON, John Edward (Lt j.g.)	USNR		
DONAGHUE, Robert Alexander	V-6	650-17-37	AS
DIXON, John James	V-6	650-16-99	AS
WOLF, Alfred	V-6	646-34-68	AS
DOYLE, Edward Thomas	V-6	650-17-30	AS
AIKEN, Tommy Charles	V-6	616-18-86	AS
ENFIELD, Pasco Buddy	V-6	616-14-05	AS
JENKINS, James Joseph	V-6	646-35-40	AS
LOFARO, Luke Ernest	V-6	646-35-46	AS
WOLFF, Robert Harold	0-1	406-39-22	GMS/c
HARRIS, Gilbert William	USN	337-33-91	RM3/c
JENSEN, Jess Lawrence	USN	386-05-11	SM (sca)

U.S. NAVY REPORT OF THE VOYAGE

SS *SAMUEL CHASE*

Molotovsk, U. S. S. R.,

July 14, 1942

From   Commanding Officer, Armed Guard Unit aboard S/S SAMUEL CHASE

To: Chief of Naval Operations.

Via: Assistant U. S. Naval Attaché, Archangel.

Subject: Report of the Voyage of the S/S SAMUEL CHASE Norfolk to Archangel, U.S.S.R.

1   I was assigned the S/S SAMUEL CHASE by Lieutenant Commander Curtin, the Port Director at Naval Operating Base, Norfolk, Virginia on April 23, and boarded her the same day. After receiving our final instructions on April 24 we sailed from Hampton Roads to Lynnhaven Roads where we anchored for the night. On April 25 we ran from Lynnhaven Roads to the Delaware River Breakwater where we again laid over for the night. On April 26 we ran from the Delaware River Breakwater to New York Harbor, and anchored over night. On April 27 we pulled up the East River, thru Hellgate to and into Long Island Sound, anchoring in Buzzard's Bay for the night. We passed through Cape Cod Canal on the morning of April 28 and sailed to Halifax arriving there on the evening of April 29. We lay at anchor in Halifax until May 7, when at 1200, in company with 56 merchant ships we set sail with the Clyde as our listed destination. The convoy was composed of eleven columns of ships, five ships to a column, and two rescue vessels. The escort consisted of two destroyers and four corvettes. We sailed without incident until Sunday May 17, when with 12 merchant ships and three escort vessels, we parted from the main convoy and headed for Iceland. However, on Monday May 18, we were told to change course again and join with the main convoy, which we did, catching up with them early on the morning of May 19. We sailed without further incident until Friday May 22 when we sailed up the Firth of Clyde and anchored in Loch Long. We remained in Loch Long until Tuesday May 26, when at 0015 in company with 22 merchant ships, and with four trawlers, we set sail for Loch Ewe, arriving at Loch Ewe the evening of May 27. On Thursday May 28, we sailed from Loch Ewe bound for Iceland, with approximately 20 merchant ships and destroyers and corvettes for escort. On Sunday May 31, the escort vessels picked up a submarine but whether or not the submarine was destroyed cannot be said as the escort vessels remained on the scene and were soon far astern. On Monday June 1, at 2100 we anchored in Hvalfjodur, Iceland, where we remained until Thursday June 27, when at 1600 we sailed with 39 other merchant vessels and more than 15 destroyers and corvettes. Murmansk was our destination. The course of the convoy was laid down to be as follows: Around the western and Northern side of Iceland to 19° W, there steer NE to 75° N, passing on the eastern side of Jan Moyon Island, then due East well past Bear Island, then head SE and finally South to the entrance to the White Sea. The speed of the convoy was to be 8 ½ knots.

2   Rounding the northwestern tip of Iceland the convoy, which was steaming in two columns, ran into heavy fog and also occasional ice floes. On Sunday, June 28, the S.S. *Richard Bland* sent out a message saying she was aground on the rocks. We later learned that the S.S. *Exford* damaged her bow in the ice and had to return to Iceland so that when the convoy formed up on

Monday June 29, we were 38 ships including three rescue vessels, nine columns abreast with four ships to a column and two rescue vessels making a fifth column. The original convoy number of the *Samuel Chase* was 93 (third ship in the 9th column) but we took position of 91, formerly the station of the *Richard Bland*. This placed us first ship in the starboard column of the convoy. We sailed without incident until Thursday, July 2 when the first German reconnaissance planes were sighted at approximately 1100. Our position was about 200 miles due West of Bear Island. The planes were Heinkels 115's torpedo reconnaissance and a Blohm and Voss reconnaissance. The Heinkels darted at the convoy on the flanks and drew fire but no attack was launched. During the entire day of June 2, the escort ships seemed particularly busy with submarines and twice on the starboard side of the convoy following the explosion of depth charges black water was seen to erupt. Later in the day our ship ran through an enormous oil slick and to all appearances these signs pointed to the destruction of three submarines, but there was no official information. The Blohm and Voss plane remained with the convoy until 0300 July 3, where we ran into heavy fog. During the day the weather cleared and a task force of four cruisers and two destroyers appeared on the port bow of the convoy. This included three British cruisers and the U.S.S. *Witchita* and two British destroyers. They moved across the convoy and were soon on the starboard bow of the convoy where they remained until they left us. The reconnaissance plane picked us up again at 1940 July 3, but we again ran into fog and lost it. The fog lifted at 0140 July 4 and the reconnaissance plane picked us up immediately. The sea was smooth there was no wind and a light fog was still present. A Heinkel 115 appeared and was seen at the rear of the convoy. The fog became thicker reducing visibility to 1000 yards and the Heinkel was lost. At 0345 she appeared out of the fog on the starboard flank of the convoy and released a torpedo which passed between the *Samuel Chase* and the S.S. *Carlton* (#92) and struck the S.S. *Christopher Newport* amidships. The plane was not heard until she was seen. All machine guns on the *Samuel Chase* opened fire and the range was so short that all guns hit but no effective damage was seen and the plane was lost in the fog. The *Christopher Newport* was #81 and was slightly behind station and received the torpedo at what appeared to be the engine room on the starboard side. The starboard life boats were gone and there was much damage to the bridge but at no time while she was in sight did she appear to be settling. The port life boats were put over and it was later learned that the crew was taken aboard the rescue ship *Analek*. Possibly she was sunk by gun fire but I cannot say this to be a fact. The fog again set in at 0700 but lifted in the afternoon. At 1700 the Blohm Voss appeared and at 1800 six Heinkel 115's and a Junkers 88 appeared. They made two complete swings from the starboard flank of the convoy to the port flank but never closed in. The ceiling was low, there was no fog on the water, and the sea was smooth. The JU 88 flew over the convoy hidden by the ceiling and when fired upon, released her bombs which did no damage. At 1900 the six Heinkels and the JU 88 disappeared. At approximately 1915 more than 25 Folke Wulke planes appeared on the starboard quarter of the convoy flying very low and made straight for us. They flew within 75 feet of the water and attacked the convoy from the rear and starboard side, releasing torpedoes, then banked, and left the scene immediately. From the *Samuel Chase* not more than 5 planes were seen to fly through the convoy, the majority banked away within 1000 yards.

Four ships were hit and fell astern of the convoy. One was identified as the *William Hooper*, the rest we could not identify. However, two of these four rejoined the convoy, two were left astern, and again I cannot say positively that these were sunk by gunfire. The *William Hooper* settled slightly at the stern but did not seem to be sinking. Three planes were seen to fall in the water, the crew from one plane being picked up were seen to fall in the water, the crew from one plane being picked up and placed aboard a former USS four stacker "Destroyer". The attack was over at 1930. At 2136 the convoy was ordered by the commodore to scatter and proceed to the port of destination. (Prior to this all ships in the convoy were told that their port of destination was Archangel.) The dead reckoning position of the *Samuel Chase* at 2136 July 4 was 76-12 N, 30 – 00 E. The cruiser-destroyer task force was evident during the entire attack but was approximately six miles away on our starboard bow. All the destroyers escorting the convoy headed south. The cruisers headed west. When these two forces joined the entire forced headed west and was soon lost to sight. When last seen, this force consisted of four cruisers and at least 9 destroyers included in this was the U.S.S. *Wainwright* and *Rowan*.

3.   The ships were to scatter according to the plan in Mersigs. The Blohm Voss remained over the convoy the entire time we were scattering and was with us until approximately 0300 July 5. The two anti anti-aircraft ships (which joined the convoy three days out of Hvalfjodur and the corvettes, sloops and trawlers, scattered with the merchant ships. All hands were on watch from this time on. The ship was steering 105° true, heading for Novaya Zemlya.

4.   On July 5 at 0500 a black dot was seen dead astern which by 0645 was identified as a German submarine. She was steaming on the surface and crossed to our starboard quarter and began to overhaul us on the starboard side. Then she disappeared from sight at 0800. A ship, which we presumed to be the *Daniel Morgan* was hull down on the horizon behind the submarine. She was seen to turn and head north. At 0830 dead reckoning position 75 – 44N 37 –00 E, the Captain ordered engines full astern and told all hands to get into the life boats. All boats were away from the ship by 0845 and they gathered and laid 600 yards from her. At 1100 the Captain and the Chief officer and the Engineers went aboard and got up steam, and at 1200, the boats were called back to the ship. At 1220 the ship was again underway steering 75 true, at 12 knots, and immediately we picked up speed, the submarine reappeared dead astern. No attack was made on the ship while the boats were in the water.

5.   The visibility was excellent, no wind, smooth sea, no clouds. The submarine again hauled to our starboard side and could be seen from the crow's nest to be paralleling our course, running on the surface. About 1400 a JU 88 bomber was seen dead astern flying high and headed north west. At that instant a fog bank appeared and we entered it and commenced zig zagging. The fog was in patches and for the next six hours we ran from fog patch to fog patch, with brilliant clear weather between, or ran through low hanging fog with a clear sky overhead. At one point in the fog a plane was heard passing our port side quite close. Machine gunners were instructed not to fire, least we reveal our position, and the plane was heard no more. At 2330 July 5 we sighted one of the A. A. ships accompanied by two corvettes. Evidently he had picked up a RDF transmission as the first thing he told us was to maintain silence. He then informed us that he was heading for any bay on the Coast of Novaya Zemlya at his utmost speed, as the *Tirpitz*, *Admiral Hipper* and six destroyers were steering a course 60° from North Cape at 22 knots. A few minutes later he told us he was heading for Matochkin Strait and advised us to do the same. To our question "Can we accompany you" he replied "My course is 150° my speed is 14 knots". As our best speed was a fraction over 12 knots he pulled ahead and was lost to sight in the early hours of July 6. We were steering 75° true when we met him but on his information we came to course 150° true and followed him. Our dead reckoning position when we changed course was 76 – 13 N, 46 – 05 E. During the afternoon of July 5, we listened in on 500 KC and heard numerous distress calls often two ships at the same time. We listened for just a short time, and then shut down, least we give away our position, but while we were receiving, the following ships were heard from:

BCR6 –*Earlston* (BR) submarine attack – 76-35N 33-41E

No call ltrs – 2 submarines attacking ship – 75-04N 37-50E

No call letters – ship torpedoed – 75-05N 38-02E

WSP0 – attacked by seven planes – 74-43N 34-20E

SAVED BY A SERIES OF MIRACLES

SS *Washington* dive bombed – 76-40N 33-41E

SS *Daniel Morgan* – aircraft attack – 75-49N 43-00E

SS *Pan Kraft* – aircraft attack – 76-50N 38-00E

We laid down the course line of the German fleet on the chart and crossed this line at 0500 July 6. At 1315 July 6 we made a land fall on Novaly Zemlya due west of Matochkin Strait. At the same time we sighted three ships headed south along the coast. They provide to be the SS *Hoosier, El Capitan, Empire Tide*. We flashed to them, our information of the German fleet. The *Hoosier* and *El Capitan* followed us but the *Empire Tide* continued south. At this point a ship was sighted heading north. She proved to be the *Benjamin Harrison*, and she too, headed in after us. At 1600 a Blohm and Voss plane was sighted heading north. The *Empire Tide* made no attempt to follow us in. She was seen to head west and tried to hoist her balloon which broke away. Then she headed south and disappeared. A Free French-British corvette came out and led us into Matochkin Strait. There we found the two A.A. ships, the corvettes , and sloops and trawlers from the convoy, the SS *Ocean Freedom* and the rescue ship *Zamalek*. We anchored at 2100.

At 1750 July 7, we sailed from Matochkin, present were the *Hoosier, Ocean Freedom, Benjamin Harrison, El Capitan, Zamalek, Samuel Chase.* two AA ships and 8 sloops, trawlers and corvettes. Our course was plotted first for heading south along the coast, heading south west passing Kolroen thence to Cape Kanin and Iokanski. On July 8 the course was changed to take us south of Kolleuv thence to Cape Kanin. The run south along the coast was made in heavy fog and the *Benjamin Harrison* was lost. Whether she was torpedoed or went aground we do not know. At 1600 July 8 we encountered heavy ice. We were steering approximately due south at this point. We worked out way through and ran clear at 2100. However at 2350 we again ran into very heavy ice, and by steering NW we succeeded in breaking clear. At 0400 July 9 when we came out, we joined with the *Ocean Freedom*, two sloops and a trawler and headed west skirting the ice field. At 1430 we headed approximately SW and maintained that course until 2230 where we came to SSW heading for Iokanski.

Subject: Report of the voyage of the SS *Samuel Chase* Norfolk to Archangel

At 0300 July 10, we heard gunfire ahead in the distance and saw heavy smoke. The mirage effect was very extreme all during the day of July 10 so that we could not see real outlines of ships. We later, learned that this was the attack on the *Hoosier* and *El Capitan* in which both ships were lost all hands being saved. At 1100 July 10 we sighted a Russian reconnaissance plane, and almost immediately afterwards we sighted German planes. There were more than six over us and seemed to be JU 88s. They dive bombed us at first pulling out quite high and not coming close with the bombs. However, as the attack proceeded and they felt out the AA fire, they came in closer and their bombing was more accurate. At this point we were still with the *Ocean Freedom* two sloops and a trawler. We received not less than six "near misses" all within 60 yards of the ship. The effect of this was to snap all our steam lines stop off the engine cut off the auxiliaries so that the ship lay dead in the water *[sic]*. The compass was knocked from the binnacle and damaged and light damage done inside the ship. We received no direct hits and at 1145 the attack was over. The *Ocean Freedom* pulled ahead and the British sloop J-42 took us in tow and soon we had steam on the steering engine. By 1500 we had effected enough repairs to proceed under our own power. At this point two more sloops joined us as escort. At 1535 we were again attacked by dive bombers but the protective fire was better, the planes were kept higher, and no further damage was sustained, the attack ending at 1615. During the attack at noon, two planes were seen to fall into the sea, and one was seen on the horizon, fighting a fire. At

1800 we sighted ships ahead. From 1900 we had Russian planes over the convoy. At 0130 July 11, we joined up with the ship which consisted of the two AA ships, *Ocean Freedom*, *Zamalek* and sloops – corvettes, and were lead into the white sea by a Russian pilot boat which had met us in the forenoon of July 10. At 1130 we anchored at the entrance to Archangel Channel and a Russian pilot came on board and we proceeded to Molotovsk. We anchored outside to await high water and at 1900 the Captain and 51 officers and men from the SS *Hoosier*, including Ensign Blackwell and nine enlisted men, were transferred to the *Samuel Chase*. On Sunday July 12 we came alongside the dock at Molotovsk.

No casualties were sustained aboard and the gun crew and also the majority of the civilian crew must be complimented upon their splendid behavior.

S/John E. Sexton

Lieutenant (jg), U.S.N. R.

NOVEMBER 13, 1942 - APRIL 1, 1943: TO NORTH AFRICA

THE SECOND VOYAGE OF THE SS *SAMUEL CHASE*,
OUTWARD BOUND

At the beginning, the second voyage seemed like a refreshing breeze after our ship survived the horrific attacks and experienced the miraculous escapes during the first voyage to north Russia. Our rumored destination to the Mediterranean Sea conjured up much more pleasant thoughts than that rough cold trip to north Russia. Even so, our new cargo was not reassuring. Our ship's hold carried war goods of all kinds, including ammunition, vehicles, and thousands of five gallon cans of gasoline. Notable were some huge bombs stowed on a bed of sand in the bottom of hold #2.

Then again, we felt good about the renewed sea worthiness of our ship, because we had limped home challenged by cracked bearings on the propeller shaft, with the Chief Engineer declaring, "We'll never make it home, never!" Fortunately, he was wrong, and we did make it home.

The crew had succeeded, and we were the most fortunate of survivors because our ship, the SS *Samuel Chase*, was one of eight survivors of the original 36 ship Convoy PQ-17.

From a crew of 36, not including the U.S. Navy gun crew, only two men returned for the second voyage: the former Chief Mate, now Master George Wilson, and I, former Third Mate, now Second Mate. One other man named Rocky, a seaman who left the ship, returned for a visit. Rocky served on the *Chase* during the six-month voyage to north Russia. At the end of the voyage Rocky received pay in the amount of $1,700 – a large sum in those days. He spent all the money on a deserved celebration. Even though he was broke he said he would never, no never, sail on the *Chase* again. He was not looking to make money. Instead, Rocky stayed with his family and shared the happiness he felt about surviving the *Chase's* voyage. For this reason Rocky became like a ghost from the past for the two of us who returned to duty on the *Chase* – we'd rather forget Rocky. So long, Rocky.

We sailed from New York traveling 9 knots in a fast convoy. That was the plan. But the reality was if the vessels that could only make 10 knots fell behind for any reason, they did not have enough speed to catch up with the convoy. When they trailed behind, they became inviting targets for the enemy. From necessity, we maintained a speed of 8 to 8.5 knots. We stayed together in our convoy and enjoyed a relatively pleasant trip without losing any vessels. There were alarms followed by emergency turns. In the daytime, those of us on the bridge suspected the Commodore imposed practice maneuvers. Nighttime was scary. All ships were blacked out except the Commodore's red and green signal lights set in a vertical line. The nearest ships were vague black shapes. The scary part was trying to determine other ships' courses. Had they obeyed the Commodore's course change or not? If not, there was the risk of collision. The sound of depth charges would have given reason for the madness of blacked out ships changing course on a black night. There was none. Much later, we realized that we were probably being routed away from danger. No attacks on a convoy headed for a war theater was a victory.

We entered the Strait of Gibraltar without incident. Where were the German subs? We would soon find out.

We were ordered, along with a few other ships, to break off from the convoy and enter the port of Oran. I was on the watch below and made my way to the port wing of the bridge that was not in use at the moment. The purser joined me and as we admired the scenery, he struck up a conversation with me. "I worked for the Boston Globe, and I've been interested in getting war stories just for my own interest, but I have not had chance to talk to you." I opened my mouth to speak, but shock silenced me, when a cataclysmic explosion enveloped the ship ahead of us. The ship disappeared in a huge black cloud when its cargo of gasoline and bombs ignited. Bits of black debris floated down around us. We steamed through the water where the ship floated only moments ago. We saw small pieces of flotsam. There were only three survivors.

After the shock of witnessing a ship full of crew blow up and sink subsided, I went in search of my binoculars and found them in the wheelhouse and scanned the steep hills of the approaching shore. Clusters of people watched the ship disappear in a horrendous explosion. I hoped that such a horrific show would be a once in a lifetime experience.

DECEMBER 1942
ORAN, NORTH AFRICA

Purser Frank Robinson and I were the involuntary participants in the horror show that had just occurred. He had just asked me about my war experiences when one ship blew up close in front of us. I guess he felt he had a story, as he did not approach me again on this subject.

I was traumatized by the sure death of that ship's crew and the U.S. Navy gun crew aboard the Liberty Ship – 56 men. After the ship's sinking so near to us, less than two ship lengths away, instant therapy was forced on us. As our ship approached the dock, our crew had the job to tend mooring lines, run docking winches, get heaving lines ready, rig the gangway, and have the cargo gear ready for discharging cargo.

The first people up the gangway were the group of port officials. They checked the ship's documents and checked off each crew member against the crew list. Knowing from a distance what we witnessed close up, they treated us kindly and with sincere deference.

A strange incident occurred after docking. We heard a brief air raid warning. An unidentified aircraft circled the port and flew in an unusual pattern. Was it possibly an enemy observation plane? Nobody seemed to know, and we were never informed. Port intelligence was none of our business. There was a language barrier with natives, including longshoremen; however, they seemed to know how to handle war cargo, and they had the proper gear for it.

PORT OF ORAN, NORTH AFRICA
WE DROPPED OUR OWN BOMB ON OURSELVES

As we neared the end of discharging cargo, two accidents happened.

At #1 hatch, the last piece to be lifted out was a six-wheel army truck, said to weigh 5 tons. The truck was hoisted to the main deck level and then swung outboard, bending the cargo boom. Tested to hold 7 tons weight, the boom should have been more than adequate to hold the cargo. Chief Mate Higgs made a quick investigation. The native hatch boss pointed to a large crate in the body of the truck containing a heavy piece of machinery. The total weight exceeded boom capacity; this ended the investigation. We had an extra boom lying on deck. After the replacement, the bent boom looked just as pathetic on deck as it had looked in place.

The time had been set for the westbound convoy home. A few ships still had to finish offloading the cargo at several North African ports. Our ship was one. We still had cargo in #2 hatch, the largest hold in the ship. The remaining cargo consisted of 2,000 pound bombs. A dozen or more remained, strongly wedged on a floor of oak dunnage, which had been laid on a bed of sand.

The sand saved us when a 2,000 pound bomb fell from its sling to the bottom of the cargo hold, pierced the oak dunnage floor, and buried itself in the sand cushion. The dunnage floor was a mass of splintered lumber, resulting in a big delay while repairs were made.

WE MISS THE CONVOY

Each shattered piece of wood had to be dug out of the bed of sand, and then thrown into a canvas sling for discharge. Then the sand had to be shoveled away so that slings could be attached to the bomb. Actual danger was minimized as plugs had been screwed into the noses of all bombs. There were no detonators; however, we still carried the vision of the Liberty ship's horrendous explosion seared into our minds. There existed an unspoken presumption that all the hundreds of bombs and all of the thousands of cans of gasoline would ignite at the same instant.

It took several hours to clear away the mess in #2 hold plus finish the off-loading of the remaining bombs. During this time, a messenger came aboard and bluntly informed us that we had failed. "Failed," he said, "to be ready to join the convoy home. Your ship's name has been deleted from the convoy plan. In a day or two, another convoy will be organized bound for the U.K.," he continued. "Good luck." It was bad news.

Instead of going directly from Gibraltar to New York, we anticipated being part of a convoy bound for England. Once there we would become part of a North Atlantic westbound convoy.

The weather difference brought on discomforting thoughts. It's not unusual on a voyage from the United Kingdom to New York to encounter two or three gales.

NO CHOICE – THE LONG WAY HOME

A few days later, we were directed to join the United Kingdom bound convoy. The reluctant anticipation became reality. Another consideration even more discomforting than mere bad weather occupied our thoughts. We had heard and read about German submarine bases located on the coast of France. The submarines docked in huge concrete pens lay ready to go out and prowl for our ships. Were they still operational? We didn't know.

However, the convoy was not attacked. It stayed well off the coast of France. Maybe that route helped keep our ships out of harm's way. We felt gratified to reach the Irish Sea without incident.

The Port of Glasgow, Scotland had several substantial bays, salt-water arms of the sea, which spread out from Glasgow Harbor and vicinity. We were boarded by a pilot off Glasgow. He conned us into a long narrow arm of the sea called Loch Long where we anchored amid a dozen other ships already there and waited for a west bound convoy to New York.

The high land on both sides of Loch Long appeared to give us shelter from strong winds. This anchorage turned out to be false. The wind swept down the sides of the hills and blew with great force against the anchored ships.

On the first afternoon, everyone who could go ashore, went ashore. After awhile, I became aware that I was the only deck officer onboard the ship. The Captain had left early to "enter" the ship, which was important ship's business. Everyone else just needed time off the ship and took it. It was a long ride by water taxi to Glasgow, and it had been a breezy day so it was a rough boat ride as well. No one appeared to mind that though. The men's first importance was getting ashore. As it turned out, they all stayed ashore and found hotel rooms because the breezy day turned into a windy night. The wind whipped the water into foam-topped waves too high for any small craft to venture out. The ship began to tug hard at the anchor chain. There wasn't enough room in the narrow bay to let out more chain, so I alerted the Chief Engineer to our plight and asked for slow ahead on the engines. Good move. That night, five ships dragged anchor ashore. Daylight showed the five ships listed over on the beach with their sterns on the beach. We were OK.

The next day, an anxious Captain and Chief Mate returned to the ship. They expressed their appreciation that the ship was afloat and not aground, like the fate of some ships near us and some in other anchorages. I pointed to the quick response by Chief Engineer Mehetra. I didn't tell them how scared I was when the ship began to yaw to port and then to starboard at the first heavy gusts of strong wind.

Some shipmate said with intentional irony, "The authorities waited for stormy weather to schedule our departure." He could have been right. We departed northern Scotland in gusty winds. Outside the protection of land, the wind became a gale, whipping the sea into short but high waves. The chop was not good for ships that were nearly empty, causing them to ride high in the water. In fact, the ship began to pound right away. The bow lifted out of the water and slammed down hard as the wave moved beneath the vessel.

Just after midnight, I was on the 12:00-4:00 A.M. watch on the bridge. Captain Wilson was also on the bridge because of the newly formed convoy and the deteriorating weather. We couldn't change course or speed, except to keep our station in the convoy diagram. We felt the bow rise high on an unusually steep wave and hang in the air for about five seconds, and then it came down with a fearsome crash that reverberated through the empty ship.

A FALSE ALARM

Three or four minutes passed, when the Radio Operator stumbled into the blacked out wheelhouse. In a panicky voice he blurted out, "I sent out an S.O.S. but I need a position."

Captain Wilson was quick to answer, "Cancel the message and get off the air."

"You mean we're not sinking?" Sparks cried. Later, Sparks explained that the bow's shattering crash woke him from a sound sleep. He was sure a torpedo had hit and we were sinking.

Storms were the norm in the North Atlantic Ocean's winter and something to be endured. Progress in miles per day was reduced sometimes by half, from 200 miles per day to 100, more or less. The fast moving storms blew to the east. Our ship steamed west. It was misery holding on while I stood watch.

During the night, the convoy sailed in mid-ocean when the Germans attacked and hit the outer column. Our ship sailed in the second column. Three ships, half of the outer column, sank. The second night, the enemy sank the remainder of the ships in the first column.

AN END TO DANGER – A NEW BEGINNING

Our ship went from the second column to the first and outer column. A strong feeling swept through the men on our ship. Were we next? A helmsman came to the bridge and relieved the helmsman on the wheel. The second helmsman was on the verge of panicking. When those of us on the bridge reassured him, he calmed down enough to concentrate on the compass course, and the ship's wheel.

Third Mate Bob Werner had a curious reaction to the danger. He said, "I have a date with my girl and I don't want to miss that." She was a Rockette, and lovely. Once, he took me back stage to meet her. WOW, I thought.

Bob made that one trip and quit. I could not blame him.

IT COULD NOT HAPPEN IN NEW YORK BUT IT DID

It was early spring of 1943 when the *Chase* experienced a rough trip home on its voyage from the United Kingdom across the North Atlantic. It seemed like this empty freighter bounced from wave crest to wave crest all the way. Finally, we reached New York's Ambrose Light Vessel and the pilot boat nearby. Our spirits were dampened by the orders to go to anchorage rather than to a dock.

In New York harbor, there was a good water taxi service. Once again, everyone that could go ashore went ashore. Once again, I was the only deck officer left on board. This was New York, not Loch Long where the windstorm drove five anchored ships ashore one night. Dragging anchor would not happen in good old New York, would it? Oh, no?

On a beautiful sunny afternoon, I lolled around the wheelhouse and chartroom, watched the passing ships, and admired early spring scenery in the nearby park. I felt just a bit sorry for myself, because home was only 200 miles away. Our ship was anchored in Gravesend Bay, leaving plenty of room for one ship to swing on the tide which ran strong, as much as 5 knots at times. I thought of a small bit of work I could do in the wheelhouse and still keep an eye open on anchor watch.

A quick trip down the ladder, one deck, to my room, I gathered the writing material I wanted, and glanced out the porthole. Amazing – the scenery was going by – scenery going by – the anchor was dragging! A hot flush charged inside me. I felt fear, dread, and the threat of severe damage to rudder and propeller. I dashed out to the boat deck, slid down the steel straight ladder to the main deck, turned and sprinted up the main deck toward the bow, thinking of what I had to accomplish: lift the pawl from the anchor chain so it could run free, grab the iron bar, slide it into the brake socket, and loosen the brake. I needed to be careful not to slack too much chain, which would cause the ship to pick up speed. The chain must lead from the anchor along the bottom to the ship and not in a straight line to the ship. Horizontally, the fluke of the anchor would dig in and stick fast.

After slacking carefully a full shot of chain, the moving ship fetched up. The anchor held. I breathed a sigh of relief. I watched closely as the full force of the tide lessened. We were safe for a few hours. The flood tide would not be as strong as the ebb tide. The Hudson River current gave impetus to the ebb-tide.

In a cold sweat of relief, I returned to the wheelhouse thankful yet chastened. The lesson I learned was to keep a careful anchor watch on the strength of the tide.

The *Samuel Chase* paid off in New York on March 8, 1943. I had every intention of staying on. The next trip sounded interesting. The *Chase* would sail to Australia from New York going through the Panama Canal and then down the west coast of South America, through the Strait of Magellan, across the South Atlantic and the South Indian Ocean to Melbourne or some other port. The port destinations of this trip were secret.

When the new crew came on board, life on board took a turn for the worse. The deck crew was mostly inexperienced and the engine gang the same. Worst of all, the cooks were from cooking school. The quality of food served lessened. Mr. Higgs, the former Chief Mate, was paid off for family reasons. The new Chief Mate was a nice elderly man, who had not been to sea for 15 years. He depended on me to answer his many questions because our ship was new to him. I was willing to help him and did, but there were many more irritants aside from his questions. Some people came to the Chief Mate with their questions, but they often came to me instead of him. Someone from the office pointed out the new reduced requirements for raising marine licenses to the next grade. It was time for me to raise mine to Chief Mate.

As hundreds of new ships came into service, operating companies searched for crews. Our government helped with new schools. Becoming a crew member on one of these new ships became an option for those who felt threatened by the draft.

THE DAY THE BELL FELL

Then the bell fell. One shot of anchor chain is 15 fathoms or 90 feet. The bell was mounted on the bow near the anchor windlass. When the anchor was hoisted, the bell sounded as the marked shots of chain appeared. Four bells meant that four shots were still in the water as the fourth mark appeared. These bells were used in the old days before telephones.

The bell hung from a stand and bracket. A bolt and nut held it together. My guess was that the repetitious pounding of the bow had loosened the nut. When the bell fell, I wondered, was the bell a signal or was it just foolishness? All the very new greenhorns, the not so good food, and the long trip that could be monotonous and consume many months were the negatives. Out of all the negatives, raising my marine license was a positive. I ran up the ladder two steps at a time to the Captain's office and told him my plan.

A SAILOR SAYS FAREWELL

The Captain sighed and said, "I cannot keep you from raising your license. Write a short letter to Captain Bain requesting a relief for your job and the reasons, and I will deliver it to him this afternoon when I go to the office." Said and done on April 10, 1943.

I informed my parents that they would have me as a boarder for a month or six weeks, and it pleased them. With glad and thankful hearts, they welcomed me home, grateful for my safe return. (I did not tell them about the miracles and dangers.) At first opportunity, my mother suggested I check in with the rationing board and the draft board, which I did.

For the raise of grade to Chief Mate, I enrolled for two weeks in the school on Long Wharf in Boston. This exam was going to be much tougher than the ones for Third Mate and Second Mate.

I was officially on vacation, but it was necessary to keep the grindstone turning, sharpening and shaping my mind for what lay ahead. One thing I did not do was spend much time reflecting on the two trips of the *Samuel Chase*. The first was horrendous. The second was merely unpleasant in light of the running battles of the first voyage. The horrifying explosion of the nearby Liberty ship *Arthur Middleton* on the second voyage was a tragic event, never to be forgotten.

Part 4: 1943 to 1944 - SS *Pennsylvanian*

The SS *Pennsylvanian*, a venerable vessel and a veteran of World War I, completed two trips in May 1943 through the dangerous waters of the South Atlantic Ocean and the Caribbean Sea. The ship, built in 1913, looked like it had come out of a Glencannon series of stories. It had an upright pipe smokestack, a straight stem bow, and a flush main deck, which meant that the main deck was almost a direct horizontal line from stem to stern. The radio shack, perched on the after end of the boat deck, seemed to me a designer's afterthought upon considering the *Titanic* disaster. What little gracefulness it boasted showed in the slight downward curvature of the deck line. It may seem disrespectful, but its straight up style reminded me of the style of a Model T Ford. Another similarity with Glencannon was with the personnel. Both our ship's caring veterans, the Chief Mate and the Chief Engineer, were wise old-timers at the same time profane and worldly wise. No one doubted Captain Vaux's ability to command. He was a Christian and in control. I came into this environment, a new Second Mate and a youngster of 22, but I had already been through the worst of the war. Knowing that I was war seasoned, Chief Mate Taggart and Chief Engineer Matheson accepted me as the new Second Mate.

When I joined this old vessel on May 11, 1943 as Second Mate, Captain E.B. Vaux was an energetic man with a cheerful disposition. He was also a Christian who voiced his strong opinions and remarked concerning life at sea, "You can survive without sex." At some period in his career, he had been an assistant to Captain Pettigrew, the company's New York American-Hawaiian Port Captain. The men who dared to make fun of Captain Vaux behind his back cupped their hands to their mouths and yelled, "Call Captain Pettigrew right away." In reality, this happened often as Captain Vaux worked the ships in port, and Captain Pettigrew stayed in the office at 90 Broad Street in New York City.

Chief Mate was Tom Taggart, a strong good looking man in his forties who about five years previously had married a young girl. When he went ashore, usually the first night in port, he had learned the hard way to be discreet when he needed to satisfy his need for alcoholic beverage. While at sea, he introduced me to the habit of having a quick "short" before supper. He provided the whiskey. It was a habit that I couldn't latch onto. I hated the taste of beer and stronger drink. When I drank the whiskey, I felt an unpleasant buzz on my empty stomach. Tom Taggart was very capable. He should have been a Master. However, I believe that his alcoholism held him back from receiving promotion.

The Chief Engineer, a veteran company man approaching retirement, usually wore greasy clothes and carried a wrench in his hands or visibly in his pocket. He served the ship and its owners well. One day while in port, the Chief went to the rail near the gangway for a breath of fresh air. A visitor came aboard and said to him. "Are you a wiper?" The Chief did not mind. The drastic downgrading didn't bother him. A wiper was usually a beginner, who kept the engine room clean. He wipes the oil and grease from the steel floor plates, handrails and ladders, hence the name wiper.

The senior officers were veterans of American Hawaiian SS Company. My record of service covered two years and seven months, including the two miraculous, eventful trips on the *Samuel*

Chase. In addition, I served briefly on eight ships. Seven of them were the aging freighters of the company's intercoastal fleets. I was familiar with the ships that worked east coast ports north of Norfolk. Other fleets from the same company worked ports along the east coast south of Norfolk. All ships visited U.S. West Coast ports.

When I joined the *Pennsylvanian*, I was the Second Mate with a Chief Mate's license in accordance with the company's conservative practice. As the old freighters became casualties of the war, they were replaced by more and more Liberty ships and later, Victory ships.

The supply of new ships began to outstrip the decreasing ability of the Germans to sink them. Accordingly, the need for crews grew. After three voyages on the *Pennsylvanian*, I was promoted to Chief Mate. It was the practice for all Chief Mates to have a Master's license. In effect, I became one of the exigencies of war. In the event that something happened to the Master while the vessel was at sea, I would become the inexperienced de facto temporary Master.

Although the *Pennsylvanian* was a strong vessel, it soon became evident that she was not a comfortable ship. Her steel plates were much heavier than those of the *Samuel Chase*, the ship I had just left. The overlapping plates of the *Pennsylvanian* were riveted throughout. The plates on the *Chase* were welded throughout. The plates survived stresses and extreme near misses from concussion bomb clusters. Those were tests that could not be imagined in a laboratory.

During the first storm at sea, when the "Pennsy" was deep loaded, green sea water often swept the main deck. The midship house, where most of the crew lived, was made of steel. The door openings were framed with wood, and the doors were fashioned with three-inch thick timbers. In spite of the best efforts of the ship's carpenter, these doors could not be made watertight. Consequently, sea water sloshed into the ship's galley and the officers' and crew's mess rooms. Only the Captain, Chief Mate, Second Mate and Radio Operator quarters, which are located on the boat deck, remained dry. The deck gang slept aft and their quarters were dry as well. When the ship rolled heavily, doors flew open. The heavy oak wood would overcome the brass latch. Our ship's carpenter spent a lot of time repairing rubber gaskets, distorted latches, and warping wood.

In broad daylight, I once ran into the edge of a door when it swung open with the roll of the ship. I was knocked to the deck, dazed but not hurt. I was also grateful I did not have to explain a visible injury. No one believes the story of a person running into a door in the dark, but running into a door in daylight?

Wartime cargos were sometimes loaded by army personnel or other men who were maybe or maybe not qualified. Usually the ship's officers and company personnel were not involved in planning of cargo stowage. Ship's gear and equipment had to be maintained by the ship's crew. So the ship's complement could readily blame the loading for heavy rolling. A slow deep roll would indicate too much weight in the upper decks. A quick roll indicated too much weight sat in the lower holds.

On an outward bound trip, all the fully loaded ships in convoy wallowed nearly in the exact trough of the northerly seas. We were moving on an easterly course. While I was on watch, I held onto the handrail under the wheelhouse windows and I watched the clinometer measure the angle of the roll. It indicated rolls of more than 30°. As the ship rolled into the wind, the noise level rose to a shriek, then lowered to a moan as the ship rolled away from the wind. One roll seemed worse than all the others. The clinometer stopped for a moment on 43°. Chairs slid across the floor and created additional noise. Everything not tied down sounded almost calamitous. It was unnerving. The steward department lost stores of jars and bottled goods.

Finally, the ship's rolling eased as the storm moved away. We realized the convoy Commodore had to follow his routing courses previously laid out by naval authorities.

As to the cause of the rolling, some bright mind somewhere invented a mechanical device called a Stabilogauge. It measured the meta-centric height of the vessel, or center of buoyancy vs. center of gravity. This instrument was about the size of a large book. It had many knobs with which tonnage figures could be entered according to any of the five hatches or tank placement. The distance in feet from the ship tipping center was automatic, identified by hatch or tank. It was accurate and invaluable. When our ship was selected to be a blockship for the Normandy invasion in June of 1944, we were ordered to load ballast to a certain draft 25 feet fore and aft, or even keel. The Stabiloguage revealed how many tons and into what hatches to load gravel ballast. The British Army personnel cut holes in certain bulkheads and placed explosive charges in strategic places, so the ship would be sunk on an "even keel." It worked, thanks to that pre-computer mechanical device. It was the most interesting wartime project of my experience.

This may be an interesting coincidence to me only. The *Pennsylvanian*, built in 1913, was the same year that my Uncle Thomas Dickie was lost from a dismasted sailing ship in a storm on the Grand Banks off Newfoundland. Green seas swept across the deck and swept him overboard when he tried to reach a less exposed position. Many years later, in the late 1930s, a neighbor showed me the *Boston Post* newspaper clipping reporting the loss of the ship and its carpenter, my uncle. The clipping was not his to give away, and there was no way for me to make a copy quickly.

On board at sea in good weather, we waged a constant and tedious battle against rust. Along with the constant rust fight, we endured the aggravating noise of chipping guns and the stench of fish oil applied to the main deck.

In port, the longshoremen removed the tarpaulins from the three hatches, and folded and piled them on one place on deck. Then they removed hatch boards, removable steel beams, and placed them on deck, which scored the deck plates, resulting in more rust and more fish oil stink.

It was inevitable that I would compare the company's aging ships with the new Liberties. The old ships had many more compartments in their cargo holds; therefore, the potential for special cargo like shoes, liquor, cosmetics, etc. meant higher revenue and more work. The new Liberties were simpler, slower, safer, and just as clumsy to maneuver with a gyro compass, which made navigation compass courses more precise.

All in all life on a Liberty ship was a bit easier, but since I liked to go to sea and I especially liked navigation, I usually took the job that was assigned. Only once I turned down a call to join a ship, and I regretted that decision.

The *Pennsylvanian* had rope-topping lifts on her 5-ton cargo booms. Four inch, four strands with heart, on the topping lift. I would never see those again. Liberty ship cargo booms had all wire topping lifts. They could be dangerous to handle, but they worked. The *Pennsylvanian* was a workhorse, and I didn't mind that a bit.

The *Pennsylvanian* arrived in Baltimore on April 22, 1943 after a long voyage to Basra in the Persian Gulf, via Cape Town. On May 11, 1943 I joined as Second Mate when the ship was loading war cargo for the U.K.

Our convoy departed New York on May 25 bound for Liverpool.

Between May 11 and May 25, I spent a lot of time on the bridge and in the chart room in order to familiarize myself with the vessel. The voyage across the North Atlantic was typical for that time of year. The ship sailed through plenty of fog that meant the need to tow fog buoys. Storms caused more misery. The curse of the wooden weather doors allowed seawater to slosh through all the main decks.

A particular cross to bear for the ship's Mates was the loss of a main deck wooden lamp locker. All the portable cargo lights were gone. U.K. ports were blacked out at night, but the cargo lights were used late in the day and down low in the holds.

Even at slow convoy speeds, the ship had a distressing tendency to plow through the seas rather than ride over the water.

There was no enemy activity on that eastbound voyage, even though it was a large convoy covering many square miles and an attractive target to tempt drooling predator subs. About this time Admiral Doenetz withdrew his subs from the Atlantic because of many losses; "effective counter measures" took their toll on his U-boats.

1943: TO LIVERPOOL

DEPART MAY 25, NOON; ARRIVE JUNE 10, 1136 HOURS

We weighed anchor at noon, and a pilot conned the *Pennsylvanian* down the ship channel to Ambrose Light Vessel. The pilot's vessel stood close in order to move nearby the vessels when needed. A two-man rowboat came alongside and ferried our pilot to the pilot vessel.

Our vessel hurried, at 11 knots, from the sea buoy to Zed position, where the convoy formed up. The convoy coursed due east at 9.5 knots, as ordered by the Commodore's flag signal.

The next morning at 0845, dense fog set in. Intermittent dense fog complicated the convoy's efforts to maintain station on each other for the next three days.

A strong gale blew in after midnight on the 29th of May. At 0400 on the 30th, our ship lost contact with the convoy and struggled against huge seas breaking over our decks. At 0800, the heavy sea took down the #1 lifeboat. At 0810, the heavy sea struck the #3 lifeboat, broke one side of the boat and bent a davit so that the boat could not be lowered. Dense fog returned and shrouded our struggles. On May 31 at 0300, the gale moderated. By 0800, we contacted an escort vessel and we rejoined the convoy at 1500. Intermittent fog continued to plague us. On June 2, another gale overtook us. The logbook stated, "Vessel laboring and taking heavy water over all." On June 3, the weather moderated.

On June 5 as planned, vessels detached from convoy bound for specified ports.

EAST BOUND FOR LIVERPOOL, ENGLAND

On June 9, 1943, the rough seas and fog continued to require a vigilant watch. On June 10, the convoy formed into a single line. At 0924, we rounded the Skerries, and at 1126, we arrived at Liverpool.

The sail from New York up to the Irish Sea to Liverpool took two weeks. Pilot and tugs warped us into a basin that protected the ship from tides and storms. Their skill and patience, developed over the centuries and handed down from pilot to pilot, moved our ship at slow speed so that no paint or rust was scraped from the hull by the stone quays.

On June 10, 1943, I didn't admire the large group of men I saw waiting on the dock. They wore suits, overcoats, hats, shirts and ties. I wondered, "Who are these men?" The boarding officials quickly processed our crew, then the waiting men swarmed aboard, rigging cargo booms and opening cargo hatches. Longshoremen! They worked hard with deliberate speed. Their attitude seemed to broadcast the importance of this cargo.

JUNE 11, 1943
IN LIVERPOOL, ENGLAND DISCHARGING WAR CARGO

At coffee time the next morning, a dock official came into the officers' mess looking for a cuppa. I explained we had plenty of coffee, but no, he had to have tea. I gave him a cup, fished out a tea bag from a carton, and pointed to the hot water urn.

He said, "What's that?" stabbing his finger at the tea bag. He took it, examined it, tore it open, and poured the tea leaves into the cup before I could stop him. It would have been OK if the urn water had been hot, but it was only warm. He had his cuppa, but never came back for another cuppa.

I was disappointed too – in myself. I wanted to tell him that I knew the man, Bill Patterson, who invented, patented and manufactured a type of tea bag. He was a deacon in my church, The First Baptist Church of Arlington, Massachusetts. I wanted to tell him how I used to watch his machinery produce tea bags by the thousands in his rented store at the Foot of the Rocks in Arlington Heights. I never got the chance.

If this was the first contact of tea bags in old England, the bag would never make it.

The second night in Liverpool, the Purser and I decided to go ashore. We sought and received briefings about where to go and what to do. However, it was the unexpected that overwhelmed us. As soon as we left the dock, we were in the city – and the city was blacked out. To our amazement, the sidewalks were crowded with people walking, I know not where. There was some conversation but not much noise. I didn't see many vehicles although an occasional taxi showed dimmed bits of light. The Purser and I wondered out loud about where were we going – where was everyone going? Someone grabbed my sleeve, "Hey, are you Yanks?" A girl's voice.

"Hey, are you a Limey?" I asked her – my accent gave me away.

"If there's two of you, come with us to our home and meet the family. It's not far."

The two girls took us to meet their parents. We talked a get-acquainted conversation about the war, and then we had some refreshments. The girls were attractive. After awhile, the parents excused themselves and left. We cuddled with the girls. The war was on the other side of the blackout curtains, far away. We had an understanding. All four of us were day workers, so at an agreed upon time, one of the girls called a taxi for our return to our ship.

In the long days of June, cargo discharge continued every day and sometimes into twilight. On June 23, 1943, all cargo was discharged, and we were to return to New York.

LIVERPOOL TO NEW YORK

On June 24, 1943, the vessel departed Sandeem Basin and became delayed waiting for locks to open. At 0700, the pilot departed at Bar L/V. The vessel proceeded through a swept channel to join convoy. At 1030 hours, we joined convoy ON-190 in position 61 (lead ship, column 6).

The convoy enjoyed good weather until July 2 at 1930 hours when dense fog shut in around us. On July 5, our #62 vessel ran over our fog buoy. We rigged a new fog buoy. At 2300 hours, the fog lifted. On July 8 at 1640 hours, we followed the line of buoys to New York Harbor entrance. At 1931, the pilot climbed the long Jacobs ladder. We had arrived at home port.

Plans for the ship had been made before our arrival so on July 13, we signed on for the next voyage, again to the U.K. I was instructed to make sure we had corrected charts of the east coast of England. The east coast of England! I listened to stories and rumors about the E-Boats the Germans used in the Channel against the east coast to sink coastal vessels.

1943: LONDON, ENGLAND

On July 22, 1943 at 2300 hours, our ship was loaded with cargo and ready for sea. Captain Vaux logged the Degaussing ON at 61 amperes and thus neutralized the ship's hull against the attraction of magnetic mines.

At 0050 on July 23, we proceeded down Ambrose Channel to sea. At 0240, engine trouble developed. Anchoring became imperative. The Commodore granted permission. The ship's engineers completed repairs at 0415, and we again hove up the anchor.

At 0454, our pilot departed and at 0500 hours, official departure was was recorded. The convoy formed on both sides and astern of the Commodore. Every ship flew its International Code Flag convoy numbers from the flying bridge halyards so the procedure of forming was orderly.

The next day, July 24, fog banks set in and intermittently lifted and fell.

On July 26 at 0900, the small Halifax section convoy joined us under clear weather.

When the convoy Commodore ordered a 45° emergency turn to port, all ships executed it in good order without knowing the reason why. We soon saw the reason for the maneuver. The convoy steamed around an iceberg and it created an exciting diversion.

Stragglers were another problem. The commodore broadcast in secret code new positions where stragglers could meet the convoy or our escorts. Even though fog caused the straggling, the Commodore had to control the stragglers. Luckily, there were no casualties among the stragglers, as they could be a tempting target to enemy subs.

We had assumed our destination was to Liverpool again, but another signal changed it to Loch Ewe, Scotland.

LOCH EWE TO METHIL
FIRTH OF FORTH TO LONDON

On August 5, 1943 we logged ARRIVAL at Loch Ewe at 1047 hours, and our vessel passed inside the boom net. At 1122, the anchor went down with 60 fathoms of chain in 18 fathoms of water. At 1142, the engine telegraph was placed on F.W.E. (Finished with Engines). We had no idea how long we would be awaiting orders. We did not wait long. At 2130 hours, the anchor was hove up and DEPARTURE was taken. Port time stops, sea time begins. We were in transit to London via Firth of Forth. On August 6, at 1103 we passed through Pentland Firth and turned south along with our coastal convoy. While in Pentland Firth, we could see the Orkney Islands to the north and mainland Scotland to the south. Within the Orkney Islands is a large, protected bay called Scapa Flow, where the British Navy sheltered capital war ships.

August 7 at 0500 hours, we logged ARRIVAL at Firth of Forth, Edinburgh, Scotland, where we waited for a pilot to take us to an anchorage. At 0940, the anchor was down. At 1100 hours a launch brought us special equipment – a barrage balloon, at the end of 300 feet of wire. The balloon looked strange and it did not reassure us.

Then the accident happened, which had nothing to do with the barrage balloon. At 1645 hours, we started to heave the anchor. The Chief Mate signaled "anchor away." The Pilot ordered half ahead.

Suddenly, the chain parted between the windlass and the riding pawl. We lost the anchor, chain, and the pawl assembly.

Now that the anchor sat on the bottom, caught on some object, it seemed to me that the moving ship broke the chain. Even though there was no immediate remedy, the cargo still had to be delivered. At 1900 hours, DEPARTURE time was logged. Coastal Pilot Jarvie arrived and piloted our vessel to the entrance of the Thames River. ARRIVAL was at August 9, 1030 hours. Our barrage balloon was removed. We almost forgot it was there.

A barrage balloon is a blimp about 30 feet long which is tethered to an electric winch by a wire at the stern of the ship. At night in a fog, we lowered the balloon to 300 feet. In clear weather it was raised to 1,000 feet. This kept enemy aircraft too high for accurate bombing. At the entrance of the Thames River, the need for barrage balloons appeared to be over. This was another quiet victory that was not celebrated by rejoicing.

We viewed London as being opened for business and Hitler as on the defensive in the eastern Atlantic.

Our ship squeezed through a lock into a basin surrounded by undamaged warehouses and sheds. English maritime personnel displayed their usual patient efficiency. When we asked about bomb damage, we were told there was some damage nearby not visible from this place.

Purser Ed Lucas and I went ashore and rode the double decker bus into London. Along the bus route, we did not see any damage from German air raids. It could have been cleaned up. We did see Trafalgar Monument and Square. The square was well populated with hundreds of pigeons and dozens of prostitutes. We saw Buckingham Palace and other historic places. It was fun being a tourist.

Cargo discharge was day work only with blackout at night. It seemed apparent that Germany was occupied in the East.

LONDON TO METHIL, FIRTH OF FORTH, SCOTLAND

Our ship was docked in the King George V locks or basin. On August 27 at 1240 hours, we undocked. At 1340 hours, we cleared the locks with the help of the tug *Sun*, which unexpectedly cast off our hawser from its towing hook. The four crew members and I hurried to heave in the hawser. Before we could lead the hawser to the docking winch to pull it in, our propeller caught the hawser in its blades.

Because communications were primitive, the navigation bridge used a large megaphone to shout to the bow or stern. As Second Mate, I was in charge of the stern and used hand signals or shouted. Finally, my shouting and screaming brought everything to a halt. The engineers in the engine room realized something was hindering the turning propeller.

A diver was called. He arrived at 1600 hours, dove down to the propeller, and cleared the hawser from the blades. He found no damage to the propeller. End of incident – except for reports we had to write about the delay and expense.

Degaussing is a means of demagnetizing the ship's hull using a cable around the inside perimeter of the hull. The degaussing range, essential to our ship's safety, interpreted how well our degaussing functioned. We made two runs over the range. Finally at 2055 hours on August 27, we anchored at South End at the mouth of the Thames River.

London was a city full of intense activities and the work related to the purpose of winning the war. We were glad to be homeward bound.

August 28, 1943, the *Pennsylvanian* was 30 years old. There were a few occasions when we appreciated the simplicity of operating the ship, such as no electronic or radio gears to maintain. There were many more times, however, when we wished for modern systems like telephones instead of speaking tubes and a gyro compass instead of magnetic compasses which needed recalibration after every cargo discharge. Our ship was empty of cargo and the magnetic compasses needed adjustment. On August 28 at 8:00 A.M., we hove anchor to adjust the compasses. It took four hours to calibrate the compasses with Degaussing ON and Degaussing OFF, as the degaussing affected them.

At 1244 hours, we anchored awaiting convoy.

At 1445, a barrage balloon was rigged from our stern. I thought balloons were unnecessary, but the authorities knew better.

At 1500 hours, Captain Vaux attended a convoy conference. Coastal Pilot Burbridge was assigned to us for our destination to Methil.

On August 29, 1943 at 0700 hours, we weighed anchor. Our convoy sailed single file at 6 knots. At 1300 hours, our convoy formed two lines at 7.5 knots. We had been given some chartlets with the route laid out on them. I had more faith in their charlets than our charts.

August 30 at 1245, a carrier pigeon landed with an aluminum message band attached and another message held under a rubber band, stating it had been watered and fed on August 29, by a ship's Second Engineer sailing in the North Sea.

August 31 at 1000, ARRIVAL was logged Firth of Forth.

At 1130, anchored at Methil Anchorage.

The carrier pigeon was turned over to local military.

METHIL, SCOTLAND TO LOCH EWE, SCOTLAND
LOCH EWE TO NEW YORK

Aug 31	1630	Up anchor – proceed in convoy with barrage balloon at 1,000 feet.
Sep 1	1353	Fog – hauled balloon down to 300 feet as per instruction in fog.
	1906	Cape Wrath abeam (Northwest corner of Scotland). Fog cleared – raised balloon to 1,000 feet.
Sep 2	0030	ARRIVAL – off Loch Ewe.
	0245	Anchored Loch Ewe – await convoy.
	0945	Up anchor – assigned position #105, in convoy ON-200.
	1100	DEPARTURE.
Sep 3	1000	Rendezvous with ocean convoy.
	1600	Received straggler's diversion via wireless telegraph from Liverpool.

Sep 4	0300	Moderate gale, rough seas continue on September 5, moderating September 6. The Captain requested permission from Commodore to change convoy position from #115 to #111, due to poor station keeping and straggling of vessels ahead of us. Permission granted.
Sep 7-8		Gale winds and rough seas. Convoy averaging about 200 miles per day.
Sep 9	1600	Dense fog-streamed fog buoy.
Sep 10		Fog plus moderate gale and rough sea.
Sep 10	2000	Fog lifted. Lost fog buoy.
Sep 11		Report from #51 "Torpedo track ahead."
	1350	Emergency turn to right.
	1402	Return to convoy course.
Sep 12		Dense fog, streamed new fog buoy.
Sep 13	0830	Fog lifted.
Sep 13	2320	Course change 45° left – alarm sounded – depth charges dropped by escort.
Sep 14	0730	Resumed convoy course, more depth charges by escort.

LOCH EWE, SCOTLAND TO NEW YORK

Sep 14	1115	Degaussing energized to 64 amperes.
Sep 15	0400	Moderate gale increasing to whole gale by 2200. High heavy seas.
Sep 16		Gale lessening.
Sep 17		Changed convoy position from #111 to #91 by order of Commodore.
Sep 18	1200	ARRIVAL, Ambrose. L/V.
	1210	Pilot boarded.

New York, New York – our home port. We received a startling surprise about a new destination, Cuba, for sugar. A more routine surprise: Captain Vaux was taking a vacation. He would be relieved by Captain Greenlaw.

SEPTEMBER 1943: TO CUBA

The ship's cargo holds needed cleaning in order to accept a full cargo of sugar. Special boxes covered with burlap were secured to the bilge strainers (or roseboxes).

There are no records for this voyage except the locater cards from National Archives which have arrivals and departures. There is only my memory. We departed New York alone on about September 25, 1943 and five days later arrived in Matanzas. We immediately loaded large bags of cane sugar. Slings were landed "in square" on a platform so that the longshoremen would not need to lift heavy the bags off the deck. Longshoremen, who weighed less than the bag of sugar, carried the bags across their shoulders and laid them into the sides, ends, and corners of the hold. Their hot, sticky work didn't end until all the compartments were filled.

The owner of the sugar plantation set up a bar near the Chief Mate's Office and served free rum and Cokes to the ship's officers.

CUBA TO NEW YORK

We survived the freebie rum and Coke. After the first drink, I found that Coke on the rocks without the rum was also free, and I managed to subsist on that.

After five hot days of work, the longshoremen topped off the ship's hold with the sweet cargo of sugar cane.

Loaded ships are much more valuable than empty ships so rather than returning directly to New York, we departed Matanzas for Guantanamo, the convoy port. Once there, we waited for a week to join a northbound convoy sailing on October 11, 1943.

The escort protected the sugar and coincidentally, the ships that carried it and the crew that manned the ship.

It was a measure of success that the Navy did not feel the need to protect every ship, especially empty vessels that left port and went to sea. The Navy had achieved a measure of control over the predator subs.

Convoy GN.89 departed Cuba on October 11 and arrived New York on October 18, 1943.

The cargo discharge began immediately at a sugar refinery dock. Captain Greenlaw departed our ship, and Captain Vaux returned. There would be no free rum and Cokes this voyage. We had another surprise: Chief Mate Tommy Taggart was paid off and I was promoted to Chief Mate.

Tom Taggart invited Purser Ed Lucas and me to a farewell drink at a nearby bar.

I demurred. They worked me over verbally. I said something like, "I'm the Chief Mate now and I'm not going." I went.

I did not like the situation. Tom Taggart, paid off, should have gone home. Instead he bought drinks in a bar for the shipmates. I nursed my second drink (one was never enough). Finally, after nearly two hours and some nagging on my part, we took a taxi to Tom's house located several miles away.

Mrs. Taggart, a pretty young woman, sat on the front steps, chin in hand. She put up a good front, having to greet her husband's homecoming in the presence of somewhat inebriated strangers. I was embarrassed and broke off the introductions as soon as possible. I had the good sense to keep the taxi. After Ed Lucas and I returned to the ship I realized that Lucas, a handsome bachelor, never quite forgave me for inhibiting a fun evening. I never saw Tom Taggart again.

NOVEMBER 1943: TO CUBA (AGAIN)

The *Pennsylvanian's* departure, I believe, was expedited by the authorities. Nevertheless, essential repairs, cleaning of cargo holds, inspection of holds by the American Bureau of Shipping, taking of stores and supplies, signing on of the crew, and all the required legal paperwork was completed on November 7, 1943.

On November 8 at 0802 hours, we passed through the harbor's protective nets near The Narrows. At 0900 hours, the log shows, "Pilot away." We proceeded down the buoyed sea channel to deep water east of New York's Ambrose Light Vessel. We were alone. After two years of being escorted by convoys on the Atlantic Ocean, we proceeded independently. It was lonely indeed. Our protection was a thick haze that turned into a gale early on the 9th of November.

Our empty ship did not take kindly to rough seas. November 9 at 0145, Captain Vaux reduced engine speed from full speed, about 72 RPM to 60 RPM. At 0900, we took another reduction in speed to 55 RPM. We needed ballast to deepen the draft. The only ballast available was salt water. This would contaminate empty fuel tanks, if we had them, and contaminate the ocean when pumped out. Unthinkable. Make the best of it.

At 1505, we were challenged by a U.S. Navy aircraft. We hoisted a three flag signal and our four flag call letters.

At 0600 on the 10th of November, we resumed full speed. November 12 at 0415 hours, we sighted Watling Island Light right ahead about 18 to 20 miles. A course change to the left was essential in order to pass the island's starboard side to a safe distance of 7 miles.

I couldn't help but think of Christopher Columbus. He sighted the high land where the lighthouse now stands 451 years ago.

We steamed on through the islands arriving at the eastern end of Cuba on November 13 at 0130 hours. At 0250 hours, we sighted a westbound convoy and passed on its south side. At 1112 hours, ARRIVAL was logged off Morro Castle, Santiago, Cuba.

Once again, the men faced five days of hard work to fill our cargo holds with bagged cane sugar, each bag weighing 200 pounds.

The harbor and narrow entrance to Santiago, bordered by high cliffs, was beautiful. The war could not diminish the beauty. We took DEPARTURE from Santiago at 0930 on November 18, 1943 and anchored in Guantanamo at 1406.

We headed to Baltimore, not New York, departing on November 19 from Guantanamo at 1800 hours.

Guantanamo was our convoy port. There had been some changes in shore facilities since I visited the port while I served on the school ship in 1939. Of course, many more merchant ships arrived and departed.

I felt no regrets departing Guantanamo. No shore leave there – except that as lower class men on the school ship we had visited the rifle range with our Springfield bolt-action rifles, where we tried to qualify as marksmen. I failed because I hit a classmate's bull's-eye once so that he qualified. I was guilty of taking my eye off my target and then finding the wrong bull's-eye.

On November 20, 1943 we departed for Baltimore from Guantanamo. Some of the crew were disappointed that we were not going to New York, because New York was their home port. Worse yet came the news that upon completion of discharging all sugar, we would prepare to load cargo in Baltimore to be delivered to the U.K.

We heard the usual "What do you expect – this is war."

Every officer and crewmember knew this trip could be the last one. If not this trip, then the next. I never shared with anyone our Lord's declaration to protect the ship on which I served. No one on our ship ever mentioned what fate might have in store for our now 31 year old ship.

We were to be selected as an ammunition vessel. It made sense because our ship had more decks in our holds than the Liberty ships which had one between deck, plus the lower hold. These old intercoastal freighters had two 'tween decks in every hold and three decks in #1 hold. #1 'tween deck was used to carry green hides from the West coast to the East coast. The hides stank, and the odor was never completely eradicated. This stink caused no threat to ammo cargo and was merely unpleasant for workers and crew.

So it happened. In Baltimore, we docked at a pier that looked like a lumber yard. Crews lowered beautiful, clear, planed lumber into every hatch where gangs of carpenters built strong lockers and compartments for stowage of ammunition of all sizes and calibers.

We were docked in Baltimore for three weeks. On December 19, fully loaded, we finally sailed and arrived in New York on the 21st. The next day, we joined the U.K. convoy and were back on the North Atlantic winter travail. It was small comfort to know that the rough seas of winter handicapped the German subs – assuming that there were some hunting for us.

On the U.S. east coast, empty steam vessels could steam cautiously in shallow water, where subs could not attack. Deep loaded vessels, usually northbound, were slow and vulnerable in deeper water.

We did not know it at the time, but the old *Pennsylvanian* would only make two more trips after this one.

DECEMBER 1943: TO LIVERPOOL, ENGLAND

On December 22, 1943 the *Pennsylvanian* sat at anchor in Gravesend Bay, New York Harbor and awaited Convoy HX.272 bound for the Mersey. At 0104, our anchor aweigh bell rang out over the nearly silent harbor. At 0115, we passed through the net "gate" in The Narrows. At 0245, our harbor pilot departed by Jacob's ladder into his two man rowboat.

Captain Vaux was responsible for his ship. However, while the ship was in the harbor, he was subject to the supervisory advice of the required harbor pilot. After leaving the harbor he was subject to the more exacting orders of the Commodore, who was responsible for the convoy.

A number of ships preceded us and more followed us out of the channel. Our position was #92. Our ship, with its sensitive cargo, had other ships all around us – as protection? On December 23 at 2000 hours, SS *Leo J. Duster*, #102 constantly crowding, came too close. The ship risked collision by crossing close ahead, without warning, from column 10 to column 8. All vessels showed a blue stern light as directed because it was difficult to see gray painted ships on a black night. A blue stern light could be seen for a few hundred feet, no more. The *Duster* denied maneuvering and said it was vessel #111, SS *James Manning*.

On December 25 at 0900 in Halifax, our group joined the convoy. The convoy enjoyed good weather for Christmas. There was no way to gift wrap the weather, except possibly with colorful sunrise and sunset, not likely in December in the North Atlantic.

NEW YORK TO LIVERPOOL
LIVERPOOL TO NEW YORK

Dec 27	2245	Emergency turn to port.
	2315	Emergency turn to starboard.
Dec 28		Gale – rough heavy sea and swell.
Dec 29		Gale moderating.
Dec 31		Passed floating mine, raised flag signal, "MQ"; gave alarm signal on ship whistle, series of A's, acknowledged by Commodore.
Jan 1		Five various courses and speeds as convoy steams in formation into Irish Sea – destination Liverpool Bay.
Jan 5	2106	ARRIVAL Bar L/V, 2256 Anchored – received orders to dock on A.M. tide next morning – Gladstone Docks.

It had been my first Atlantic crossing as a Chief Mate. It was an exceedingly rough, slow trip. Arrival on January 6 in port was a relief from the discomfort of storms at sea.

THE HANDSOME STRANGER

The handsome stranger had to come up the gangway, but he never said from where. He joined me for coffee without an invitation. Most of our conversation took place in the officers' pantry. He was affable, outgoing, and obvious. He wanted something. When he asked a couple of personal questions I realized he was angling for an invitation. He wanted to come to the States and stay with his host, me.

Thanks, but no thanks. Maybe I should have been flattered. I was not. Something was not quite right. How was it that a handsome, well dressed civilian in his thirties in wartime was in a restricted area? Curious. If he was an intelligence agent, what was his point? He was gone. All he got was a cold shoulder and a cold stare.

LIVERPOOL TO NEW YORK

On January 22, 1944 at 1100 – all cargo off-loaded, ship ballasted and ready for sea – we let go lines proceeding to anchorage off Bar Light Vessel. At 1411 hours, we let go the starboard anchor with 65 fathoms of chain at water's edge in nine fathoms of water. A strong breeze blew on January 23, and at 0730 we received the message, "Convoy not sailing." At 0850, we eased out 90 fathoms of anchor chain. The wind increased to a moderate gale. On January 24 at 1100 hours, we began heaving anchor. At 1120, anchor aweigh. Our vessel proceeded on northerly courses under a whole gale and rough, heavy, confused seas.

Jan 26	1500	Convoy forming up – our vessel in position #103. Reason for delay – adverse weather, poor visibility.
Jan 27		Fresh westerly gale, heavy rough sea.
Jan 28-30		Retarded clocks 3 nights to zone 2.
Feb 1-2		Fresh to whole gale to storm force. Precipitous seas. Vessel laboring heavily.
Feb 2		Distance made, only 52 miles.
Feb 3		Change convoy position from #103 to #102.
Feb 6		Convoy over Grand Banks.
Feb 6	0800	Degaussing ON +62 amps.

Whenever our vessel found itself in less than 100 fathoms of water (600 ft), it was the Captain's duty to have the degaussing (D/G) turned ON. A special heavy electric cable circled the hull on the inside of the hull's steel plates. It neutralized the magnetic attraction of the hull to magnetic mines.

Feb 7	0700	Clear of Grand Banks D/G OFF.
Feb 7	1000	Fog set in. Fog buoy streamed.
Feb 7	1100	Fog lifted.

A CURIOUS COURSE CHANGE

Feb 10	1200	Commodore: "All ships to reverse direction." All ships turned 90° together, then all ships turned 90° again. Now the convoy was steaming east instead of west.
	1630	All ships ordered to reverse course again. This slowed arrival time eight hours. No reason was given, but another convoy departing New York at our original arrival time was the likely reason.
Feb 11	1210	We received orders to anchor ESE of Ambrose L.V.

1400   Anchored 90 fathoms of chain holding vessel in heavy snow squall.

Feb 12   Docking destination, Bayonne, NJ.

The convoy had survived the terrible winter weather of the North Atlantic. Apparently the delay was longer than anticipated. The thought of two convoys meeting at the mouth of New York harbor? Unacceptable!

While at sea, the port of New York City was a refuge in my mind. After docking, it was a different story. Traveling from outlying places like Port Newark, the Brooklyn shipyards were daunting. Staten Island was the worst, while the Hudson River was the easiest. Booking a flight out of New York or New Jersey was a nightmare. It was easier to stay on board and go crazy. I hated to go ashore alone in New York City. Dinner and a movie did help. Alcoholic beverages were not my thing. Some career seamen had a thirst for them. Many years later, they were banned from freighters.

FEBRUARY 1944: TO LIVERPOOL (AGAIN)

AN AMMUNITION SHIP
DEEPLY LOADED, ATROCIOUS WEATHER

On February 27, 1944 at 1018, we let go lines and left the Caven Point dock at 1143 and passed through the nets. At 1245, pilot away. At 1300, DEPARTURE – sea time began in poor visibility; our convoy was HX.281, position 92. Bad old North Atlantic Ocean in winter. It was essential to keep the routine. Four hour watches, eat, sleep, keep clean and hold on. There were hand rails in every alleyway (corridor). Advance the clocks – do not forget to also advance wristwatches.

The March 1 logbook described weather: "Whole gale, NXW (North by West) 10-11 force, precipitous seas." Our Commodore changed speeds from 9 knots to 8 knots, then 6 knots to ease the struggle.

Mar 2		We made 95 miles.
Mar 3		We made 113 miles.
		Whole new gale hit us. We fought heavy confused sea and swell.
	1030	Heavy seas carried away the port after raft . The vessel labored heavily. Only three vessels were visible in the convoy at times. (Ships of convoy unable to stay together.)
Mar 4	1000	Contacted escort and 12 vessels of convoy. Ordered to remain with flat top from escort.
Mar 5	1500	Position changed to 82.
Mar 6,9,11&13		Advanced clocks one hour.
Mar 13		Changed position to 83.
Mar 14	0105	DETENTION – Engine stopped to repair throttle valve. Vessel in Irish Sea – took position 4.
	0235	Resumed.
	1948	Liverpool section of convoy breaks off.
Mar 15	0130	ARRIVAL, Bar Light Vessel.
	0200	Let go anchor, 60 fathom chain. Ready to off-load our full load of munitions (7,000 tons) to swell huge ammo dumps preparing for invasion of Europe.
Mar 30	1500	DEPARTURE, Bar L/V 1813. At end of swept channel, ships form up in two columns.
Mar 31		Form up cruising position, ours was 22.
Apr 1		Convoy drills on "emergency turns. Our position changed to 23.
Apr 2,3,6,9&16		Retarded clocks 60 minutes.
Apr 9		Captain Vaux requested Commodore to change our position to 22 as 23 constantly falling behind forcing rest of column out of position. Reply – 22 is in position.
Apr 16	1600	Convoy forming single column.
	1830	ARRIVAL, off Ambrose L/V, New York.

Weather on this homeward bound crossing was so much improved after the travails of previous voyages. Captain Vaux didn't mention it in his Skerries. For four days our distance run was only 160 average. Empty ships were held back by moderately rough weather.

Our last voyage was unrecorded, except that the locater card from the National Archives shows our DEPARTURE was May 19.

In port for one month as gangs of carpenters rebuilt the interior of all cargo hold spaces for secure stowage of munitions of all kinds and sizes.

The ammunition ship *Pennsylvanian* loaded its munitions cargo at Bayonne, New Jersey. I could see the back of the Statue of Liberty from the loading dock.

On May 19, 1944 our ship, loaded to its Plimsoll Mark WNA, (Winter North Atlantic), departed for U.K., arriving June 3, 1944 at – once again – Liverpool where we received news, the greatest surprise of all.

THE GREATEST SURPRISE OF ALL

Winter in the North Atlantic Ocean was tough. Constant attention was essential to maintain the ship's position in the convoy formation. The bridge officer and the engineer officer on watch were in frequent communication. The bridge officer made small changes in the ship's course and speed in order to keep position. The engineer adjusted the throttle to change revolutions per minute by one or two as ordered.

The bridge rolled through an arc in high seas, while the engine room tipped from one side to another.

The month of May was fog month. For hours on end, the mate on watch saw none of the other ships in convoy, only the spout of the fog buoy the ship ahead towed. Never was he to lose sight of that fog buoy, as it was our only visible connection to the convoy. On June 3, 1944, after a tension-filled trip, we arrived in Liverpool.

Captain Greenlaw heard the news first, regarding the imminent invasion of France. How did it affect us? The *Pennsylvanian* had been selected to be a block ship at the beachhead!

FIRE IN THE AMMUNITION MAGAZINE

It was much too late, we thought, to take part in the actual invasion. Our cargo of munitions had to be discharged. The U.S. Army preferred the term "off-loaded." In any event, once the cargo was off-loaded, the ship had to be prepared for scuttling at the beachhead. This would take perhaps four or five weeks.

Our cargo was off-loaded rather quickly because the long days of June provided about 16 hours of working time each day.

When we got news of the invasion of Normandy, much of our cargo still remained to be put ashore. On the 12th of June, we received rush orders to proceed to Glasgow where the ship was stripped of all equipment and prepared for its last resting place.

If there was such a thing as a faithful ship, the *Pennsylvanian* was one. It was strong. Its main engine almost never broke down. During the seven voyages I was on the *Pennsylvanian*, it never ran aground or collided with any object or other ship.

First we removed the guns, the gun crew, and all the ammunition. Everything went ashore, except food and fuel for the short voyage to the beachhead.

Somehow, a fire started in the empty ammo magazine. We could only speculate whether the fire started with a spontaneous combustion or a carelessly discarded cigarette. The Naval Petty Officer of the gun crew reported the fire to me, the Chief Mate, because the gunnery officer was not on board. The Petty Officer and I decided we could not enter the empty magazine because we had no oxygen mask equipment, so we called the Glasgow Fire Department. After the fire was put out, the gun crew cleaned the magazine. Fortunately, no other space on the ship was affected by the fire.

A SHORT VOYAGE – AN EPIC VOYAGE
NEVER TO BE FORGOTTEN

On the morning of June 19, 1944, we sailed from Glasgow, Scotland, dropped the pilot, and joined a small convoy of six ships bound south to the English Channel. Although this leg of the voyage down the Irish Sea was uneventful, we looked forward to our arrival at the Normandy beachhead where two weeks ago, the greatest invasion in history had taken place. Our anticipation seemed to increase with every turn of the screw.

After we found the first buoy off the Isle of Wight, we followed a string of buoys that led us to the Normandy coast, and then the fog set in.

A double problem faced us. The strength of the ebb tide flowing out of the channel pushed us sideways and off course. Because of this, we looked through the fog for the next buoy four miles ahead. We had to adjust our course at each buoy. The largest adjustment was 21° on the maximum strength of the tide. I reckoned the new course as we found the next buoy. Captain Greenlaw checked my plotting. We sounded the steam whistle with its hand lever and used Morse code to send out the number of the buoy as we sighted it. With the buoys behind us, we headed on a new course for an appointed position.

JUNE 1944
THE SHIP AHEAD IS SUNK BY A MINE

In the final miles of the SS *Pennsylvanian*, visibility was improved but we still could not see the French Coast.

Suddenly, we heard a muffled explosion from the ship ahead. We watched the ship slow and turn to the right and stay on an even keel as it drifted off into the light fog. We presumed it sank, because it lost propulsion and steering. It was important to concentrate on our own problems and not dwell on the casualty of the ship ahead of us. The weather cleared, and that was a blessing because we were able to sight the launch that came alongside our ship. An Army lieutenant climbed aboard and told us where to anchor.

As Chief Mate, my station was on the bow with the ship's carpenter manning the anchor windlass. We communicated with the bridge by hand signal and/or by megaphone. When the Captain held up his right hand and arm then dropped it quickly, I signaled the carpenter to take the brake off the starboard anchor.

ITS LAST RESTING PLACE

The anchor fell into the water and the chain rattled noisily behind, leaving a small cloud of rusty dust. The anchor did not have far to fall, as the water was only about 30 feet deep. The ship was finally anchored over its last resting place.

When we arrived at the beachhead, all was quiet ashore. We were told that the next day we needed to gather our personal gear and be ready to leave the ship at 10:00 A.M. when a launch would arrive to take us ashore. Partway to shore the launch would stop, allowing us to watch the sinking of the SS *Pennsylvanian*. After that, we could go to the citadel for the night.

Before we left the ship, we had dinner and then breakfast onboard. After dinner while doing last minute packing and clean up, we heard many aircraft roaring overhead. We rushed outside and were greeted by a shower of aluminum foil chaff. The foil chaff was to jam enemy radar. Hundreds of four engine bombers were to bomb the hedgerows used by the Germans to help contain our troops from breaking out to the south and east.

We learned later that our General McNair had been killed in the bombardment.

Much later, I thought about the ship ahead that struck a mine. Our ship led the way across the English Channel, because we found all the buoys in the fog and signaled to the other ships. I could not remember how the ship that struck the mine got ahead of us. It triggered the mine and therefore saved us. I had to believe that it was God's action. God promised that I would never be on a ship sunk by enemy action. This was His doing. This was the 11th miracle that protected me during the war.

JUNE 19, 1942
THE LAST HOURS

I had divested myself of every possession I did not want to carry home, except a windup portable Victrola with many 78 RPM records. After the anchor went down, I went to the bridge and spoke to the lieutenant who directed our anchorage. I approached him about giving him a gift of the Victrola and many records. He was overjoyed. He explained that the troops had found a place to use as a rec hall but there was nothing in it. Voila! Now they had music and did not need a nickel or quarter to play it.

I assumed he meant the troops had captured some place like a farmer's barn or a meeting place in a village, but he did not explain. It did not matter. The consequences of the gift were more interesting.

Late that afternoon two American civilians came aboard. They identified themselves as Intelligence Officers. They came aboard to personally thank me for the gift of the phonograph/Victrola with records. I was surprised and somewhat chagrined, because they woke me up from a nap that I needed before I went on watch at 4:00 P.M.

AT THE BEACHHEAD – UTAH BEACH

A sober realization came over us. The ship would never sail again. The navigation equipment would never be used again. Someone suggested the officers could take home souvenirs. The Captain took dividers from the chart table. I took the heavy brass parallel rulers used for drawing course lines from one point to another point. They looked like the ship's original equipment. Someone took compasses out of the lifeboats. I decided to take home a compass. Set in its original wooden box, I carefully wrapped it and put it with my other things to carry with me.

The next morning we boarded the launch to watch the preset charges set off on our ship. Because we were too far away to hear or see anything except a slight haze of dust, the sinking of the Pennsylvanian was a visual disappointment. The ship had served its purpose. The Army was moving into Germany.

As to the sad ending of ship, I heard many months later about a terrific storm broke the ship's back.

In wartime, when a ship is sunk, the crew's pay stops. However, our pay continued until we were returned, as passengers to New York.

LIFE ASHORE – FREELOADING

The launch took us to an American troopship that had been converted from a new C-2 freighter. Our officers' quarters were excellent. For dinner, we ate capon with lots of trimmings. Overnight the troopship returned to England. From a port I could not identify, we were taken by bus to a citadel for another overnight. What a place! It could have been hundreds of years old. We walked into a huge hall with rows of pedestals, each about seven feet long, three feet high, and three feet wide with thin mattresses stuffed with straw. Each of us had a blanket from our ship. (I still have mine.) It was an uncomfortable night but we survived it. In the morning, we were served something like creamed chipped beef, known in my school ship days as "SOS." Then we were taken to a hotel.

It was a resort hotel and had been luxurious. The military had effectively downgraded its luxurious condition, but for us it was a giant step up from ship environment. Captain Greenlaw showed up to give us money for a cash advance. He told us we would all be there for a while.

JUNE 24 – JULY 14, 1944
OUR TIME IN TORQUAY, ENGLAND

The officers and crew of our ship now enjoyed a paid vacation, including meals and rooms. It turned out to be a three week vacation, as the saying goes – foot loose and fancy free. We had no daily responsibilities. It seems that only the Captain was responsible to keep us supplied with money.

Since Torquay was a resort town, there were plenty of recreation possibilities. The most obvious was the beach. The Purser and I went to the beach and relaxed on a blanket under the sun. We rejoiced to have good weather, for which England is not noted. The beach was crowded with the young and elderly because all the able bodied people were occupied by imperatives of war. Except us. We were waiting for transportation home.

Meanwhile, we made friends with girls who were also enjoying the beach. They were nearly all teenagers, so there were no lasting relationships. We spent our time at the movies and play houses and restaurants. We walked and talked, and read the news.

Remarkably, there were no crew troubles or problems reported to me as Chief Mate. If there were any problems, they were probably financial, such as crew members overdrawing wages. Money was the Captain's responsibility and Purser's work.

JULY 1944: HOME ON THE SS *ARGENTINA*

OUR CREW WAS REPATRIATING HOME

It had been a fortuitous vacation. We had not known when it was to end. Typically, the end came on short notice. The vacation came to an abrupt end, as it had the time we received the notice that our ship was requisitioned for a beachhead block ship. We were told to board the SS *Argentina* the next day. Another bus trip took us to Southampton where the *Argentina* was docked. The *Argentina* had been a luxury passenger ship turned into a troop ship. Our bunks were in an open area, so there was not much privacy. Other passengers on board were mostly civilians, families, dependents, immigrants, war brides, and children, and they were quartered in other spaces. The daily routine was pleasant enough. At ten, we enjoyed morning coffee and pastry. My crew grouped together in one of many lounge areas. Our carpenter had purchased a radio on which he found loud jazz music.

One morning at coffee time, I sat down at a mess table with some other passengers, including a mother and her daughter, who was quite lovely with dark hair and ivory skin. Mother proceeded to extol the eligibility of her daughter to me. I listened in some surprise, never dreaming of the real surprise that lay ahead.

Later, the ship's Second Officer, dressed in uniform, approached me and asked if I would like to see his living quarters. I said yes. He gave me directions to his room because the ship was very large. He told me to walk right in. The door was not locked.

I walked into a large room with a double bed set against one wall, all nicely decorated, as befitting a luxury passenger ship. Standing on the far side of the room was the lovely daughter of the sales lady mother. I was stunned. I had closed the door behind me, but I suddenly remembered that I had some responsibilities. Without a word, I turned and walked out. I never saw the Second Officer, the mother, or her daughter again.

Later on reflection, perhaps the Second Officer thought my desires were supposed to overcome any scruples. After all, this was a passenger ship, and it can be said that each passenger ship has its own de facto morals set by those who happen to be on board. I had to look on this experience as an entanglement avoided.

It sounds like naiveté on my part, that I struck up a conversation with a very attractive strawberry blond. She had a voluptuous figure that she tried to hide with a sweatshirt and baggy slacks. It didn't work. We met as the ship approached New York, and we talked while we walked around the ship. We liked each other, but there wasn't time to get to know each other better.

Our Captain Greenlaw reached New York before the *Argentina*. When we arrived he was already prepared to pay us. That expedited our leaving that big ship and fed our eagerness to get back home.

I walked down the gangway and stepped onto the dock to see my new friend waiting for me. Her smile of recognition told me she was waiting for me. I liked her, but I did not want to make a commitment because I was intent on going home. Her smile broadened to a smile of expectation and then disappeared when I explained I was intent on getting home to Boston. I didn't know her well enough to exchange addresses, so we parted with some disappointment, perhaps mutual.

I did not tell her the strong reason I was unwilling to commit to a relationship with her. I had a girl back home. My affection for her kept me loyal to the relationship we had from high school.

The other reason was food. After months of eating good and indifferent cooking from ships galleys, I looked forward to my mother's cooking.

ANOTHER CAVEAT

The *Pennsylvanian* led a charmed life. It made two trips to the Persian Gulf via the long way around the Cape of Good Hope. The ship sailed alone and without incident through waters infested by German surface raiders and German and Japanese submarines. After that trip, the ship was assigned to North Atlantic convoys to supply Europe in May 1943.

At this time, I joined her as Second Mate (trip to U.K.). Later, after another trip to the U.K. and two trips to Cuba, the *Pennsylvanian* made a trip into the Mediterranean. Part of this voyage Captain Vaux omitted from his secret log.

My promotion to Chief Mate had taken place previously; some vivid memories have remained through the years of Bari, Italy.

Before arriving at the Port of Bari, we had stopped in the Port of Ancona and discharged our deck load.

The Port of Bari, on the Adriatic Sea had been attacked with great success by the German Air Force. Many allied ships had been hit by bombs and sunk in the shallow water. One ship was an Italian cruiser, capsized about 135° from vertical. Judging from its gracefully shaped bottom, painted a bright red, it was once a handsome vessel. Lesser vessels, mostly merchant freighters, sullied the harbor waters. We were told an ammunition ship had exploded and killed more than 1,000 men.

Our ship offloaded its cargo onto an open dock because so many structures such as dock sheds had been destroyed.

In these two ports we did not see much of the beauty of Italy. There was one major exception – opera. I managed to take in three operas, *Tosca*, *La Traviata* and *Madame Butterfly*. I had never been to an opera, and I was enthralled at these performances. One performer's name was William Dickie; his last name the same as mine. He had a strong baritone voice. I admired all the singers' exuberant, practiced voices.

When all cargo was offloaded, the decks were a mess of dunnage, pieces of rough lumber used in the stowage of cargo. As the longshoremen walked down the gangway, one man picked up a small piece of cut lumber and asked me if he could take it off the ship. When I nodded my head yes, a loud yell came from the deck above. "Nothing, nothing leaves this ship," yelled Captain Vaux. I threw up my hands. The longshoreman departed, sorrowfully and empty handed. On reflection I realized if one man did it, many would follow.

OUR PATHS CROSSED 6,000 FEET APART

Recently, my wife Barbara and I enjoyed dinner in the dining room of the Sugar House at the Sugar Hill Retirement Community in Wolfeboro, NH. Somehow I was led to tell of an incident that took place during WWII at Utah Beach, Normandy, France. I related how our ship, the

SS *Pennsylvanian*, anchored one afternoon in the exact spot where it was to be purposefully sunk the next morning in shallow water. The ship was to be used as a dock and breakwater. After supper on the ship, I returned to my room and packed all my belongings. The next morning after breakfast, our last meal on board, the growing roar of many aircraft engines sent me out on deck to find out the source. Hundreds of B-24s heading south into France, flew in close formation and dropped great quantities of silver foil in order to confuse the German radar. We knew the B-24s' purpose from listening to the news. They were to bomb the hedgerows from which the Germans used to delay the invasion.

A dining companion, Cliff Jennings spoke up. "I remember that. I was a pilot on one of those aircraft." Those planes belonged to the 8th Army 491st Bomber Group, Second Division, and had dropped thousands of bombs to help the army troops to break out of their perimeter.

The coincidence of the two of us eating together and comparing notes gave the story a personal touch which interested all present.

On June 19, 1944, Cliff flew his plane accompanied by the entire 491st Bombardier Group over the SS *Pennsylvanian* at Utah Beach, Normandy on their way to bomb the German's protective hedge rows.

In the year 2009, I, the former Chief Mate on the *Pennsylvanian*, and Cliff, both now residents of Sugar Hill, traded war stories. I told how I was writing this book and how God protected the ships I served on throughout the war.

He told of a remarkable incident while he flew in a group bombing run over Germany during March 1944. When they flew over and attacked the target, they received anti-aircraft fire. An 88 mm shell came up through the bottom of his B-24 just behind his pilot seat. The shell rolled up the protective armor on the back of his chair like a scroll and then exited the top of the plane without exploding. Cliff was not injured. The four engines were not affected, and his plane made it back to base without further incident. Cliff stated that his plane had to be flown to another place to have the holes and seat repaired. When the plane came back, the damage was invisible. The plane was as good as new. It seemed likely, he said, that the shell's explosive charge had been set to explode at an altitude higher than the plane was flying. Cliff told the story as a matter of fact. I regarded the story as a miraculous incident.

A SLOW LEARNER, A QUICK LESSON
WHY ME?

I was always a slow learner, but when I prayed a prayerful question to our Lord, He soon answered my prayer.

"Why only me Lord. Were there others who had or received the assurance that I did, the assurance of safety in perilous circumstances and assurance of safety during attacks by deadly enemy?"

The answer was succinct. It was not my business. It was the Lord's business.

Previously, I had speculated that the Lord uses human weakness to display His Glory. In grammar school I was one of the weakest and smallest in my class. I developed a talent, I learned to play a piano quite well, but I dropped it in favor of baseball. A willful mistake.

No doubt while at sea, there were many praying for me – family, relatives, an entire congregation of a large church, and others. I had to be content knowing that.

My original declaration of the indwelling of the Holy Spirit was a very personal, very intimate communication with my God. It was to be more than 60 years before I shared it with anyone.

Part 5: 1944 to 1945 - SS *William J. Worth*

This Liberty ship signed its crew on foreign articles September 27, 1944 in Philadelphia, where the ship loaded war cargo.

Captain Murwell E. Ryder, the Master, and I had never met nor had I ever heard about him. No doubt he had been briefed concerning me, as he asked me no personal questions. He was the scruffiest officer I had ever seen. Unruly black hair covering the top of his head stuck up and his unshaven facial hair stuck out. His rumpled clothes sagged along with his frown. I never saw him hurry. He knew his job and treated me well. On occasion he laughed. The Bos'n was experienced and old enough to be my father. Scruffy or old, these men kept our ship well cared for and ready to go to sea.

MORE ON LIBERTY SHIPS – SS *WILLIAM J. WORTH*

One feature of passing interest was the large skylight placed amidships on the after end of the boat deck. It ventilated the ship's galley. When the skylight was opened in good weather, I looked down on the large stove in the galley and watched the cooks stir the meals in pots or fry the meat on the hot surface of the range. Odors wafting up through the opening attracted the curious. Steaks laid out in rows whetted our appetites. The most delicious odor of all came from frying liver. I didn't like the taste, even though it smelled good. Apparently, many on board liked the stuff.

In rough weather, a simple system of short vertical stanchions and horizontal bars kept the pots and pans from sliding off the top of the stove.

The Stewards department personnel were the only ones allowed in the galley, except during Captain's inspection.

Generally, the food was good. Complaints were minor.

The *William J. Worth* completed loading cargo and undocked at 1815 hours, September 30, 1944. Towboat captain Marvel, with the aid of his tugs *Triton* and *Neptune*, assisted.

As Chief Mate, I stood on the bow with six crew members. Second Mate Otto Postel, with five crew members, stood on the stern. Third Mate Alfred Whitehead stood on the bridge along with the helmsman, Captain Ryder, towboat captain Marvel, and the river pilot.

Down came the order from the bridge. "Take in all mooring lines." When all the lines were on board, the two tugs began to push the ship. Nothing happened. The ship did not move! We were stuck in the mud. Captain Marvel ordered an astern bell on the main engine. The reversed propeller began to turn. The tugs continued to push. The ship began to move, but with obvious reluctance. Instead of backing directly out of the slip, the mud and the tide pushed the ship toward the adjoining pier. In spite of the tugs' efforts, the ship struck the corner of pier 100. The impact did not damage the strong pier.

However, our gangway stowed in a recess of the main deck sustained damage. I wondered if this mishap was an omen for the trip.

After Captain Marvel spent 25 minutes maneuvering the ship out of its berth and into the river, he departed and river pilot Dunlop took over.

PHILADELPHIA TO ANCHORAGE, DELAWARE BAY

In prewar, a junior officer or cadet from the ship's personnel took the soundings around the docked ship using a hand lead and line. He then made a chart in the shape of the ship which showed the depth of water around it. The eight or ten soundings he took on both sides of the ship were sufficient. The basis of the soundings was mean low water, so he had to consult the published tide tables and apply the difference in height to his charted soundings. The chart then showed depths of water at low tide.

However, we did not take soundings and did not know the depth of water at our dock. In wartime, we docked and departed as ordered.

Pilot Dunlop conned the ship cautiously. The ship crept down the river. All the ships docked parallel to the river as well as the ships tied up to docks perpendicular to the river, were affected by the great volume of water moved by our deeply loaded ship passing by them in close proximity.

I received permission to stow all the mooring lines below. The lines would not be used again until our discharge port, an unknown place and time.

The next morning while the ship was in Delaware Bay, Captain Ryder made arrangements to have a compass adjuster come aboard. I received the order to drop anchor.

DELAWARE BAY TO NEW YORK

I found dropping and heaving the anchor to be one of my most interesting duties.

At 0425 hours Chips, the ship's carpenter, released the brake and the anchor splashed into the water. The deafening percussion of the chain rattling through the deck opening, over the windlass, and through the hawse pipe was music to my ears. The anchor chain's violent passage left a cloud of dust and rust from dried mud and oxidation. Two shots of chain (15 fathoms or 90 feet) were enough. Chips applied the brake and lowered the pawl in place on the chain. The ship was anchored in Delaware Bay awaiting the compass adjuster.

At 0720 hours, the adjuster came aboard and we hove up the anchor. He climbed aboard quickly and began his work. Captain Ryder and the three deck officers gobbled breakfast and took turns assisting the compass adjuster. At 0927 hours, the magnetic compasses and the radio compass were calibrated. The adjuster climbed down the Jacobs ladder into his boat bound for the distant shore of the bay.

OCTOBER 1, 1944
PHILADELPHIA TO NEW YORK

We were on our own – no pilot, no convoy, no commodore, no escort. After three years of war, our orders were to proceed alone to New York. It seemed like some kind of victory. No subs, no danger. Even the ship channel out of Delaware Bay was marked on the chart "swept" – no mines.

At midnight, without incident, we arrived at New York's Ambrose Light Vessel. At 0030 hours, Pilot C. Lowe clambered up the short pilot ladder to the deck. He piloted many Liberty ships and knew the best route up three decks to the navigation bridge. He piloted our ship up Ambrose Channel to anchorage #23. Pilot Lowe departed.

We remained at anchor in sight of the Statue of Liberty, from early on October 2 to 0832 October 5 until Pilot Bauzler took us back out through Ambrose Channel and out to sea. At 1046, our pilot climbed down the Jacobs ladder into his rowboat. Two oarsmen rowed him to the pilot boat.

OCTOBER 1944: TO EUROPE

The *Worth* steamed down the buoyed sea channel to Buoy A where the convoy was to form up. Our position was #121, the leader of column 12. Once all the ships were in position, the convoy steered east toward the United Kingdom and Europe in fine weather.

NEW YORK TO THE U.K.

The fine weather continued through October 9. We advanced ship's clocks one hour at night. This served to keep the time near 12:00 noon when the sun was on the meridian, and it permitted the navigators to obtain a noon latitude.

I wondered if our convoy was becoming bored. We enjoyed good weather, excellent formation, no problems, no attacks. Great! Let's have convoy 45° emergency turn drills. Could it be possible our convoy Commodore was getting bored as well? The turns started at 1100 hours and finished at 1545 hours. They were called exercises. The entire convoy participated. It was October 12, 1944.

It was as if the Commodore had excited the weather gods. On October 15, the storm swept in and overtook us. The wind blew, the seas built, and heavy rain doused the convoy. Fresh breezes helped us along. By October 17th, gale winds and heavy seas sent green seas sweeping across our main deck.

After dark on October 18, a mountainous rogue wave slammed over our starboard side. The force lifted #1 lifeboat out of its moorings and plucked it away.

There was nothing we could do to retrieve the boat, but we hoped to find a replacement in the next port.

On the same night, the Commodore was obliged to alter course 20° to the right using colored signal lights as printed in our secret signal book. A position report, most likely from ashore radar installation, warned the Commodore of the need to change course.

ARRIVAL U.K.
ANCHORED FIRTH OF FORTH, SCOTLAND

The next morning, the south coast of England, Start Point was abeam of our ship. Rough seas plagued us right up to the time the next pilot boarded the ship at 0700 on October 20. Pilot Bray took us to anchorage at the south end, a place called Warp, 1500 hours off Southampton. We were happy to relax while we waited for orders.

On October 22, 1944 at 0742, when Pilot Bray returned to us, we departed and steamed north up the east coast of England and Scotland. The pilot conned us into the Firth of Forth, Edinburgh, Scotland on October 23, 1944. At 2240 hours, we anchored and waited for daylight. At dawn, we weighed anchor and steamed to a convoy anchorage to wait for orders.

On November 17, strong gales beat on the *Worth*. The authorities decided to move our ship to a more sheltered anchorage. Both anchors were holding, but it seemed prudent to move, which we did, twice. Again, it was necessary to use both anchors. We steamed slow ahead to relieve the strain on the chains and prevent dragging the anchors. It was a rare occasion when it was necessary to use both anchors to hold the ship in place.

I wondered how long it would be before this gale ended. The Captain's secret log read, "November 19-December 2, Vessel at anchor in Methil Roads, experiencing numerous gales. Vessel riding to two anchors and steaming. Vessel holding. Forty two days at anchor. That last 17 days with constant gales. Days of standing alert anchor watches on the bridge, waiting for orders."

METHIL, SCOTLAND TO SOUTHAMPTON, ENGLAND

We didn't hear much news, because the only radio on the ship was in the radio shack. Only the radio operator occasionally heard a broadcast. Anything dramatic he passed on to others or us. Captain Ryder repeated some non-confidential items to us when he garnered some information from authorities.

Finally, on the morning of December 3 we received a message, "The pilot will board at 1300 hours."

Pilot Floakhart boarded at 1320. Twelve minutes later, we weighed anchor. 1332 hours was the official DEPARTURE time – time port time ends and sea time begins. The *Worth*, part of a small convoy, breasted heavy head seas and pitched its way down the east coast of England. On December 5 at 1000 hours, the *Worth* received orders, along with seven other ships, to proceed to the Downs anchorage. We arrived at 1700 hours. A launch visited each ship to collect its pilots.

SOUTHAMPTON TO LE HAVRE

On December 6, 1944, we weighed anchor at 1331 hours, Master conning, bound for the recently opened French port of Le Havre. The weather, typical for winter in the English Channel, was overcast and squally. Our ship joined a convoy crossing the channel. On December 7 at 0400 hours, the *Worth* detached from the convoy and, with an escort vessel, followed a buoyed channel to Le Havre. At 1536 hours, we let down the port anchor with 90 fathoms of chain. We thought that should hold our vessel in place for awhile – but for how long?

The anchor held for six days. On December 13 at 0830 hours, Pilot Emile Perrault climbed aboard. We hove up the anchor at 0840 hours and steamed into Le Havre harbor. Two U.S. Army tugs assisted us into berth #4. It was necessary to tie up to mooring buoys, because the harbor ruins included the loss of dock bollards. We used the port anchor to help hold the ship in place.

Cargo discharge began as soon as the gangway was rigged and the longshoremen could get aboard.

Because we saw that the structures along the waterfront had been bombed and destroyed, there seemed to be no point in going ashore. However, some enterprising crew members managed it and found some grog shops, pubs. The crew needed some relief after many weeks of waiting at anchor. After three years of North Atlantic crossings, storms, and sinkings, the stress of waiting seemed to me almost like a vacation.

Was the entire German Air Force involved in the defense of Germany? At night no enemy aircraft appeared while we were offloading cargo under brightly lighted decks and holds. At 0600 on December 21 all cargo was offloaded.

At 1120 hours, Pilot Lonthoon boarded and the unmooring began. After all lines were hauled aboard, the anchor windlass heaved on the anchor. Nothing happened. The bottom of the harbor continued to hold the anchor in its grasp. The faithful steam anchor windlass strained and groaned trying to haul up the anchor. The anchor chain shook and trembled under the strain. The pilot ordered the engines ahead. Still nothing happened. The pilot ordered the engines astern, the rudder left, then right. Nothing helped. For one hour, these maneuvers had no result, until something broke loose. Ever so slowly, the windlass hoisted a great weight. A mass of rubble broke the surface of the harbor water in a wild tangle of steel beams, rods and concrete wrapped around the anchor. Captain Ryder and the pilot conferred. "Unlock (disengage) the windlass, release the brake, drop the anchor, and maybe the rubble will come off." Again nothing happened.

For another hour, the windlass strained with desperate maneuvers. Suddenly, all was quiet. The windlass easily cranked in the anchor chain until the bitter end showed the anchor was not there. The anchor and the rubble remained on the bottom of the harbor. The ship was released. The ordeal was over!

I leaned against the bow bulwarks clinging to the cap rail and exhaled with relief. It was not a triumph, only a release. The *Worth* steamed out of the harbor. Au revoir, Le Havre. The pilot departed into his launch at 1525 hours, no doubt glad to see us go.

Now the *William J. Worth* lacked one of four lifeboats and one of two bow anchors.

As Allied forces drove retreating German forces from southeastern France, the Allied command hastily opened such harbors that became available. Le Havre, for instance, was not clear of debris and safe for ships. Yet the U.S. Army was outrunning its supplies and had to use every resource it could, even bombed out harbors like Le Havre.

LE HAVRE TO SOUTHAMPTON

On December 21, 1944 Captain Ryder ordered the time of DEPARTURE as 1527 hours.

It was my bridge watch at 1600 hours. To my surprise, the *Worth* was proceeding independently with no escort, no pilot, and no enemy opposition. A buoyed route directed us back to Southampton area.

One hazard slowed us – FOG. Nab Tower stood nearby, but the fog became so thick we needed to anchor. Once again the Bos'n, carpenter, seaman on watch and I trudged up the empty deck to the bow. There was only one anchor – the starboard – and at 2355, our carpenter Chips released the brake on an order from the Captain on the bridge.

It was December 22. (I remembered, "It's my Dad's birthday – he's 48 and I'm 24 – he's just twice my age.")

At 0915, the fog cleared. It took only 14 minutes to run to the windlass, purge water from the cylinders, and heave up the anchor. However, it was one of those patchy fog days. At 1007 hours, down splashed the anchor again. At 1243 hours, we had an anchor drill once more in the fog. At 1344 hours, Pilot Brown boarded. He had been expecting us and told us the news. The *Worth* was to be the Commodore ship in a convoy. Big deal? No. The convoy's route was to be from Nab Tower around the corner to Barry, Wales – the corner being the south tip of England – a day and a half voyage. Barry or Bristol Channel was the storage anchorage for ships awaiting orders on convoys or ballast.

SOUTHAMPTON (ST. HELENS ROADS) TO BARRY, WALES

At precisely 1600 hours on December 22, 1944, Commodore of the convoy Commander MacMillan and his staff climbed up the long Jacobs ladder and made themselves at home.

The next morning, December 23, the Commodore's staff took over the flying bridge to man the flag hoist halyards and signal flags. At 0627 hours we weighed anchor, Master conning, and the *Worth* led the way. When our ship passed other ships at anchor, they responded to our signal flags and/or orders previously issued. It was like being a maritime Pied Piper.

The following morning, when the convoy passed Falmouth, more ships joined the procession.

BARRY FOR BALLAST

On Christmas Eve day, at 2136, the *Worth* arrived at a place called Mumbles in Bristol Channel where we anchored. At 2300 hours, a boarding officer ordered us to proceed to Barry at once. The Commodore and his staff hustled home.

We weighed anchor and proceeded independently to a place called Breaksea Light Vessel. We anchored and awaited orders.

I felt as if someone was passing our ship from one place to another because no one wanted us. However, there was a purpose, and it had nothing to do with the fact it was Christmas Day. The harbor was full to overflowing with ships and we had to wait for berthing space!

Our vessel had anchored at 0225 Christmas morning. At 1425, Pilot Edmunds boarded and conned us through a breakwater and into locks which protected the port of Barry.

The *Worth* went through locks into the Port of Barry and tiered with two other ships. There the *Worth* waited its turn to load ballast. The ballast was gravel said to have been dredged from the bottom of the Thames River.

PREPARATIONS FOR HOMEWARD BOUND TRIP

The only obvious sign of Christmas celebration appeared on our printed menu headed "Merry Christmas." The cooks prepared roast turkey for the noon meal and sirloin steak for the evening meal, plus ice cream.

To my dismay, the *Worth* was not only tied up to buoys fore and aft, but the ship was tiered between a British vessel and the American vessel SS *Samuel Nelson*.

However, because the locks system kept the harbor waters motionless, the tiered ships did not chafe against each other. Our turn at the ballast loading dock came a few days later.

On December 29 at 1035 hours, Pilot Thoring and two tugs, *St. Barack* and *Benson* pulled our ship out of the tier and alongside the loading dock, which had been a coal tipple and now was a gravel ballast tipple.

Experience proved many times that empty freighters in the North Atlantic were at the mercy of the strong winds and high seas. Fifteen hundred tons of ballast in the wintertime was a necessity to keep the propeller and rudder in the water.

Captain Ryder, officers, and the crew were thankful for the replacement of the lost anchor and the lifeboat. Those things were the nearest we had to Christmas presents.

The loading of the ballast only required five hours, but the ship remained there at the coal tipple over New Year's Eve.

However, there was little or no celebration. Someone spoke of the obvious, "After all, we are still at war." That statement was supposed to be a consolation.

All on the ship knew we would soon be homeward bound. That was the real consolation.

On January 1, 1945 at 1645 hours, Pilot Benson and two tugs undocked our vessel and took us through the locks to the anchorage at Barry Roads, where we anchored at 1910 hours.

On January 2, Captain Ryder, ordered a compass adjuster. We received the adjuster on board at 0920 hours. All the officers and a pilot who came on board helped the Captain complete his job.

I stood by the anchors because it was necessary in the restricted waters to turn the vessel in a wide circle. Our gyro compass had proven to be less than 100% reliable. Because we were sailing in winter across stormy waters of the North Atlantic, we anticipated a rough trip home.

Our orders sent us to Milford Haven but were immediately countermanded to remain at Barry Roads. It was just another anchor, let go, and heave up drill – or in this case, heave up the anchor and let it go again drill.

January 2 was a false alarm as to our departure, but January 3 was for real. At 1600 hours, a boarding officer arrived with routing instructions.

On January 3, 1945, the boarding officer was followed by a Vice Commodore of the Barry section of the convoy. At 2050 hours, we weighed anchor and at 2054, DEPARTURE was logged.

The *Worth* was homeward bound. It steamed south out of Bristol Channel and past Milford Haven where other sections joined us. Somewhere before the convoy turned west into the Atlantic Ocean the Vice Commodore departed. It was January 4, 1945 and our position in the convoy was #111. The *Worth* was the first ship in the 11th column of the now full convoy, the last contingent joining on the morning of January 5.

My philosophy concerning the weather of the North Atlantic Ocean was to expect the worst and hope for the best. The reality was in between. Three days of fog brought heavy rain squalls. The sea and swell were bad news for the crew in a vessel still riding high in the water despite the added ballast. Under the wintry and rough weather, our vessel pitched and rolled heavily, reacting to every irregularity of the sea surface by riding over it rather than through it. Although our vessel rolled heavily at times, counter measures that were employed helped. The messmen wetted the tablecloths. That measure prevented dishes from sliding off the tables, but did not prevent liquids from spilling. We placed life preservers under our mattress edges to keep our sleeping bodies inside our bunks.

But – we were on our way home and the weather had moderated considerably!

With all our meanderings in and out of many anchorages and ports, long days and seemingly endless weeks of waiting, hundreds of miles of convoys as well as running alone (only when empty!) – we met no enemy action of any kind in port or at sea until the afternoon of January 5. At 1518 hours our escorts and aircraft began dumping depth charges on an unseen enemy.

At 1520 hours, the convoy was ordered to make an emergency 45° turn to port (the left) followed by another 45° turn to port again. Now the convoy steamed south instead of west. At 1600 hours, the convoy began two emergency turns to starboard (the right) and resumed the original course.

When the convoy executed two successive 45° turns, the ship that had been ahead in the column was now on the starboard side. The ship that had been astern in our column was now on the port side. The ships that had been beside us in the respective columns were now ahead and astern. Reorientation was complicated by different turning circles. One ship could use 10° rudder, another 20° rudder. Did all bridge officers give their helmsmen orders at the same time? Probably not. On a dark night, nearby ships became black blobs. Distances were hard to judge. Hopefully, they maintained the same course and speed as the other ships.

Ironically, if the weather had been bad, it was likely no attack would have been attempted. But the moderating weather had make an attack feasible. Fortunately, the countermeasures were effective. The convoy had steamed about six miles south and escaped by going around the position where the depth charges were dropped.

This was the only obvious threat of the entire voyage. The convoy steamed on. After we escaped the threatened attack, we enjoyed three days of good weather.

Our homeward bound seamen grew impatient. Usually heading against wind and sea, the crossing of the North Atlantic seemed slower heading west. Worst of all, the clocks were retarded four times. At those points, each of the three night watches had 20 minutes added. If a four hour watch on a stormy night seemed long, a four hour and 20 minute watch seemed like it would never end. For that reason, labor union seamen have been known to seek overtime pay for that extra 20 minutes until they recognize that on the eastbound voyage, the clocks are advanced, so the night watches are only three hours and 40 minutes. Then those 20 minutes seem like a free gift.

Day after day, we sailed a little closer to home. The Second Mate posted a chart in the messroom to plot the noon position every day. Our convoy made good time, averaging a distance of about 240 miles or 10 knots per hour.

Our eagerly anticipated ARRIVAL came at 0654 hours on January 18, 1945 when New York's Ambrose Light Vessel came into view. In turn, our pilot boarded at 0950 hours.

We were home!

HOME PORT: NEW YORK

January 18, 1945. The New York pilot boarded our ship on ARRIVAL, and we steamed up Ambrose ship channel into New York Harbor. Docking in home port after a long hard trip was a happy time. Everyone on board was anticipating a loving reception at home. Parents, wives, children, girl friends and relatives were waiting on the dock or at home.

First a boarding party marched up the gangway, including a doctor, immigration officials, the port authority checking crew members to crew list, and customs who were checking declarations and likely searching quarters. Crew members with long hair got special attention. As soon as this procedure was finished, the ship was declared cleared. There was a rush to get ashore. The mate on watch was the first man down the gangway to read the draft markings fore and aft. All the men looked for telephones. Some were quick to find transportation home locally.

Company representatives met with the Captain and as soon as possible announced the date and time of "payoff." Wages were paid in cash only, by law. If the payoff was considered large, a bank representative was present to sell traveler's checks. The officers and crew lined up on a first come, first served basis to be paid by the Purser. A Company representative, the Captain, and Shipping Commissioner were witnesses. While waiting in line, the men's happy anticipation was tempered by goodbyes. This was a bittersweet time. Most crew members split ASAP with a hot pocket full of cash, if they had not already spent it in foreign ports.

TRIP # 2 AT HOME PORT, NEW YORK
AND
NEW YORK TO BOSTON

January 18 - 31, 1945. The wartime intensity of events and life on a freight ship preparing to load cargo and sail away while in the port of New York defies brief description. In the midst of the organized turmoil of repair, resupply and manning, and loading cargo, we received news that our ship would top off cargo loading in Boston and then return to New York to join a convoy bound for Europe.

Officially, our Voyage #8 began at 0000 hours on January 31, 1945. At 1125, two Moran tugs, *Alice* and *Agnes* under the orders of a docking master, undocked our ship from its loading berth. Pilot Coan directed our ship up the East River, under Hellgate Bridge, and into Long Island sound.

The pre-war practice of American-Hawaiian Steamship Company of going around Cape Cod did not apply here. We were to transit Cape Cod Canal; the safest and shortest route in wartime from New York to Boston.

Many of the following entries were taken from the Captain's "Secret Log," which has been transcribed in full in the Appendix.

Feb 1	0300	We anchored off the western end of Cape Cod Canal. Pilot Syverton conned us on this inland route.
	1048	Anchor aweigh.
	1150	West end reporting station.
	1223	East end reporting station, a 33 minute transit.
	1600	ARRIVAL at BOSTON LIGHT VESSEL, Pilot M. R. Jackson conned us through the nets and by the examination vessel.
	1857	Tugs *Luna* and *Ares*, with tug Captain Sullivan, took us into the old Army Base, now B.P.O.E. (Boston's Port of Entry).

BOSTON, MASSACHUSETTS, FEBRUARY 2, 1945
HOME FRONT WELL ORGANIZED

As a Chief Mate, I was the designated first aid person. I kept a medical logbook of all crew members who asked for help in dealing with colds, lacerations, indigestion, constipation, diarrhea, and chest pains, in which was recorded names, dates, places and the treatments. All this was routine. Then came the surprise! A message for me came aboard. I would give all the crew members an inoculation! The next day, I would be provided with the inoculation materials.

For me, it was not panic time, not quite anyway. I had never used a hypodermic syringe. I sought the Captain's advice, hoping that he had experience in this procedure and offer to take over.

However, Captain Ryder advised me to go to the Chief Steward and obtain an orange to practice on. An orange to practice on! The Chief Steward was amused as he went below decks to the large walk-in cool room where perishables were kept. He broke into a full crate of oranges, gave me one, and took one for himself.

The hypodermic supplies were in the hospital room. The large room consisted of two sets of tiered bunks and a row of locked lockers that were filled with supplies including jars of creams and ointments, tubes of remedies, and a plethora of medical emergency gear, like rubber sheets and bed pans as well as the hypodermic syringes and needles. I found the necessary items and went back to my office room, where I practiced sticking the needle in the orange. At first my attempts were awkward. As I became more confident in my skill injecting an orange, I also realized that the tough epidermis of an older seaman might be different than the softer orange peel.

The next morning, I set up in an unused room, with disinfectant, cotton swabs, and a row of throw away syringes. The syringes were pre-loaded with serum against a half a dozen diseases, such as typhoid. I tried to choose the first victim carefully, but the Purser volunteered. The improvement in my skill, as well as my confidence, was fast. I completed all the inoculations in less than an hour, including stragglers and those on watch.

BOSTON TO NEW YORK

New York was the ship's legal home port, but Boston was my home port because my family and I lived in suburban Arlington. I hoped to get home for at least a quick visit.

Feb 2   0800   Vessel commenced loading cargo.

Feb 6   1800   Vessel completely loaded.

My hope was delayed. Second Mate Eric Pierce lived in Boston. Third Mate Alfred Whitehead lived with his wife in Fall River. There was no night relief mate. It was my decision, and I stayed the first night.

Late in the evening, the ship was quiet. A stranger knocked on my open door while I read at my desk. He introduced himself and subjected me to a hard sell – to join the Navy! I was astonished!

All graduates of Massachusetts Nautical School, later renamed Massachusetts Maritime Academy who passed the test for their third mate's license received a provisional commission as an Ensign in the United States Naval Reserve. In October of 1942, when I returned home from the disastrous trip to North Russia with Convoy PQ-17, I found a pile of mail which included a discharge as an Ensign in the U.S. Naval Reserve. Being at sea almost continually since graduation, I had failed to verify the commission. The provisional time had expired while I was being attacked by German bombs and torpedoes. I was angry at the Navy! The stranger departed, disappointed because I refused to join.

It took five working days to load our cargo, so I did get home.

FEBRUARY 1945
TO GIBRALTAR

1945

Feb 7   0700   Tugs, *Ares* and *Mercury* alongside, Tug Captain H. A. Pits, conning. Our vessel was delayed because of many lighters (barges) in our slip.

0803   All lines aboard.

0833   Vessel in channel. Harbor Pilot E. A. Martin now conning us through nets.

0915   Magnetic compasses undergoing adjustment. Coast Pilot C.H. Lawrence now conning.

BOSTON TO NEW YORK TO GIBRALTAR

1945

Feb 7   1042   DEPARTURE – Boston.

1127   Boston Light Vessel abeam. Our vessel proceeding to Cape Cod Canal.

1515   Anchored, awaiting canal transit.

1710   Anchor aweigh.

1726   East end reporting station.

1814   West end reporting station. Transit time 48 minutes. The tidal current was strong against us. We steamed down Long Island Sound.

Feb 8   As we approached the vicinity of Hellgate, heavy snow squalls closed down the visibility. We anchored twice. The second time, we awaited the Hellgate Pilot W. B. Morse, who boarded at 1045.

1245   Under Hellgate Bridge assisted by tug, *Sheila Moran*.

1341   Passing Battery.

1350   Passing Statue of Liberty.

1430   Anchored in #23 anchorage near Staten Island.

Feb 9   Vessel at anchor awaiting convoy.

Feb 11   1130   Anchor aweigh. Pilot C. Huns conning. Tug *Madelyn J. Mesick* assisting us out of crowded anchorage.

1230   Through nets.

1314   Pilot away.

1315   DEPARTURE, Ambrose Light Vessel. Taking position #11 in convoy (lead vessel in first column.)

Feb 12   Convoy enjoying good weather.

Feb 13-20   Weather overcast, strong breeze to moderate gale. Convoy averaging 220 miles per day.

Feb 21-27   Fine weather – gentle breeze, slight sea.

Feb 28   0237   Cape Spartel in sight.

| | 0420 | Passing through Strait of Gibraltar. |
| | 0925 | Our convoy position changed to #32. |

GIBRALTER TO U.K.

1945

Feb 28	1930	Received message over BAMS radio: "Return to Gibraltar forthwith, advise receipt and E.T.A. Gibraltar." Notified Commodore.
	1935	Broke from convoy and turned west.
Mar 1	0900	ARRIVAL Gibraltar.
	0915	Pilot Viale on board.
	0930	Passed over degaussing range.
	0953	Let go port anchor in 50 fathoms.
	1550	Anchor aweigh. Vessel proceeding to sea in Convoy MKS 86.
	1600	DEPARTURE.
Mar 2	0740	Convoy forming front, steering west. Our position assigned as #64 changed to #63. Convoy turning from west to northwest.
	1702	Commenced series of emergency turns. Eight in all. Resume course of 340°. No reason given. Weather partly cloudy, gentle breeze, and slight sea.
Mar 3	1230	Emergency turns, six in all.
	1510	Resume course of 0010.
Mar 4	1200	Moderate gale, heavy seas. Only made 181 miles today.
Mar 5	1200	Weather moderating – 131 miles.
Mar 6		Changed course to an easterly course picking up stragglers. Our position changed to #62.
Mar 7	2330	Lizzard Head abeam. (South coast of England).
Mar 8	2300	ARRIVAL, St. Helens Roads, Southampton.
	2315	Pilot A.D. Howe aboard, conning.
Mar 9	0110	Let go port anchor. Vessel at anchor off Cowes, Isle of Wight.
	1737	Anchor aweigh.
	1915	Exit nets.
1926		Pilot away – joining convoy.

SOUTHAMPTON TO CHERBOURG
TO SOUTHAMPTON TO BARRY ROADS (BRISTOL CHANNEL)

1945

Mar 10	0200	Our vessel detached from the convoy – our destination Cherbourg, France. One escort vessel accompanied us.
	0400	Cape Barfleur near.
	0645	ARRIVAL – Off Cherbourg. Pilot J. Costel aboard and conning.
	0830	Tugs *Cherbourgois #3* and *Cherbourgois #4* alongside.
	0850	We passed through the inner breakwater.
	0918	First line on dock.
	0930	All fast to dock, berth #30.
	0930	Ordered to move to berth #32.
	1005	All fast to berth #32. Cherbourg.
Mar 11-12		Discharging cargo.

Another Liberty ship docked in berth #30. Chief Mate was Jocko Carlson, a school shipmate of 1939-1940. We had a fond reunion recounting the bad old days when we were sailing ship cadets. He was also Fourth Mate on the SS *Arkansan* July 8 - December 15, 1941. Jocko was always liked by his shipmates.

Mar 12	1200	Finished discharging cargo.
	1400	Pilot F. Perrigault aboard. Tugs *Cherbourgois #3* and *Abella* alongside.
	1418	All lines gone.
	1425	Clear of pier.
	1452	Clear of breakwater. Let go port anchor.
	2138	Anchor aweigh, Master conning. Steering north, weather fine and clear.
Mar 13	0439	Vessel following buoys to Nab Tower, Southampton. Distance 90 miles.
	0635	Pilot Vigaro aboard and conning.
	0710	Let go port anchor – awaiting orders.
	0845	Anchor aweigh. Master conning.
	0916	DEPARTURE, vessel bound around southwest England into Bristol Channel.
Mar 14	2206	ARRIVAL Barry Roads.
	2223	Vessel at anchor off Breaksea Light Vessel awaiting orders – Fine weather.

A CAVEAT

Spring, 1945. There was a discrepancy in the recounting of the SS *William J. Worth's* itinerary for the voyage from January 31, 1945 to April 30, 1945.

In fact, a whole leg of the voyage in the Mediterranean was omitted from the Captain's log.

The *Worth* anchored in the bay at the port of Leghorn, Italy sometime in the month of March 1945. I have a photograph taken at the Leaning Tower of Pisa, undated but likely taken in March as we all wore jackets. The ship's Officers were in the picture. Their names were on the crew list for that voyage only and not for the previous voyage. The following voyage was to the Philippine Islands.

I have a vague recollection of Captain Ryder telling the Chief Engineer in my presence, that he had a lot of catching up to do on his personal log. This turned out to be the secret log required by the government.

Another indication that the port of Leghorn was omitted from the Captain's secret log was that our only port of discharge, according to the secret log, was Cherbourg, for two days only. The loading of that cargo had spanned seven days. It would have been nearly impossible to offload a cargo in two days that had taken seven to load. Therefore most of the cargo must have been discharged at anchor in Leghorn, Italy.

Subsequent to the offloading in Cherbourg, the *Worth* loaded cargo in Avonmouth, England and later discharged in Ghent, Belgium.

IN LEGHORN, ITALY

The DUKWs often provided transport for shore leave. A group of us made a trip to Pisa as tourists: the Gunnery Officer, Lt. Williams, the Purser, the Third Engineer, the Army driver, and I. Purser Hank Koch arranged the trip. It was an interesting interlude in a beaten country where some places of beauty and history remained untouched.

Our offloading was slow. The cargo was offloaded into DUKWs which had a capacity of one ton only. It seemed to me that there were so many loaded ships that needed to be offloaded and all that cargo had to be used, stored or moved. Had the enemy submarines failed? A resounding YES. This was a proven fact, as we steamed homeward bound north off the French coast from Gibraltar to the Irish Sea. There was no apparent danger from the infamous submarine pens, possibly now bomb damaged beyond usefulness. But we were homeward bound.

BARRY, WALES TO AVONMOUTH, ENGLAND

1945

Mar 15	0642	Pilot A.W. Garrett aboard.
	0652	Anchor aweigh, proceeding into port of Barry through locks to coal tipple.
	1006	Vessel fast to dock under coal tipple.
	1640	Pilot J. Booker and tugs *Windsor* and *St. Barack* assisting (vessel took fuel and fresh water.) Pilot Cler takes us through locks. Vessel anchors overnight.
Mar 16	1800	Pilot C. Roland now conning.
	1800	DEPARTURE. Vessel proceeding northeast farther into Bristol Channel.
	2120	Off Avonmouth locks, await transit. Tugs *Merrimasic* and *West Wind* alongside. Pilot H. Canby on board.
	2242	Vessel fast to S Shed, Avonmouth.

Mar 17-18		No cargo worked.
Mar 19	0800	Commenced loading cargo.
Mar 20-25		Vessel loading cargo.
Mar 25	1700	Completed loading.
Mar 26	0405	Dock Pilot G. Canby, tugs *Triton*, *Bristolian* assist vessel.
	0442	Clear of dock.
	0445	Locking through.
	0517	Clear of locks. Pilot Hunt conning, tugs away.
	0518	DEPARTURE.
	0804	Vessel slows to permit pilot to depart.
	0827	Let go port anchor.
	0840	Commodore Gross and four men aboard.
	0907	Anchor aweigh – steering westerly courses out of Bristol Channel in convoy.
	1510	Convoy into Irish Sea, south bound.
	1515	Escort investigating contact – no results.
Mar 27		Convoy steams around southwest point of England. Overcast hazy light airs.
Mar 28	0625	Thick fog.
	0723	Let go port anchor.
	0845	Anchor aweigh – fog cleared.

AVONMOUTH TO SOUTHAMPTON TO GHENT, BELGIUM

1945

Mar 28	0908	Nab Tower abeam.
	0930	Pilot A.E. Billett aboard.
	0908	Let go port anchor St. Helen's Roads – awaiting orders.
	1015	Pilot, Commodore, and staff away.
	1658	Anchor aweigh. Master conning.
	1742	Nab Tower abeam. Vessel following buoyed route to Trinity Bay, northeasterly courses. Weather overcast, hazy to thick fog.
Mar 29	0412	Pilot L. A. Couves on board, conning.
	0730	Vessel at anchor in Trinity Bay. Weather overcast, fresh breeze, moderate sea.
Mar 30	0358	Anchor aweigh. Vessel proceeding to Belgium Coast.

	0540	Pilot Couves away – Belgian Sea Pilot aboard. Small convoy proceeding toward Western Schelde.
	1120	Opened fire on black object making way through water. Fired several rounds of four inch and 20 mm guns until our escort orders us to cease fire.
	1525	Entering Western Schelde.
	1555	Pilot C. Heives now conning.
	1700	Let go port anchor. Vessel at anchor off Terragon awaiting canal transit.
Mar 31	1450	Anchor aweigh. Pilot Bloem conning. Three tugs assisting vessel through locks into canal.
	2027	Vessel secured to canal bank awaiting daylight.
Apr 1	0555	All mooring lines taken aboard. Tug *St-513* assisting.
	0800	Vessel fast to Berth #27 Ghent.
	1000	Begin discharging cargo.
Apr 7	1230	Completed discharging cargo.
	1310	Pilot Verheist aboard. Tugs *U.S.A. 725* and *U.S.A. 504* alongside.
	1355	All lines on board.
	1422	Coming alongside SS *Joseph I. Kemp*.
	1705	Began pumping fuel to *Joseph I. Kemp*.
	2035	Finished pumping fuel to *Joseph I. Kemp*.

BELGIUM BOUND – HURRY UP AND WAIT

The SS *Pennsylvanian* had been an aid to the Normandy invasion in June 1944. Now the *William J. Worth* was to be a close supply ship for the U.S. Army rolling across Europe. We were to go to a designated U.K. east coast port and wait for orders. Proceeding at full speed around the top of Scotland, we dropped the anchor in the Firth of Forth, and there we waited.

Even before we anchored, we heard and read of Hitler's desperate counter attack pushing back U.S. forces, he hoped, into the sea. Day after day of dense fog forced our Air Force to stay on the ground in the U.K. while the fighting in the Ardennes region of Belgium was indecisive. We remained at anchor waiting. We were waiting for a decision that would open harbors in Europe.

We knew our troops had won the Battle of the Bulge. We wondered why we waited, and found out we were waiting for the cleanup, for the unglamorous work of making ports ready and finding the mines in harbor approaches by sweeping all the waterways.

Finally, after being at anchor for three weeks, we were ordered into Ghent, Belgium. We entered a canal system just wide enough and deep enough for a Liberty ship.

There was no room for steering error through those narrow canals. My guess was that the canal to Ghent was built wide enough for self-propelled canal barges to pass one another and for coastal steamers to transit comfortably, but transit for 400 x 50 ft. ocean going ships was not practical without assistance.

All the bridges and walkways over the canal had been destroyed. All the debris and obstructions were removed. We were supplied with a towboat to keep our ship strictly on course. Our draft was more shallow than usual because much of our cargo was measured by space and not by weight. Our cargo was relatively light and included vehicles, crates, some food, and supplies of all kinds.

The quay where we docked had electric cranes that survived the war. A young couple who were our interpreters boarded with the harbor officials, a doctor, and immigration. They spoke French, Flemish, English and, no doubt, German. They told us that when they realized American ships were coming they took an eight day crash course in conversational English. They learned quickly, spoke well and were a big help.

GHENT, BELGIUM – A CITY IN RECOVERY

The Germans had not been gone long. Maybe two to three months. Our cargo was slowly discharged in March 1945.

Because I did not go ashore very much, I did not have any souvenirs to bring home except for one brass ash tray. The passage from Ghent to the North Sea was easier because of experience plus a light draft.

The trip home was relatively peaceful because the stormy season had ended and the enemy submarines were absent. While the potential menace remained, the German Admiral Doenitz had withdrawn his submarines from the Atlantic because of their unacceptable rate of losses. However, we didn't know that. We looked for a periscope behind every wave.

When we completed the voyage from Ghent to homeport, another surprise greeted us. Wartime cargoes and destinations were full of surprises. This time we were to go to the Philippines. The cargo on deck consisted of four USCG cutters. They were 83 feet long, made of wood, and set in cradles. Their crews lived on board. I worried that a tumultuous trip on a crowded ship might cause friction between ships' crew members, Naval gun crew, and Coast Guard cutter crews. Whatever could happen may happen.

1945: TO THE PHILIPPINES

REPRISE? ANOTHER LONG TRIP ON A SLOW SHIP

New York to the Philippines was another long trip on a slow ship. The first one was 28 days on the *Arkansan* from New York to Cape Town during the peace time summer of 1941. Four years later on the *Worth*, I spent the second long voyage, 31 days in the late months of WWII.

If personality conflicts existed on this trip, they did not surface. It seemed to me that the four young officers, U.S.C.G. Ensigns assigned as commanders of the cutters we were carrying, had been carefully selected and well trained to command. Plus, the U.S. Navy Gunnery Officer with his gun crew seemed to be wonderfully compatible.

And why not? Many of us were experienced in the art of war on merchant ships. Both we and the military personnel knew our jobs and knew how to get along. In addition, the expectancy of victory was tangible. The Germans were in retreat in Europe. The Japanese were being driven back to their homeland islands. We were not exultant or joyful, but our morale was high and it stayed high.

After we left the Panama Canal, two of the cutters' officers started up a bridge game between 9:00 and 11:00 A.M. most mornings. The Gunnery Officer, two of the ship's engineers and I, a learner, made up a table. Sometimes I kibitzed, as there was often a spare player. I learned the that Gunnery Officer, a lawyer in civilian life, was an excellent player – the best in our group. The worst player was the First Engineer, a little guy from Brooklyn, New York, who had a loud foul mouth but was not perceived as a threat because of his small size and because he could also be funny. He habitually overbid his hand and played badly. The Second Engineer picked up the cards he was dealt and fanned them, but did not redistribute them by suit. This led to an occasional error on his part, like miscounting trumps or miscounting cards in a suit. I learned two things. I wasn't the worst player, and the better the player, the better the cards.

My morning watch on the bridge was from 4:00 - 8:00 A.M. Usually I was relieved by the Third Mate before the end of the watch. Then I wound the chronometers, had a brief conference with the Bos'n, and sat down for breakfast about 8:10. Often the Captain, the Chief, First Assistant Engineers, and I had breakfast together. Sometimes the Purser, and Sparks the Radio Operator would join us. In the course of the conversation we would solve ship and world problems, resolve mistakes, note ship speed and weather, and on and on.

One morning, while westbound approaching the Marshall Islands, Captain Ryder dropped a verbal mini-bomb on us. He said, "My routing instructions order me to stay at least eight miles off the Marshall Islands as the Japs there have been bypassed and there is a possibility they have artillery and ammunition."

I said, "Star sights this morning put us north of the course line, and that line is about 10 miles south of the Marshalls." The Japanese were to the north.

The Captain and I bolted for the chartroom. He won, because I let him go up the ladder first.

No sweat. We would not be passing the islands until later.

We knew that from our vantage point on the bridge, the horizon was about eight miles away. The Sailing Directions stated the Marshall Islands had a low silhouette. As it turned out, all we could see was an irregular bluish line barely above the horizon, which confirmed that our position was as ordered. We did not expect gunfire, and there was none.

It was a "tough" war. Thirty-one days of fine weather, no enemy opposition and no problems, while we covered 250 to 260 miles a day.

We had no great expectations for our port of arrival, a SeaBee port in a small harbor on the south side of Luzon or another nearby island. The water was relatively shallow and crystal clear. I could see the anchor and all the chain after we anchored. The chain snaked out to the anchor 180 feet away (two shots of chain).

When we docked we discovered a large Naval Command presence. Many U.S. Naval Officers watched our deck cargo. A huge floating crane came alongside our ship and lifted the Coast Guard Cutters from our deck. Before we could say goodbye to the Coast Guard crews they were gone. We never saw them again. Then the cutter cradles were removed and we never saw them again. We wondered briefly what was in the stacked storage boxes – some covered, some not. Much later, I thought it probable that the preparations for the invasion of the Japanese Islands had begun and the stockpiles were supplies for that invasion.

There were no entertainment facilities in evidence.

This was in contrast to our previous port of call, Cristobal, Panama, where we had docked to top off fuel oil for the long journey to the Philippines and there was shore leave for one evening.

I went ashore in Cristobal with two of the cutter commanders, both young and handsome ensigns in white uniforms. I was dressed in a khaki shirt and trousers and no tie, but with an officer's visored hat, the obvious veteran mariner at age 25. We stopped at a nightclub where there were girl hostesses and we ordered drinks for all. The alcohol mixed with the heat of Panama affected the three of us. I stopped at one drink. Not so the two ensigns, who had chugalugged three drinks. I felt it was essential to consider that the next day we would be transiting the canal and my station was on the bow standing by the anchors in the hot sun. I left the nightclub, returned to the ship and worked the next day during the transit. I never saw those two all day long. As shore leaves go, Cristobal was a bust, but at least it was shore leave.

At our Philippine SeaBee port, the Commander invited the ships' officers to dinner at his battalion headquarters dining room. He had been a ship captain for American Hawaiian S.S. Co. for many years.

THE GOOD OLD DAYS
AND GERMANY SURRENDERS

Captain Sonborg, the Commandant of the construction battalion, had a delicious meal served to us. We all reminisced, that is, the senior officers did. The junior officers ate and listened for the most part. Many American-Hawaiian S.S. Co. names were brought up, mostly from San Francisco and vicinity where Captain Sonborg was based. One of the people we discussed was Captain Bamforth. I learned that he was a Pilot in Honolulu and Pearl Harbor.

Before the war Captain Charles Nathaniel Bamforth was Master of the SS *Pennsylvanian* in 1938 and of Master of the SS *Honolulan* when it was torpedoed in 1942. He also served the American-Hawaiian S.S. Co. as a pilot on the NY - Boston - Philadelphia loop. He volunteered for the Navy and was assigned to Pearl Harbor. He was known as Iron Jaw and later co-wrote *Iron Jaw: A Skipper Tells His Story,* Captain Charles N. Bamforth. Pittsburgh, PA: Dorrance Publishing Co., 2002.

The setting was almost idyllic. The dining room was screened in on three sides. The fourth side was the kitchen. The almost flat roof had a large overhang of more than three feet, so no rain splattered the diners. Trees shaded the area and a gentle breeze dried perspiration. It was hot, but endurable.

Our cargo was offloaded with unusual swiftness. We were ordered back to the States to Los Angeles where we docked in Long Beach on May 7, 1945. The next day was V-E Day, Victory in Europe Day, the joyous day of celebration. The day that the Allies formally accepted the unconditional surrender of Nazi Germany. Jubilant crowds walked, jumped, shouted, hugged, kissed and thanked God. I was part of the crowd. Everyone was a friend. There were no more enemies. It was incredible.

What about Japan? Oh, well, they were still enemies, but it was only a matter of time!

BACK IN NEW YORK

The cnd of war at last! Japan surrendered August 14, 1945 – V-J day. I was still a Chief Mate on the *Worth*. The ship languished in a shipyard in Brooklyn, New York.

I heard the news and the noise.

Charlie, the foreman of the cleaning gang American Hawaiian used for cleaning the holds on their ships, ran to my room and demanded I sound the ships whistle. I debated if I should sound the whistle and decided there was already plenty of other whistle noise. I knew the whistle was full of water and would make a cacophony of sound. I ran to the flying bridge and tried the hand lever. Water and steam hissed from the stack whistle just over my head. After a few seconds, the whistle began to squeak, stutter then blow, the way it should. We joined the chorus of joyful noise.

It was the end of the MIRACLES. Our Lord had been faithful to His Promise "YOU SHALL NEVER BE ON A SHIP SUNK BY ENEMY ACTION."

Our Lord's promises are as good as the fulfillment. Fulfillment is inevitable. Praise, Thanksgiving and Blessing to Our Lord.

Final Thoughts

LIST OF MIRACLES FROM GOD'S PROMISED PROTECTION

A strong, clear message from the indwelling Holy Spirit, these 11 words: *"You shall never be on a ship sunk by enemy action."*

1. SS *Arkansan*, Egypt, September 19, 1941. A cluster of three bombs straddled our ship; shrapnel pierced the hull above the water line; repaired the next day. It happened during an air raid by the German Air Force.

2. SS *Samuel Chase*, steaming north of Iceland in convoy on July 4, 1942 received a German air torpedo attack. A torpedo headed toward our ship, changed course and missed our ship, as if directed by a giant hand.

3. On the same day, a submarine at the rear of our convoy fired a torpedo which converged on our bow but never exploded. Our #1 hatch in the bow held 50 tons of dynamite.

4. By order of the British Admiralty, the convoy scattered leaving the *Chase* running alone in crystal clear weather. Fog suddenly enveloped our vessel as enemy planes flew low overhead. We were not sighted. The fog shield lasted about two minutes. No Allied air force bases were within many hundreds of miles.

5. Captain Martin ordered us to abandon ship as an enemy sub closed in for the attack. Seeing lifeboats in the water, the sub Commander perhaps sensed a trap. He aborted his attack. His periscope was seen; then it disappeared. We climbed aboard our ship and resumed our voyage.

6. Six times dive bombers attacked the ship. Each dropped a cluster of three bombs. All the clusters straddled the ship and exploded in the water.

7. Violent concussions from the bomb explosions cracked every shaft bearing except one. The Chief Engineer despaired and declared, "We'll never make it home, never." A great storm, with waves 65 feet high and 1,300 feet from crest to crest protected us from attack on part of our voyage home. The propeller shaft bearings held together.

8. Homeward bound in the Barents Sea, our convoy of 11 ships, the remnant of convoy PQ-17, suffered. Two more ships were sunk at night. Again, our ship was spared.

9. Oran, North Africa. In early January, 1943, the *Samuel Chase* and one other ship were ordered to leave the convoy and enter the port of Oran. As we headed for port, a cataclysmic explosion sent the SS *Arthur Middleton* to the bottom of the sea. There were only three survivors. We were spared again. God's promise held true. The *Samuel Chase* delivered her cargo to the U.S. Army in North Africa, and she once again made it home to New York.

10.   In May 1943 after raising my license to Chief Mate, I was assigned to an older ship, the SS *Pennsylvanian*. From then until June 1944, the *Pennsylvanian* made seven voyages from the east coast of the United Stated to various ports in U.K. and Italy. The Lord's protection seemed obvious. When the ship was loaded with cargos of ammunition, no attacks came. Twice during the homeward bound voyage after delivering our cargo, our convoys were attacked but our ship was not hit.

11.   The final destination of the *Pennsylvanian's* 31 year life was Utah Beach, Normandy. It and five other ships were all to be scuttled in shallow water and used as instant docks and breakwaters. As we approached the *Pennsylvanian's* last resting place, the ship ahead struck a mine and was lost. We were supposed to be the first ship in the line. Once again our ship was spared.

12.   I was on the SS *William J. Worth* from September 1944 - May 1945. This ship sailed three voyages into war torn areas: Cherbourg, France; Leghorn, Italy; Ghent, Belgium; and Tacloban, Philippine Islands without encountering any attacks. God's protection was complete, but His miracle of timing was not obvious until later. The *Worth* arrived in Los Angeles on the eve of the German surrender and then arrived in New York just before the Japanese surrender. All the crew joined the celebrations. It's unlikely that any other ship arrived in an American home port on the eves of the surrender of both Germany and Japan so that all the crew could join in both ecstatic celebrations.

August 14, 1945 – V-J day. God fulfilled His promise, *"You shall never be on a ship sunk by enemy action."* The war ended and God completed His protection.

THE ANATOMY OF A MIRACLE

"It is impossible for God to lie." (Hebrews 6.18)

An omniscient God sees and perceives the intent and actions of men. God has the power to turn that action into a miracle that glorifies Himself.

It may take only a moment, or it may take a length of time to accomplish.

For instance, the German torpedo dropped by an aircraft came directly towards the center of our ship, the engine room. Suddenly the torpedo made a drastic course change as if guided by a giant hand and the torpedo passed close under our stern, missing by a narrow margin. Only a touch, a momentary touch, changed a disaster into a miracle.

Or consider the torpedo fired by a German submarine from a position astern of the convoy. The torpedo was sighted by our alert Chief Mate on a nearly parallel course headed for the bow portion of our ship. The #1 hatch held 50 tons of dynamite, potentially able to destroy our ship and other nearby ships also.

The helmsman failed to carry out the shouted order, "Hard right." Instead, Mr. Wilson ran the dozen steps into the wheelhouse, pushed aside the panicked seaman and turned the wheel hard right. Did the torpedo scrape along the side of the ship and propel itself into the open sea ahead? Or did it miss entirely? It failed to explode, though it took a few seconds for the Chief Mate to turn the ship away while expecting the explosion that never came.

Did God prevent the explosion? God had to prevent it in order to keep His promise to me. "*You shall never be on a ship sunk by enemy action.*"

Or again consider the miracle of the instant fog in clear weather. That fog came out of nowhere and lasted only about 20 seconds, just long enough for a squadron of German aircraft to fly over without sighting us. They controlled the skies around us within a radius of hundreds of miles.

The miracle of the dividing bomb clusters took much longer, an hour or more. The trajectory of the bomb clusters appeared certain to hit amidships, yet every bomb exploded in the water on both sides of the middle of the ship. The concussion of the many near misses caused the ship to react with great violence. All the pedestal bearings which held the propeller shaft in place cracked except one.

Our Chief Engineer declared, weeping, "We'll never make it home."

Homeward bound a great storm with mountainous seas pushed our vessel southward sagging through deep troughs and hogging over high crests. The bearings held. We made it home. Was it a miracle? The cracked bearings were caused by enemy action. God's protection was in force.

Finally, God's Watch Care miracle on the SS *William J. Worth* from September 27, 1944 through September 10, 1945, during which time the vessel made three long trips: one to Italy, one to the U.K. and western European ports, and one to the Philippines – all areas devastated by war. Our ship was not threatened by any perceived danger. God kept His promise throughout the war.

The miracles were God's actions alone. There was no worship, thanksgiving, prayer or praise involved. There was blessing. The miracles were a collective blessing. They all were God's initiative, accomplished in order to fulfill God's promise to me, *"You shall never be on a ship sunk by enemy action."*

But what activated the miracles other than God's initiative? I believe that many millions of people praying, some general prayers and some specific, flooded all of heaven. God heard and chose these miracles as part of His response to this multitude of prayers.

Afterword

A TALE OF THREE LOVES

Dad's book ends at the close of World War II, but his life continued and we wanted to briefly recount his life after the end of the book. It is a story of his love for his God, his wife and family, and of the sea.

After the war, he continued his life as a merchant seaman with long voyages interspersed with vacations at home in Arlington, Massachusetts and in Wolfeboro, New Hampshire.

On one such vacation in 1949, he stopped by to see his mother who was working as a teller at the Arlington Cooperative Bank. She introduced him to a co-worker, Barbara Sexton. The story is that they were both smitten. A beautiful young woman and a handsome man in uniform. They were married on June 15, 1950, earlier than planned because Dad's ship arrived in port ahead of schedule. In May 1951 Sara Louise was born.

Dad's career at sea continued and for the next eight years, life was a series of separations and reunions, both requiring lifestyle adjustments for all three. Barbara and Sara travelled up and down the east coast to meet Rod's ships when they returned to port after voyages to distant places. He was home when daughter Pamela Ruth was born in December of 1957, and then at sea for many months after her birth.

In 1959, Dad made the decision that his duty was to leave the sea and be at home with his family. He held a series of low paying jobs, finally ending up with a clerical position with the Bank of Boston. Dad never gave up his love for the sea and maintained his licenses and union membership the entire time by working as the night watch for ships in port in Boston and New York.

Throughout his years at home, he was actively involved in the First Baptist Church of Arlington, where he served as Deacon, Choir Member, Sunday School Teacher, and on many other boards and committees. He was also active in the Gideons International and helped place Bibles in many hotels and motels in New England. He also travelled to Brazil to give out Bibles in Rio de Janeiro and Brasilia.

When his daughters were grown up and on their own and Barbara was working as the Chief Financial Officer of the New England Institute in Boston, Dad made the decision that he would go back to sea. He went back to school to learn about the technological changes that had taken place in 20+ years since the 1950's.

From 1981 to 1986 life for Dad and Mom, their children, and now their grandchildren, became once again a series of goodbyes and reunions.

Dad finally retired in 1986 and he and Mom moved to his beloved Wolfeboro NH.

In 1991, the Russian government presented him and 116 other survivors of PQ-17 with a citation signed by Mikhail Gorbachev and a medal commemorating "The 50th Anniversary of the Victory in the Great Patriotic War" in a ceremony at the Soviet Embassy in Washington, DC. Daughter Pam accompanied him on this special occasion.

Dad never spoke much about his adventures during the war and his belief that he had been saved by God's miracles until late in life. When his sister-in-law, Claire, commented that he should write down his stories, he began to do just that. His effort to put his thoughts down on paper began as a series of short stories that he would write out by hand and mail to Claire, who would type them and mail back. So the book grew over the years. As you read through the book, you can still detect the hints of the short stories, interspersed with log book entries. The transition from narrative to log entry and back again parallel the life of a sailor at sea, days of routine interspersed with adventures.

Now in 2012 as the book is nearing completion, Dad is 91, dealing with macular generation that makes reading difficult. Mom, age 86, is in a nursing home and Dad visits her every day. Dad holds on to his faith as his strength to continue his life that was Saved By A Series of Miracles. We are grateful to have been able to be a part of his effort to proclaim his faith and his witness.

Sara and John Buttrick

May 2012

APPENDICES

GLOSSARY OF TERMS

Abeam: Beside.

Astern: Behind the stern or back of the ship. In some contexts, to back up.

Bear: Built in Scotland in 1874, the *Bear* had a varied career which in addition to being on Admiral Byrd's second Antarctic expedition, included being a sealer or a museum ship (known as the *Bear of Oakland*); doing a tours of duty in the US Navy as the USS *Bear* and the Coast Guard as the USCGC *Bear*; and a role in the 1930 film *The Sea Wolf*.

Chartlet: A small navigation chart that highlights a particular geographical feature.

Degauss: To demagnetize by means of electrical coils

DUKW: Pronounced as Duck. A six-wheeled amphibious truck designed for transporting troops and materials over both land and water.

Dhow: A lateen-rigged coastal Arab sailing vessel with one or two masts.

Dunnage: Rough wooden planking formed into crib structures or loose packing material, both used to protect a ship's cargo from damage during transport.

Emergency Change of Course: Usually 45° port or starboard.

Ensign: The most junior commissioned officer in the Navy. Previously the rank Passed Midshipman referred to an Ensign who had passed the Lieutenant exam and was eligible for promotion to Lieutenant as soon as there was a vacancy in that grade.

Fetched up: Stopped.

Firth: Scottish term for a long, narrow inlet of the sea.

Halyard: A rope used to raise or lower a sail, flag, or yard.

In Square: Refers to the area in the hold directly under the deck hatches. The cargo is lowered through the hatch into the hold. From there it is redistributed within the hold in accordance with a loading plan.

Light Vessel: Also called a Lightship. Abbreviated as L/V or L.V. A ship used as a lighthouse in a place where building a permanent structure would be impractical. The ships themselves were identified by number but were known by the name of the place they were located. For example, frequent references in this book are made to the Ambrose Lightship, which was located at the Ambrose Channel off Sandy Hook, New Jersey leading into New York Harbor.

Paps of Coyuca: Also known as Cerro Tetas De Coyuca, twin mountain peaks north of Acapulco used as a navigation aid by mariners. They are located in the Sierra Madre del Sur mountains, which is part of the American Cordillera sequence of ranges that extend from Alaska to the tip of South America and includes the Rocky Mountains in the United States.

Pawl: A hinged or pivoted device adapted to fit into a notch of a ratchet wheel to impart forward motion or prevent backward motion.

Plimsoll Mark: The load line mark on a ship. Named after Samuel Plimsoll (1824-98)

Port: The left side of the ship. Specifically refers to an opening in the side of a ship that is fitted with a watertight door, for access to the holds.

Scotch Boiler: A fire tube boiler in which hot flue gasses pass through piped within a tank of water; used used primarily on ships.

Secret Log: Official logbooks that were issued to the masters of American registered merchant vessels operated by the War Shipping Administration at the beginning of each voyage. They were turned in to the United States Commissioner at the port where each vessel ended its voyage. These logbooks were maintained by the ship's master and were separate from the ship's deck logs maintained by the watch officers.

Shot of Chain: A unit of measurement for anchor chain = 15 fathoms = 90 feet.

Skerries: A small group of coastal islands in North County Dublin, Ireland.

SS: The SS stands for Steamship and precedes the name of a ship.

Sparks: A general nickname for a ship's radio operator, derived from the use of a spark-gap transmitter to generate electromagnetic waves in early radio telegraph devices.

St. Helens Roads: No contemporary reference could be found for St. Helens Roads; however there is a village of St. Helens located on the Isle of Wright which protects the harbor of Southampton. A roads (or roadstead) is a partially sheltered anchorage.

Starboard: The right side of the ship. From the Old English, meaning "steering side" in that boats were formerly steered by a paddle held over the right-hand side.

Tipple: An apparatus for unloading freight cars by tipping them.

'Tween decks: A space between two continuous decks of a vessel.

Watling Island Light: Known today as San Salvador, the island name was changed from Watlings Island in 1926, but it probably took some time for all the maps to be updated. The lighthouse is known today as Dixon Hill Light.

Watch Below: Time when not on duty.

AMERICAN HAWAIIAN STEAMSHIP COMPANY VESSELS - 1940

In Intercoastal Trade
*Dickie Served

	Ship Name	Year	Place Built	Disposition
1	SS *Alabaman**	1921	Shanghai, China	Broken up Japan 1959
2	SS *Alaskan*	1918	Sparrows Pt., MD	Sunk, November 1942
3	SS *American*	1916	Philadelphia, PA Cramp	Sunk June 11, 1942
4	SS *Arizonian*	1920	SUN – Philadelphia, PA	Broken up, Japan, 1959
5	SS *Arkansan**	1921	Shanghai, China	Sunk, June 15, 1942
6	SS *Californian*	1922	Chester, PA	Sold to England,1940 Empire Seal Sunk February 1942
7	SS *Carolinian*	1921	Shanghai, China	Scrapped 1960
8	SS *Coloradan*	1920	Japan	Sunk October 1942
9	SS *Columbian*			Survived the War
10	SS *Dakotan*	1912	Sparrows Pt., MD	Broken up, Croatia
11	SS *Delawarean*	1920	San Pedro, CA	Sunk as Empire Hawkesbull July 1942
12	SS *Floridian*	1921	Shanghai, China	
13	SS *Georgian*	1921	Sun, Chester, PA	Broken up Hoboken 1959
14	SS *Hawaiian*	1919	Camden, PA	Broken up Italy 1958
15	SS *Honolulan*	1921	San Pedro, CA	Torpedoed July 1942
16	SS *Illinoisan*	1926	Osaka, Japan	Scuttled, Normandy, 1944
17	SS *Indianan*	1919	Seattle, WA	Scuttled, Normandy, 1944
18	SS *Iowan*	1914	Sparrows Pt. MD	Broken up 1969
19	SS *Kansan*	1918	Cramp, Philadelphia, PA	Broken up, Italy, 1944
20	SS *Kentuckian**	1910	Sparrows Pt., MD	Scuttled, Normandy
21	SS *Louisianan*	1919	Seattle, WA	Foundered (As it left Rio) 1958
22	SS *Mexican*	1907	San Francisco, CA	Broken up Brunswick, ME 1948
23	SS *Minnesotan*	1912	Sparrows Pt., MD	Broken up, Bari, Italy, 1952
24	SS *Missourian*	1922	Chester, PA	Broken up Taiwan 1970
25	SS *Montanan*	1917	Chester, PA	Sunk, Japanese Sub, June 1948
26	SS *Nebraskan*	1917	Chester, PA	Sunk, last U.S. Ship torpedoed, May, 1945
27	SS *Nevadan**	1915	Camden, NJ	Wrecked as Oakley, Alexander, ME 1947
28	SS *Ohioan**	1920	Vancouver, WA	Sunk by German Sub, May 1944
29	SS *Oklahoman*	1920	San Francisco, CA	Wrecked, So. Africa, July 1942
30	SS *Oregonian*	1917	Cramp, PA	Torpedoed, Convoy PQ18,1942
31	SS *Panamanian**	1904	Camden, NJ	Broken up, Hong Kong,1948
32	SS *Pennsylvanian**	1913	Sparrows Pt. MD	Scuttled Normandy, June 1944
33	SS *Puerto Rican*	1919	Vancouver, WA	Sunk, One Survivor, 1943
34	SS *Texan**	1902	Camden, NJ	Sunk, German Sub, March 1942
35	SS *Utahan*	1919	Seattle, WA	Broken up, Pakistan, 1960
36	SS *Virginian*	1903	Sparrows Pt. MD	Broken up, Philadelphia 1948
37	SS *Washingtonian*	1919	Japan	Sunk by Japanese Sub April 1942

Thanks to Eric Stone for compiling the above information.

SS WILLIAM J. WORTH VOYAGE # 1 ITINERARY

FROM THE CAPTAIN'S SECRET LOG

DATE   TIME   ACTION

DEPART FROM PHILADELPHIA TO NEW YORK TO U.K. PORTS AND RETURN

1944

Date	Time	Action
Sep 30	1815	Depart dock, proceed to Delaware Bay.
Oct 01	0425	Anchor Delaware Bay for daylight transit and compass adjustments, Pilot Dunlap.
Oct 01	1055	Proceeding to sea bound for New York.
Oct 02	0004	ARRIVE Pilot Love. Ambrose Light Vessel, NY.
Oct 02	0255	Vessel at Anchor, New York Harbor. Await orders.
Oct 05	1040	DEPART New York, join convoy. Position #21. Convoy steaming east at nine knots.
Oct 06-09		Good weather – advance clocks one hour.
Oct 11		Good weather – advance clocks one hour.
Oct 12	1105	Emergency turns by convoy as an exercise. Finished practicing emergency turns.
Oct 13-14		Good weather. No enemy attacks.
Oct 15		Strong winds and rain – advance clocks one hour.
Oct 16-17		Fresh breeze, moderate increasing seas.
Oct 17		Advance clocks one hour. 1232 Vessel detached from main convoy. Gale winds and heavy seas boarding vessel.
Oct 18	1945	Heavy seas and swell, #1 Lifeboat lost.
Oct 19	1320	Portland Light abeam.
Oct 19	1905	St. Catherine L/H – sea moderating.
Oct 20		Clocks advanced one hour.
Oct 20	0700	Pilot aboard – W. E. Bray – proceed to Southend.
Oct 20	1459	Let go port anchor. Vessel at anchor. Await orders.
Oct 22	0742	Anchor aweigh, proceeding North to Scotland.
Oct 23		Arrive Michel Bay. Firth of Forth, Scotland.
Oct 24-Nov 16		Pilot L. MacAcallister. Vessel at anchor. Awaiting orders.
Nov 17	1130	Heave anchor, move to more sheltered anchorage from gale winds. Pilot V. Westioster.
Nov 18	1102	Change anchorage again.

Nov 19		Vessel uses two anchors and steams slow ahead, anchors holding against gales.
Dec 3	1332	Heave anchor. DEPART Firth of Forth. Pilot Flockhart.
Dec 4		Steaming south in English Channel in convoy.
Dec 5	1006	Detached from main convoy, now Worth commodore of seven ships bound to Downs, England.
Dec 5	1650	Anchor at Southern Anchorage, Downs.
Dec 6	1331	Weighed anchor. DEPARTURE for Le Havre, France with escort.
Dec 7-12	1530	Anchor off Le Havre – await orders.
Dec 13	0840	Heave anchor proceeding into harbor.
Dec 13	1124	U.S. Army tugs assisting. Vessel moored to buoys at berth #4 and commence discharging cargo.
Dec 21	0600	Vessel completed discharging cargo.
Dec 21	1120	Undocking from mooring buoys, port anchor fouled on harbor bottom debris.
Dec 21	1426	Lost port anchor, proceeding to sea.
Dec 21	2355	Anchor in dense fog in English Channel.
Dec 22	0929	Anchor aweigh – fog cleared.
Dec 22	1007	Dense fog – let go stbd anchor.
Dec 22	1243	Anchor aweigh.
Dec 22	1334	Pilot Brown aboard.
Dec 22	1351	Let go starboard anchor in St. Helen Roads.
Dec 22	1600	Commodore MacMillan, R.N.R. and staff aboard.
Dec 23	0627	Anchor aweigh. Commander MacMillan Commodore of convoy on bridge. Master Conning – Captain Murwell Ryder. Vessels proceeding to sea. Convoy forming up.
Dec 24		Proceeding in convoy to Barry Roads, England.
Dec 24	2300	Anchor – off Mumbles – Commodore and staff away.
Dec 24	2321	Weigh anchor and DEPARTURE – destination still Barry Roads.
Dec 25	0210	ARRIVAL at Barry Roads. Anchor there.
Dec 25	1440	Moving to dock, anchor aweigh. Pilot H. A. Edmunds.
Dec 25	1612	Vessel fast to SS Samuel Nelson and a British vessel at dock #1, Barry, England.
Dec 29	1059	Tug pulling vessel out of tier. Pilot T. S. Thoring.
Dec 29	1145	Our vessel fast to loading dock #2.
Dec 29	1500	Commence loading ballast (1500 tons).
1945		
Jan 1	1740	Depart dock, tug assisting. Pilot A. H. Denning.

Jan 1	1903	Let go port anchor. Barry Roads.
Jan 2	0935	Anchor aweigh. Pilot Lan Flear. Vessel adjusting compasses.
Jan 2	1232	Compass adjustments finished – Let go anchor.
Jan 2	2254	Anchor aweigh, proceeding to Milford Haven.
Jan 2	2300	Orders received to return to Barry Roads.
Jan 2	2359	Let go port anchor.
Jan 3	2050	Anchor aweigh – DEPARTURE – our vessel is Vice-Commodore.
Jan 4	1700	Main convoy formed up – all on station.
Jan 5	1518	Escorts and planes dropping depth charges. Convoy executing emergency turns.
Jan 5	1645	Convoy on course of 242°.
Jan 6	0000	Retard clocks one hour – good weather.
Jan 7	0000	Retard clocks one hour. Commodore exercises convoy in changing course by whistle signals. Vessel rolling heavily immoderate swell.
Jan 8-9		Moderate weather, overcast, fog banks.
Jan 10	0000	Retard clocks one hour.
Jan 11-12		Thick fog.
Jan 13-15		Fresh breeze, vessel rolling heavily.
Jan 16	0000	Retard clocks one hour. Heavy rain squalls, strong breeze, rough sea, rolling heavily.
Jan 17	1400	Convoy forms two columns.
Jan 18	0654	ARRIVAL off New York.
Jan 18	0950	Pilot aboard – proceeding into harbor.

SS WILLIAM J. WORTH VOYAGE # 2 ITINERARY

FROM THE CAPTAIN'S SECRET LOG

DATE   TIME   ACTION

NEW YORK TO BOSTON TO NEW YORK THEN TO U.K. (VOYAGE NO. 8)

1945

DATE	TIME	ACTION
Jan 31	0000	Voyage No. 8 begins.
Jan 31	1132	Tug and tug captain undock vessel. Pilot Conn, N. Y. Harbor pilot through Hell Gate to Fort Schyler.
Jan 31	1355	Pilot Conn ashore. Pilot Syvertsen now conning. Proceeding up Long Island Sound.
Feb 1	0300	Vessel at anchor awaiting Cape Cod Canal transit.
Feb 1	1048	Anchor Aweigh, proceeding through canal.
Feb 1	1227	Clear of canal.
Feb 1	1600	ARRIVAL Boston L/V Pilot M. R. Jackson.
Feb 1	2000	Tugs and Captain Sullivan dock vessel, B.P.O.E.
Feb 2	0800	Commence loading cargo.
Feb 6	1800	Vessel completely loaded.
Feb 7	0800	Tugs and Captain A.A. Pitts undock vessel.
Feb 7	0833	Pilot Martin conning from dock to nets.* *Nets are in place to stop enemy subs entering harbor and opened and then closed for ships.
Feb 7	0915	Adjusting compasses (magnetic).
Feb 7	1034	Compass adjuster leaves. Pilot Lawrence conning.
Feb 7	1127	BOSTON L/V abeam, proceeding to Cape Cod Canal.
Feb 7	1515	Anchor awaiting canal transit.
Feb 7	1710	Anchor aweigh. Proceeding through canal.
Feb 7	1819	Exit canal, bound through L.I. sound to New York.
Feb 8	0615	Heavy Snowstorm.
Feb 8	0736	Let go port anchor near Execution Park.
Feb 8	0801	Anchor aweigh.
Feb 8	0830	Let go port anchor – Await Hell Gate Pilot.
Feb 8	1045	Pilot W. B. Morse aboard and conning.
Feb 8	1120	Anchor Aweigh.
Feb 8	1239	Tug *Sheila Moran* assisting through Hell Gate.

Feb 8	1430	Let go anchor – off Stapleton – await convoy.
Feb 11	1130	Anchor aweigh, Pilot Huns conning.
Feb 11	1315	DEPARTURE, AMBROSE L/V .
Feb 11	1641	Taking position No. 11 in convoy (Front Left Corner).

NEW YORK TO GIBRALTAR, TO U.K.

1945

Feb 12-13		Vessel in convoy, various courses and speeds, weather fine and clear.
Feb 14	0200	Advanced clocks one hour – rough sea.
Feb 15-17		Weather overcast, rough sea.
Feb 18	0200	Advance clocks one hour – rough sea.
Feb 19-20		Overcast, strong breeze, rough sea.
Feb 21	0200	Advance clocks one hour, fine weather.
Feb 22-24		Good weather.
Feb 25	0200	Advance clocks one hour – change position in convoy three times to position No. 42 by order of commodore.
Feb 26		Good weather.
Feb 27	0200	Advance clocks – good weather.
Feb 28	0100	Land in sight.
Feb 28	0237	Cape Spartel abeam. Proceed through Strait of Gibraltar.
Feb 28	1930	Received orders through BAMS to return to Gibraltar.
Feb 28	1935	Broke from convoy – (notified Commodore).
Mar 1	0900	ARRIVE at Gibraltar. Pilot O. Viale aboard.
Mar 1	0953	Let go port anchor in Gibraltar Bay.
Mar 1	1550	Anchor aweigh, DEPART Gibraltar in convoy.
Mar 2	0000	Retard clocks one hour.
Mar 2	1702	Commence emergency turns by colored lights.
Mar 3	1230	Emergency turns by signal flags.
Mar 4-5		Steering northerly courses in moderate seas.
Mar 6		Changing courses and speeds to pick up stragglers.
Mar 7	1435	Detached from main convoy for Southampton.
Mar 8	0000	Advance clocks one hour.

Mar 8	2300	ARRIVAL – St. Helen's Roads.
Mar 8	2315	Pilot A. D. Howe aboard and conning.
Mar 9	0110	Let go port anchor, Corves. Isle of Wight.
Mar 9	1530	Pilot Hutchings aboard.
Mar 9	1730	Anchor Aweigh – DEPARTURE.

NEW YORK TO GIBRALTAR TO ISLE OF WIGHT, CHERBOURG, AVONMOUTH

1945

Mar 9	1915	Through nets – Weather fine and clear.
Mar 9	1920	Pilot away – joining convoy. Proceeding to Cherbourg, France.
Mar 10	0200	Detached from convoy. Proceeding independently with one escort vessel.
Mar 10	0645	ARRIVAL off Cherbourg.
Mar 10	0805	Pilot O. Costel aboard and conning.
Mar 10	0830	Tug *Cherbourgois No. 3* and *Cherbourgois No. 4* alongside.
Mar 10	0850	Through breakwaters.
Mar 10	1005	Vessel fast to Berth 32.
Mar 11		Discharging cargo.
Mar 12	1200	Finish discharging cargo.
Mar 12	1200	Pilot F. Perriguilt aboard – tugs *Cherbourgois No. 3* and *Abelle* alongside.
Mar 12	1425	Clear of pier.
Mar 12	1452	Let go port anchor in Outer Rack.
Mar 12	2138	Anchor aweigh. Aster conning. Proceeding to Isle of Wight. Weather is fine and clear.
Mar 13	0620	Pilot Vigaro aboard and conning.
Mar 13	0710	Let go port anchor – await convoy.
Mar 13	0840	Anchor aweigh. Master conning proceeding.
Mar 13	0916	DEPARTURE Isle of Wight.
Mar 14	2206	ARRIVAL, Barry Roads.
Mar 14	2223	Vessel anchored awaiting orders.
Mar 15	0645	Pilot A.W. Garrett.
Mar 15	0652	Anchor aweigh.
Mar 15	0720	Let go anchor off entrance to Barry Roads.
Mar 15	0856	Anchor aweigh – Tugs *Blazaor* and *S. Ross*.

Mar 15	0935	Through locks to dock – Pilot Booker and tugs.
Mar 15	1006	Vessel under coal tip No. 5 – to take fuel and water.
Mar 15	1648	Vessel leaves coal tip. Pilot C. Roland.
Mar 15	1800	DEPARTURE – Vessel proceeding to Walton Bay awaiting order.
Mar 15	1949	Let go anchor – in Walton Bay – awaiting orders.
Mar 16	2030	Pilot C. Roland aboard.
Mar 16	2045	Anchor aweigh.
Mar 16	2120	Tug *Merrimac*, *West Wind* alongside.
Mar 16	2210	Pilot H. Canby – locking through to "S" Shed.
Mar 16	2242	ARRIVAL Avonmouth. Vessel fast to loading dock.
Mar 17-18		No cargo worked.
Mar 19	0800	Commenced loading cargo.
Mar 20-24		Loading cargo.
Mar 25	1700	Completed loading cargo.
Mar 26	0405	Pilot G. Canby, Tugs *Triton*, *Bristolain*. Depart dock and locks. Pilot Hunt conning.
Mar 26	0518	DEPARTURE Avonmouth.
Mar 26	0804	Pilot Hunt ashore.
Mar 26	0840	Commodore Gross and staff of four men aboard.
Mar 26	0907	Anchor aweigh. Coastal convoy proceeding southwestward.
Mar 26	1515	Escort investigating contact – no result.
Mar 27		Good weather - proceeding south and east around south England.
Mar 28	0625	Thick fog.
Mar 28	0723	Let go port anchor.
Mar 28	0830	Fog cleared.
Mar 28	0845	Anchor aweigh.
Mar 28	0930	Pilot A. T. Billett aboard and conning.
Mar 28	0957	Let go port anchor in St. Helen's Road. Await orders. Pilot, Commodore and staff away.
Mar 28	1658	Anchor aweigh – Master conning.
Mar 28	1942	Thick fog – proceeding northeast.
Mar 29	0412	Pilot L. A. Couves aboard conning.
Mar 29	0730	Let go anchor in Trinity Bay.

Mar 30	0358	Anchor aweigh. Pilot Couves conning.
Mar 30	0540	Pilot Couves ashore. Belgian Sea Pilot aboard.
Mar 30	1120	Opened fire on black object moving through water. Fired several rounds four inch gun. Escort ordered cease fire. Pilot Ross conning.
Mar 30	1525	Entering West Schelde.
Mar 30	1555	Pilot C. Heiss conning.
Mar 30	1700	Let go port anchor – Off Terragon. Await canal transit.
Mar 31	1450	Anchor Aweigh. Pilot Bloom conning. Tugs assisting through locks into canal.
Mar 31	2027	Vessel fast fore and aft to canal bank, await daylight.
Apr 1	0555	Take in lines – tug assisting in canal transit.
Apr 1	0805	Vessel fast to Berth #27 Ghent, Belgium.
Apr 1	1000	Begin discharging cargo.
Apr 7	1230	Completed discharging cargo.
Apr 7	1310	Pilot H. Verheld aboard and tug assisting vessel to go alongside SS *Joseph I Kemp* to fuel him.
Apr 7	2035	Finished fueling SS *Joseph I Kemp*.
Apr 8	0745	Pilot V. Vlietinch aboard.
Apr 8	0835	All clear of Kemp Begin canal transit to sea.
Apr 8	1315	All clear of locks. Let go starboard anchor.
Apr 8	1332	Anchor aweigh – received orders to proceed. Sea Pilot Moreels, to south end anchorage.
Apr 8	1337	DEPARTURE - Various courses and speeds to Pilot station.
Apr 8	2353	Pilot L.A. Couves aboard. Weather fine and clear, smooth sea.
Apr 9	0248	Vessel at anchor in WARP, Firth of Forth – East Scotland. Awaiting daylight.
Apr 9	0900	Anchor aweigh.
Apr 9	0928	Let go starboard anchor, await permission to pass though nets.
Apr 9	0934	Anchor aweigh.
Apr 9	0955	Through nets.
Apr 9	1013	Vessel at anchor off Southend Edinburgh.
Apr 10-11		Vessel at anchor, South End.
Apr 12	1023	Anchor aweigh – Pilot P.S. MacDonald conning. Proceeding south, on East Coast of England. Overcast and thick fog.
Apr 13	0729	Let go port anchor – fog.
Apr 14	0230	Fog cleared.

Apr 14	0245	Anchor aweigh.
Apr 14	0509	Let go port anchor – await daylight.
Apr 14	0629	Anchor aweigh – proceeding into St. Helen's anchorage.
Apr 14	0740	Let go port anchor – Pilot away.
Apr 14	1224	Anchor aweigh – proceeding to sea – join convoy.
Apr 14	1718	Commodore orders emergency turns.
Apr 15	0030	Last emergency turn – Convoy steering west. Weather overcast, foggy.
Apr 16	0715	Sighted floating mine.
Apr 16	0845	Thick fog (ships straggling).
Apr 16	1300	Clearing, ships out of position, reforming.
Apr 16	1500	Our position is #24, now in position.
Apr 16	2045	Thick fog.
Apr 17	0000	Clocks retarded two hours. Vessel rolling heavily in moderate swell.
Apr 18		Convoy speed 9.7 knots – weather overcast.
Apr 19	0000	Retarded clocks one hour.
Apr 19	1600	Emergency turns.
Apr 20-21		Overcast weather – vessel rolling heavily.
Apr 22	0000	Retard clocks one hour.
Apr 23		Weather partly cloudy, moderate sea.
Apr 24		Moderate to fresh gale, heavy seas, rolling heavily.
Apr 25	0000	Retard clocks one hour – gales, rolling heavily.
Apr 26-27		Gale moderating.
Apr 28	0000	Retard clocks one hour.
Apr 30	1335	ARRIVAL – Ambrose L/V .
Apr 30	1625	Vessel at anchor off Statue of Liberty.

INDEX

Luna (Tugboat), 104
Luzon, Phillippines, 114
Lynnhaven Roads, VA, 54

M

MacMillan, Mr. (Commander), 101, 128
Madagascar, Republic of, 22
Madelyn J. Mesick (Tugboat), 106
Maloney, Shawn, 38
Marshall Islands, 113
Martin, Joe (Seaman), 25
Martin, Mr. (Captain), 38, 43, 46, 47, 50, 51, 106, 117, 130
Marvel, Mr. (Captain), 95, 96
Massachusetts Maritime Academy, 105
Massachusetts Nautical School, 1, 5, 105
Masters, Mates and Pilots, 26
Matanzas, Cuba, 77
Matochkin Strait, 41, 42, 44, 52, 56, 57
McNair, Lesley James (General), 87
Mecca, Saudi Arabia, 26
Mediterranean Sea, 20, 59, 91, 108
Mehetra, Mr. (Chief Engineer), 62
Mercury (Tugboat), 106
Merrimasic (Tugboat), 109
Methil Roads, Scotland, 73, 74, 75, 99
Milford Haven, Wales, 102, 129
Molotovsk, Russia, 44, 46, 47, 48, 49, 53, 54, 58
Morro Castle, Cuba, 79
Morse, W.B. (Pilot), 106
Mt. Desert Island, ME, 11
Mumbles, Wales, 101
Murmansk, Russia, 54

N

Nab Tower, 100, 108, 110
Nantucket, SS, 2, 3, 4, 5, 6, 8, 9, 10, 47
Narrows, NY, 79, 81
Nassau, Bahamas, 13
Nebraskan, SS, 12, 16, 49, 126
New Bedford, MA, 11
New York, NY, iii, 10, 11, 13, 16, 18, 20, 28, 29, 31, 34, 47, 51, 52, 53, 54, 59, 61, 63, 64, 67, 69, 71, 72, 76, 77, 79, 80, 81, 82, 83, 88, 90, 97, 103, 104, 105, 113, 115, 117, 118, 127, 129, 130, 131, 132
Norfolk, VA, 10, 34, 54, 57, 68
Normandy invasion, 69, 84, 85, 86, 92, 111
Normandy, France, 69, 86, 91, 92, 111, 118, 126
North Cape, Norway, 40
North Sea, 75, 112
Novaya Zemlya, 32, 41, 56, 57

O

Ocean Freedom, SS (British vessel), 57, 58

Ohioan, SS, 12, 126
Oran, Algeria, 59, 60, 117
Orkney Islands, Scotland, 73

P

Palomares, HMS, 42
Pan Kraft, SS, 57
Panama Canal, iii, 13, 14, 64, 113
Paps of Coyuca, Mexico, 14, **124**
Paris, France, 6
Pearl Harbor, HI, 29, 114, 115
Pennsylvanian, SS, iii, 67, 68, 69, 71, 75, 79, 80, 81, 85, 86, 87, 88, 91, 92, 111, 114, 118, 126
Pentland Firth, Scotland, 73
Perrault, Emile (Pilot), 99
Perrigault, F. (Pilot), 108
Perriguilt, F. (Pilot), 132
Petrofsky, Mr. (Captain), 33
Pettigrew, Mr. (Captain), 67
Philadelphia, PA, 48, 95, 114, 126, 127
Philippine Islands, iii, 109, 112, 113, 114, 118, 119
Pierce, Eric (Second Mate), 105
Pisa, Italy, 109
Pits, H.A. (Tugboat Captain), 106
Ponta Delgada, Portugal, 6
Port Elizabeth, South Africa, 22
Port Newark, NJ, 83
Port of Aden, Yemen, 27
Port Sudan, Sudan, 23, 24
Port Tawfik, Egypt, 24, 25, 26
Portland, ME, 10, 127
PQ-17, 34, 37, 38, 40, 44, 47, 59, 105, 117
Prinz Eugen (German cruiser), 41

R

Raley, Fred (Second Mate), 31, 32, 36, 38, 39, 41, 43
Red Sea, 19, 20, 23, 24, 25, 26, 27
Reykjavik, Iceland, 36, 37, 52
Richard Bland, SS, 54
River Mersey, 81
Robinson, Frank (Purser), 60
Rockport, MA, 3, 4
Roland, C. (Pilot), 109, 133
Rounds, John (Lt. Commander), 8
Rowan, USS, 56
Russia, 33, 34, 48, 51, 53, 59, 105
Russian (Soviet) Army, 33
Ryder, Murwell E. (Captain), 95, 96, 99, 100, 102, 105, 109, 113, 128

S

Samuel Chase, SS, 31, 32, 33, 34, 35, 36, 37, 38, 39, 40, 43, 44, 45, 47, 51, 52, 53, 54, 55, 57, 58, 59, 63, 64, 65, 68, 117

ILLUSTRATIONS

Illustrations - Table of Contents

Illustration 1-1 - School Ship USS *Nantucket* in Gloucester

(Reprinted with permission of the Boston Herald)

BOSTON TRAVELER, MONDAY, MAY 20, 1940

NANTUCKET AT GLOUCESTER — The Massachusetts nautical training ship is shown in Gloucester harbor shortly before leaving there for the annual cruise of instruction for cadets. The ship is due in Washington on Wednesday. In the foreground is the Fishermen's Memorial monument, dedicated to the many Gloucester fishermen who have lost their lives at sea.

Illustration 1-2 - School Ship USS *Nantucket*

(Source Unknown)

Illustration 1-3 - Graduating Class

(Source Unknown)

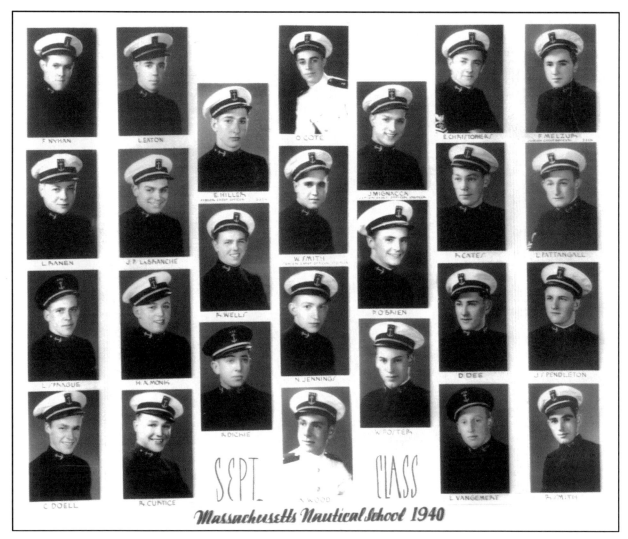

Illustration 2-1 - SS *Arkansan*

(Photo courtesy of The Steamship Historical Society Archives, www.sshsa.org)

Illustration 2-2 - Crew list of the SS *Arkansan* on her last completed voyage

May 28, 1941 to December 15, 1941.

Ports of Call were New York; Capetown, South Africa; Port Sudan, Port Tewfik and Cairo Egypt; Aden, Arabia; Vizagapatem and Calcutta, India; Capetown, South Africa before returning to New York. The *Arkansan* then made a long trip to the Middle East and was sunk June 15, 1942 in the Caribbean on the way home.

(Taken from Eric Stone's website S.S. Arkansan (http://www.ssarkansan.com/) with permission)

1. Paul R. Jones (Master)	20. Austin Ford
2. Thomas N. Lewis	21. Joseph E. Fowler
3. Jaffrey Blackett	22. Arthur G. Robinson
4. Rodman L. Dickie	23. Henry Firth
5. John G. Carlson	24. Perry C. Hinkley
6. William L. Brewer	25. Leo L. Dietz
7. Kornelies K. Stam (Dutch)	26. Karl E. Tederson
8. Albert J. Walker	27. James McKee (British)
9. Paul T. Schmolke	28. James J. Butler
10. Daniel A. Azarov	29. Angelo N. Pagonis
11. Joseph L. Martin	30. John Chilburger
12. Howard E. Nutt	31. Antonio A. Munoz
13. William C. Lewis	32. William L. Lenk
14. Thomas K. Kahele	33. Andy O. Bogardus
15. Fred E. Greenland	34. John V. Varos
16. Rufus G. Hurley Jr.	35. Sai yun Young
17. Joseph R. Vasi	36. Robert F. Trost
18. Charles F. Tabrett	37. Richard R. Reed
19. John B. Bianchi	38. Gabriel W. Schwartz

Illustration 2-3 – *Boston Globe* Account of Suez Raid

(Reprinted with permission of *The Boston Globe*)

THE BOSTON SUNDAY GLOBE—SEPTEMBER 14, 1941

S. S. ARKANSAN, damaged at Suez during raid.

Winchester, Arlington Youths on Arkansan

Two Greater Boston youths were third and fourth officers aboard the S. S. Arkansan. They are Rodman L. Dickie Jr. of 51 Ronald road, Arlington, and John G. Carlson, 45 Mystic Valley parkway, Winchester

Dickie graduated from Arlington High in 1938 and from the Nantucket Training School a year ago. He took a technical course at the Sperry Compass School in New York, then

RODMAN L. DICKIE JR., aboard SS. Arkansan hit during raid on Suez.

signed on the Arkansan. His father is connected with the First National Bank. There are two other children in the family, Ruth, a student at high school, and Paul, 12. Rodman Jr., is 20 years old.

Illustration 2-4 - The Author in Suez, Egypt September 1941

I was Third Mate on the SS *Arkansan*, in Port Tewfik, Cairo, and Egypt. It was September 14, 1941. The *Arkansan* brought war materials to the British General Wavell, who with his army, had been driven across North Africa by General Rommel and his advancing army. General Wavell and his army made a stand just west of Cairo. Many shiploads of war materials plus the American army helped the British drive the Germans out of Africa.
I hired guides to take me to the pyramids. I was so sick I could hardly sit upright on the camel, so after the experience I returned to my ship. This picture shows all that I saw of the pyramids.

(Source unknown)

Illustration 2-5 - SS *Arkansan*

From Captain Arthur R. Moore's book *A Careless Word, A Needless Sinking.*

(Used with permission of the Dennis A. Roland Chapter of the American Merchant Marine Veterans of WWII.)

SS Arkansan

Home Port: New York, NY

Company: American Hawaiian Steamship Company, New York, NY
Master: Paul R. Jones
Built: 1921 @ Hong Kong
Dimensions: 429' x 55'x 27'

Gross Tons: 6997
Former Names: (a) CELESTIAL (b) MARGARET DOLLAR

The Freighter, SS ARKANSAN, was torpedoed by the German submarine U-126 (Bauer) at 2030 EWT on June 15, 1942, about 70 miles west of Grenada (12-07 North/62-51 West), while en route from Trinidad to New Orleans, Louisiana with a general cargo composed mostly of coffee. The ship had a complement of 38 crew members and 2 passengers. Of this number, 4 crew members were killed in the explosion. Photo courtesy of SSHSA Coll'n, U of B Library

At 2029 EWT, the submarine was seen 3 points forward of the port beam. The Captain, in an attempt to evade the sub, ordered hard right rudder, but a minute later the ship was struck by two torpedoes. The radio antenna was damaged so no distress signal could be sent. The ship developed a port list and was seen to sink at 2105 EWT.

The ship was abandoned by the 36 survivors despite the difficulties experienced by an extreme list to port. They were picked up by the USS PASTORES (AF-16) at 1700 EWT on June 16, 1942 and landed at Trinidad.

The U-126 (Kietz) was bombed and sunk by a British Liberator equipped with a Leigh Light in the North Atlantic on July 3, 1943. There were no survivors.

Illustration 2-6 - SS *Arkansan* Blueprints #1

From the National Archives and Records Administration, College Park, MD

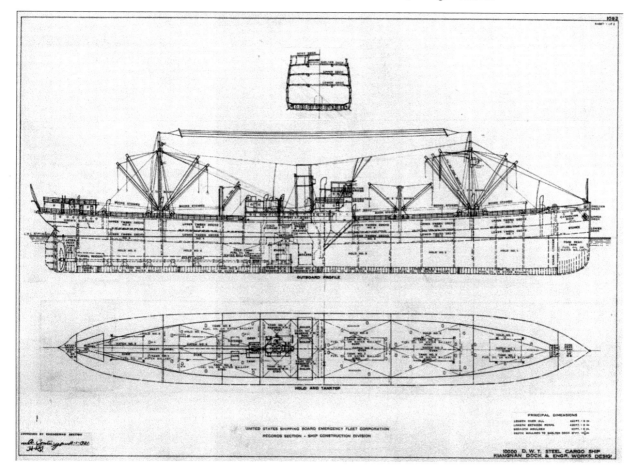

Illustration 2-7 - SS *Arkansan* Blueprints #2

From the National Archives and Records Administration, College Park, MD

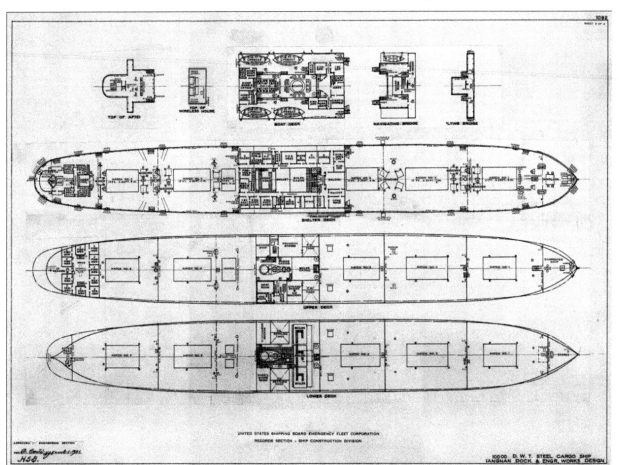

Illustrations 2-8 - 2-16 - Excerpts from Author's Log Book

Three-ring notebook a gift from Aunt Lydia M. Gore

On Arrival at New York
Find out ship's schedule from Master
and about vacation & time for examination
    Passport Photos
Get a continuous discharge book
Also application for Original 2nd M. License
Get latest Rules of the Road Rules & Reg.
Rules gov. steamboat insp (Tanker ships etc

Call for R.R. express agency & send chest home
Buy sea bag

S. S. Arkansan
Voyage #1 charter

Daily Noon Positions

Left dock 8:29 pm D.S.T. July 19, 1941

Date	Latitude	Longitude	Distance	Speed
July 20	37°-45 N	72-51 W	171 mi	11.97
21	33-41	70-21	273	11.44
22	29-15½	68-35	279	11.68
23	25-39	65-26	280	11.76
24	22-24½	61-44½	281	11.83
25	19-20	58-12	273	11.48
26	16-26	54-52½	259	10.9
27	13-18	51-47	261	10.96
28	10-17	48-37	260	10.92
29	6-59	45-24½	275	11.55
30	3-59	42-18½	260	10.92
31	1-28 N	39-22½	233	10.21

Ship crossed Equator this day July 31 at 11:12 pm (Local apparent time 39°15'w) In Long 38°11'W

Date	Latitude	Longitude	Distance	Speed
August 1	1-28 S	36°-41 w	241	10.11
2	4-52	34-21	251	10.53
3	8-37½	32-18½	258	10.80
4	12-15½	30-02½	256	10.73
5	15-54	27-56	252	10.55
6	18-46	24-47	250	10.50
7	21-49	21-24½	264	11.07
8	24-01½	16-59	283	11.94
9	25-40	12-10	281	11.85
10	27-11	07-53	249	10.50

Date	Latitude	Long	Dist	Speed	
Aug 11	28-15 S	3-11½ W	258	10.88	
12	29-27½	2-01 E	285	12.00	
13	30-22	6-47	255	10.78	(storm action)
14	31-13	9-52	167	7.00	
15	32-54	14-18	248	10.46	
ARRIVAL AT CAPETOWN 1 PM Aug 16					
DEPARTURE CAPETOWN 12 PM Aug 17					
CAPETOWN Towards ADEN, ARABIA					
Aug 18	36-28 S	21-30 E	265	10.90	
19	35-21	25-53½	224	9.45	
20	33-45	29-42	217	9.13	
21	30-23	33-00	263	11.05	
22	26-27	35-16½	265	11.11	
23	22-34½	37-15	260	10.92	
24	18-29	39-38½	284	11.89	
25	14-33	42-12½	296	12.42	
26	09-30½	43-04	302	12.58	
27	04-55	42-51	291	12.15	
28	01-18 S	45-39	274	11.51	
29	02-32½ N	48-29½	288	12.10	
30	07-23	50-46½	321	13.48	
31	12-06	50-55	325	13.54	
Sept	NORTH	EAST			
1	12-32	46-45	249	10.24	
2	6⁵³ AM ARRIVAL at ADEN, ARABIA (Oilers)				
	10³⁰ AM DEPARTURE				
3	14-53	42-11	260	10.74	Entered Red Sea
4	18-43	39-43	272	11.26	

156

SAVED BY A SERIES OF MIRACLES

Date	Latitude North	Longitude East	Dist	Speed
Sept 5				

5am Arrival Port Sudan (Anglo-Egyptian Sudan

Sept 6 Dropped a Douglas "Boston" Bomber on deck seriously damaged.

Sept 7 9¾am Departure				
8	21-34	38-08	147	10.27
9	25-15	35-49	256	10.66
10				

Lat 27-45 N Ship blacked out at midnite
to 33-54 E 8²¹am Arrival at Tor village (for orders)
signalled with anti aircraft ship.

| 11ᵗʰ Departure | | | | |
| 11. | 29-00 | 32-51 | | |

4³¹pm Arrival Suez

| 12 | | | | |

2⁴⁵am Air Raid Warning
Slight damage to ship during raid
5³⁵am all clear

Sept 23 6⁴⁸am Departure				
24	24-48	35-44	296	12.43
25	20-24	38-20	302	12.66
26	16-17	41-10	296	12.43
27	12-26	43-39	277	11.62
28	12-31	48-03	266	11.22
29	13-17	52-50	282	11.89
30	12-18	58-01	314	13.27
October	North	East		
1	10-41	62-53	304	12.83
2	09-12	67-26	285	12.02
3	08-17	72-25	303	12.79

Friday, July 25 (1941)

Day started as usual with Geoff, the second mate calling me at 5:30 with a loud "Hey" and some obscene expression. Then John Cilberger, the steward, came in with a comment on my appearance and some amusing yarn or anecdote (Don't we all look lousy in the morning!) After a hasty wash I donned coat & went to saloon, greeted Captain & others as usual. After a breakfast of scrambled eggs, bacon, toast, coffee with fruit as a beginner, I hung around my radio for a few minutes (smoking a cigarette and then went up and took a sight. It came out O.K. (3 of them) but not so good as Jocko's (4th Mate)

Capetown	Aug 16	for 20 hours
Aden	Sept 2	for 3 hours
Port Sudan	Sept 5	for 3 days
Suez	Sept 11	for 13 days

An ideal trip to Capetown except for a bad blow just out of that port. Capetown with its very English South Africaans & very Dutch South Africans. Good weather around the Cape of Good Hope, seeing navigation lights 60 to 70 miles at the southern tip of Africa

Cool weather until around Madagascar
Strong currents against us veri + with
us up near the Gulf of Aden,
Poor conditions for obtaining fixes
at landfall on the Eastern tip of Africa
Deep sea soundings all night with
the Purser assisting.
Almost unbearable heat the first
day in the Gulf of Aden and until
the Gulf of Suez.
The terrific heat of Aden.
The Question of whether we would
receive bonus (45°) for Aden.
The trying hop to Sudan through
the Straits of Babel Mandeb.
Everybodys guess is to our secret
destinations
    Seeing Port Sudan and meeting the
Americans mechanics who were to
assemble the airplanes we brought over.
the English drop one + ruin it.
the only decent hotel
the shopping district
the taboo food ashore.
Finally docking to remove
airplanes (Powder instruction)
Everyone disappears at sailing time
Hearing about the "Steel Trap" after
getting away.
Blackout

The Camoflaged Oil Tanks
Anchorage at an village after
anchoring in the straits of Jubal
Arrival at Suez in the evening
right on time
Short time at anchor and moving
into the dock without lights
First air raid warning.
Everyone watches first bombing
and the worst one at Suez.
The near hit and flying fragments,
One seaman badly picked, 1st mate
& Purser blown flat.
Feelings & observations from the bridge
White paint conspicuous
Arab stevedores, atrocious.
The hell of discharging.
Meeting and hearing adventures
of British Empire forces.
Successive air raids.
Entertainment and nights ashore.
Trip to Cairo
Damage to docks by first air raid.
  Study & conclusions concerning Egyptian
The Treaty between Egypt & England.
The last night at anchorage.
The past the moon phase.
War correspondents aboard inspecting damage.
Damage in detail.
Thanking God that Suez was behind us.

The Barrage balloon & its function

Sept 25 Thursday Clear & hot. Temp
of sea water up to 91. NE monsoons dying out
and ventilation through ship poor. Several
of the black gang sick from heat as top ventilators
were closed for blackout. Now that we're
a day's run south of Shadwan Is. where
the "Star Seafarer" went down there is no
more blackout. I live outside the Radio
Shack. The mate ripped my cot with his
great weight and he gave me one he covered
himself with canvas. It is too rough to
sleep on without bed clothes & it's not taut
but it's better than nothing. I am reading
a book "Outline of History by H.G. Wells in three
volumes. It looks like a long haul.
Passed Port Sudan about 2 P.M. That's good.
The sooner we leave this continent behind us.
the better. We've been waging a constant
battle with hordes of flies with spray guns
+ swatters.

Sept 27. Saturday We're through
the straits of Babel Mandeb and
into the Gulf of Aden. There is a gentle
S'ly breeze to cool things off although the
mercury 90°. The Radio Oper. & the
Purser are having a hell of a time developing
+ printing snapshots. I'm trying

to catch up on the laundry pile.

Sept 28. Sunday   Uneventful 4-8
watch. good weather.   Stayed up till
5 A.M. to get news but didn't hear any.
Consequently overslept breakfast. Felt
very irritable.   The Master hasn't
been coming up at noon lately which is
good. Citer has Master Jr. which is better.
Fricasee chicken for dinner cabboiled with
a white sauce plastered over it. Something new.

    The temp of the sea water went up to 97°
but is cooling as we near the mouth
of the Gulf of Aden.

Sept 29   Very damp & cooler early A.M.
Passed through patch of fog about 1½ A.M.
Called Master but cleared up before he
reached bridge.

Illustration 3-1 - Author's SS *Samuel Chase* Certificate of Discharge 10/21/1942

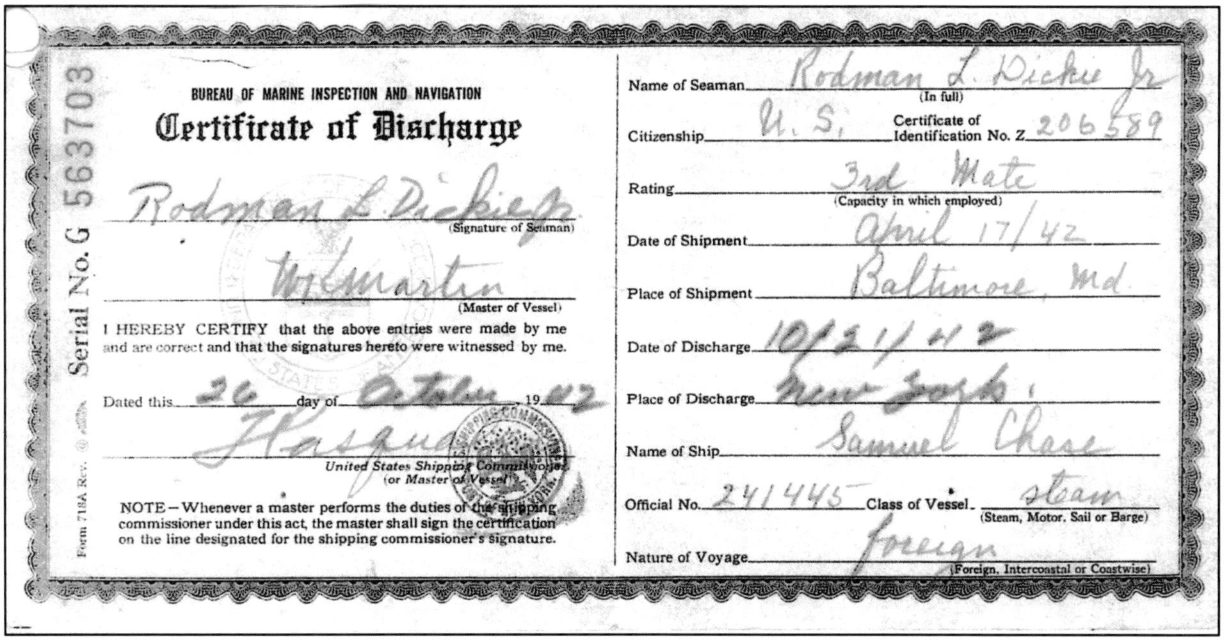

Serial No. G 563703

BUREAU OF MARINE INSPECTION AND NAVIGATION

Certificate of Discharge

Rodman L Dickie Jr.
(Signature of Seaman)

W. L. Martin
(Master of Vessel)

I HEREBY CERTIFY that the above entries were made by me and are correct and that the signatures hereto were witnessed by me.

Dated this 26 day of October 1942

United States Shipping Commissioner (or Master of Vessel)

NOTE—Whenever a master performs the duties of the shipping commissioner under this act, the master shall sign the certification on the line designated for the shipping commissioner's signature.

Form 718A Rev.

Name of Seaman Rodman L. Dickie Jr (In full)

Citizenship U. S. Certificate of Identification No. Z 206589

Rating 3rd Mate (Capacity in which employed)

Date of Shipment April 17/42

Place of Shipment Baltimore, Md.

Date of Discharge 10/21/42

Place of Discharge New York

Name of Ship Samuel Chase

Official No. 241445 Class of Vessel steam (Steam, Motor, Sail or Barge)

Nature of Voyage foreign (Foreign, Intercoastal or Coastwise)

Illustration 3-2 - Third Mate's License

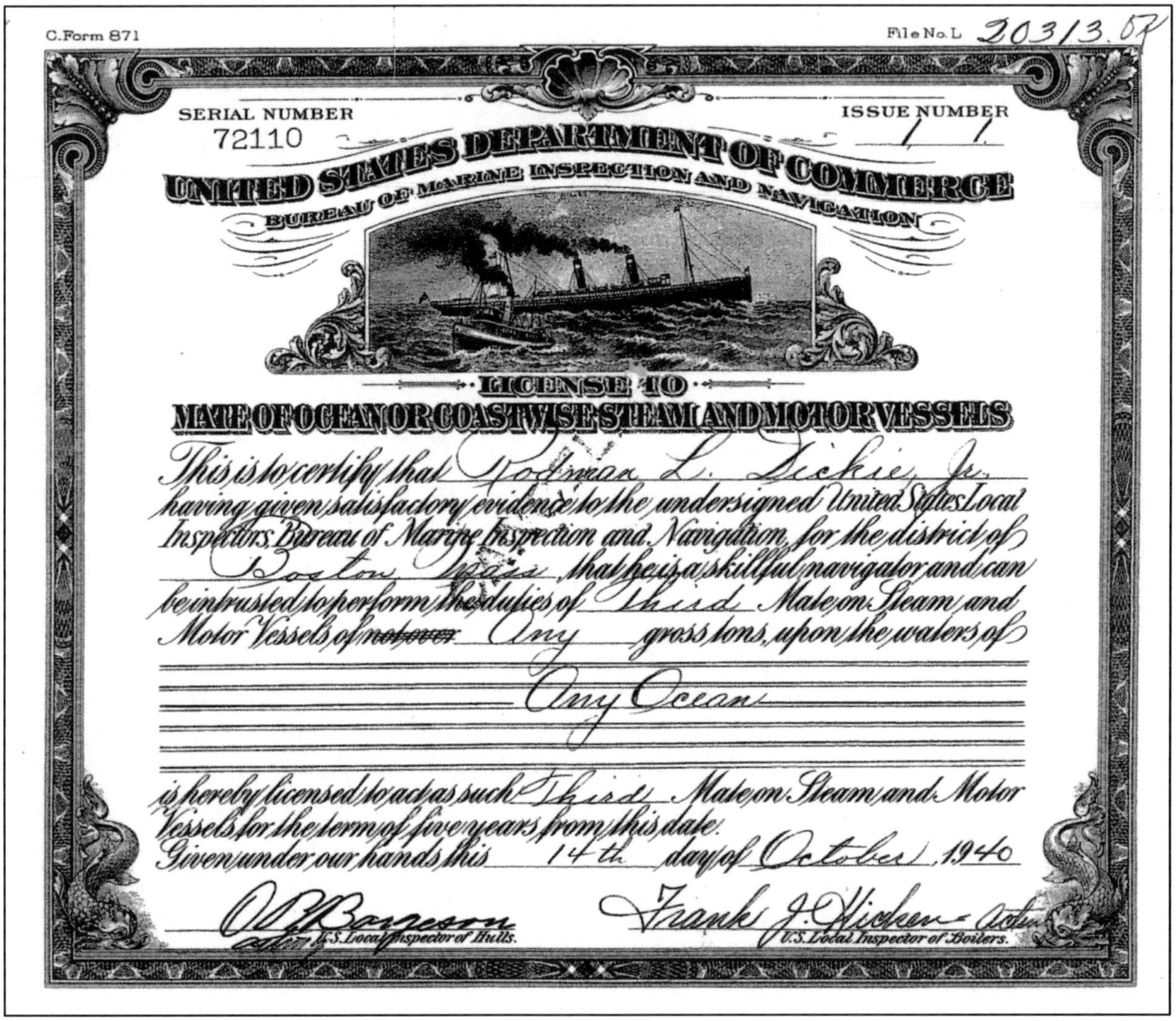

C.Form 871

File No. L 20313.07

SERIAL NUMBER 72110

ISSUE NUMBER 1 1

UNITED STATES DEPARTMENT OF COMMERCE

BUREAU OF MARINE INSPECTION AND NAVIGATION

LICENSE TO

MATE OF OCEAN OR COASTWISE STEAM AND MOTOR VESSELS

This is to certify that Rodman L. Dickie Jr. having given satisfactory evidence to the undersigned United States Local Inspectors, Bureau of Marine Inspection and Navigation, for the district of Boston Mass, that he is a skillful navigator and can be intrusted to perform the duties of Third Mate on Steam and Motor Vessels of ~~not over~~ Any gross tons, upon the waters of

Any Ocean

is hereby licensed to act as such Third Mate on Steam and Motor Vessels for the term of five years from this date.

Given under our hands this 14th day of October, 1940

O. P. Borgeson
U.S. Local Inspector of Hulls.

Frank J. Hicken - Actg.
U.S. Local Inspector of Boilers.

Illustration 3-3 - SS *John W. Brown*

This liberty ship was built in Baltimore and launched on Labor Day 1942. She participated in the rest of WWII as a troop ship and took part in the invasion of southern France and at the Anzio beachhead. Later she served as a maritime high school for 36 years. The ship was kept in good condition by its instructors and students and as a result was the natural selection for restoration. The work was beautifully done by a large group of volunteers. Her home port is Baltimore and occasionally departs on excursion cruises. She is shown here returning home from Portland, Maine through the Cape Cod Canal.

The author sailed on four different liberty ships during and after WWII, The SS *Samuel Chase*, SS *William J. Worth*, SS *John Morton* and SS *M.E. Comerford*. They all proved durable. The *Samuel Chase* had the longest useful life and was sold to the breakers in 1968.

From a postcard photo by Richard I. Weiss

Illustration 3-4 - SS *Christopher Newport*

From Captain Arthur R. Moore's book *A Careless Word, A Needless Sinking.*

(Used with permission of the Dennis A. Roland Chapter of the American Merchant Marine Veterans of WWII.)

SS Christopher Newport

Home Port: Baltimore, MD

Company: Calmar Steamship Co., New York, NY
Master: Charles E. Nash (MARORE)
Gross Tons: 7176

Built: March 1942 @ Baltimore, MD
Dimensions: 441' x 57' x 37'

The Liberty Ship, SS CHRISTOPHER NEWPORT, was torpedoed by a German Heinkel Torpedo Bomber about 0315 local time on July 4, 1942 in the Barents Sea, about 35 miles Northeast of Bear Island, while in Convoy PQ-17 before it had been ordered to disperse. The ship was en route from Baltimore, Maryland to Archangel via Halifax, Reykjavik and Hvalfjordur, Iceland, loaded with war supplies. Her complement was 38 merchant crew and 12 Naval Armed Guard. Three men were killed in the engine room by the explosion.

The ship was struck by a torpedo about 0315 local time on the starboard side amidships, tearing a large hole in the hull, completely demolishing and flooding the engine room, but the ship did not sink. After the crew abandoned ship, HMS P-614, a submarine which was part of the convoy escort, put a torpedo into her but she still remained afloat. The German submarine U-457 (Brandenburg) came across the ship and gave her the coup de grace in position 75-49 North/22-25 East.

The crew abandoned ship in the #2 and #4 lifeboats. The starboard boats were destroyed in the attack. Forty-seven survivors were picked up by the SS ZAMALEK, a British rescue ship, and taken to Archangel.

The U-457 (Brandenburg) was sunk north of Murmansk on September 16, 1942 by the HMS IMPULSIVE (I-11). There were no survivors.

Illustration 3-5 - PQ-17

En route from Reykjavik, Iceland to Archangel, Russia on July 4, 1942, the convoy consisted of 36 ships. One ran aground and missed the convoy. There were nine columns of four ships with three rescue ships at the rear of the columns and two anti-aircraft ships sandwiched in between the two outer columns. The British Admiralty was in charge. The Commodore vessel was #51.
Taken from *The Destruction of Convoy PQ-17* by David Irving, who meticulously researched the subject.
Published in 1968 by Richardson & Stierman.

(Used with permission of the author)

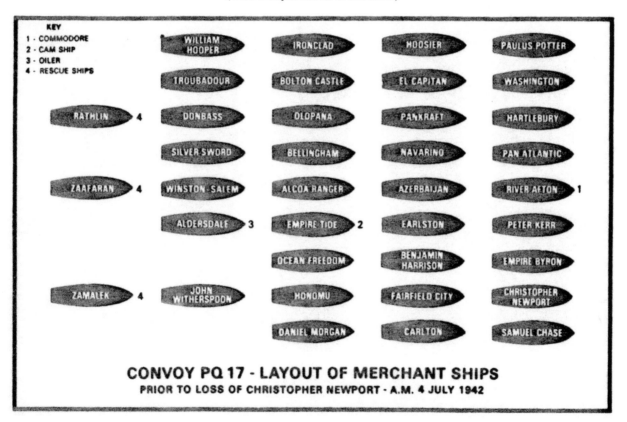

Illustration 3-6 - PQ-17 Before the Scatter

Taken from *The Destruction of Convoy PQ-17* by David Irving, Published in 1968 by Richardson & Stiermaan

(Used with permission of the author)

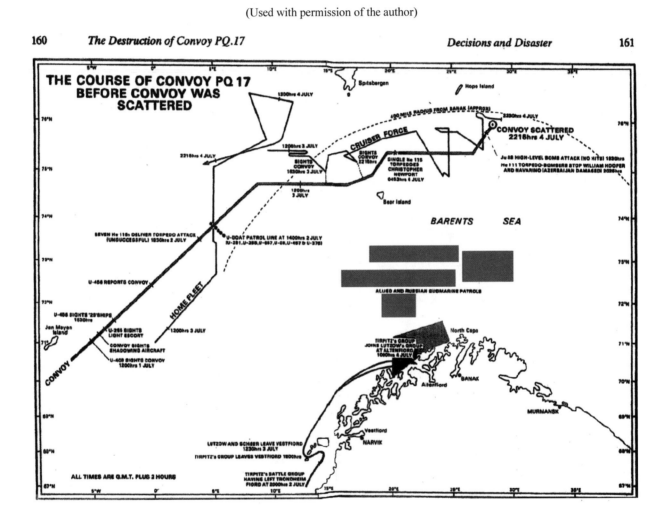

Illustration 3-7 - PQ-17 After the Scatter

Taken from *The Destruction of Convoy PQ-17* by David Irving, Published in 1968 by Richardson & Stiermaan.

(Used with permission of the author)

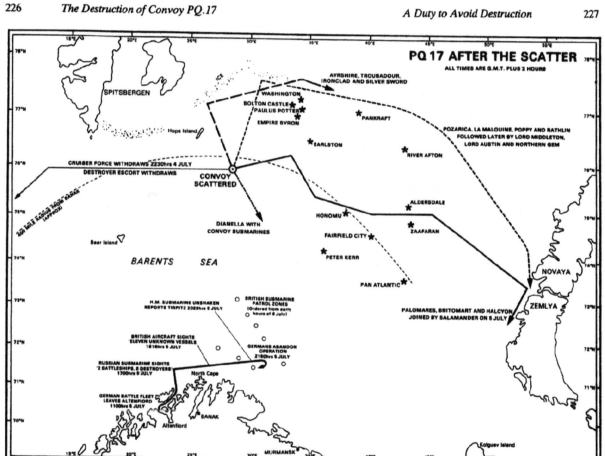

Illustration 3-8 - Sinking of SS *Hoosier*

Commander Friedrich-Karl Marks of U-376 watches his torpedoes give a coup de grace to the abandoned Hoosier.
Taken from *The Destruction of Convoy PQ-17* by David Irving, Published in 1968 by Richardson & Stiermaan.

(Used with permission of the author)

Illustration 3-9 - Crew of the SS *Samuel Chase*

From the National Archives and Records Administration, College Park, MD

Form 608
U. S. DEPARTMENT OF JUSTICE
IMMIGRATION AND NATURALISATION SERVICE

Sheet No. 1

LIST OR MANIFEST OF ALIENS EMPLOYED ON THE VESSEL AS MEMBERS OF CREW 255

Required under Act of Congress of February 5, 1917, to be delivered to the United States immigration officer by the representatives of any vessel having such aliens on board upon arrival at a port of the United States.

Vessel "SAMUEL CHASE", arriving at New York, OCTOBER 20th, 19 42, from the port of Molotovsk U.S.S.R. 9/13/42

(1) No. on list	(2) Whether member of crew on last voyage to U.S.	(3) Name in full — Family name	(3) Given name	(4) Length service at sea (Years)	(5) Position in ship's company	(6) Shipped or engaged — When	(6) Where	(7) Whether to be discharged at port of arrival	(8) Whether able to read	(9) Age	(10) Sex	(11) Race	(12) Nationality	(13) Height	(14) Weight	(15) Physical marks, peculiarities, or disease	(16) Remarks	(17) Action of Immigrant Inspector
1	NO	Martin	William K.	52	Master	4/17/42	Baltimore	Yes	Yes	64	M	English	USA	5-10	200	None		
2	"	Wilson	George A.	22 14	Chief Off.	"	"	"	"	32	M	"	"	5-09	160	"		
3	"	Baley	Fredrick R.	10	2nd Officer	"	"	"	"	28	M	"	"	6-01	200	"		
4	"	Dickie	Rodman L.	4	3rd Officer	"	"	"	"	21	M	"	"	6-08	140	"		
5	"	Oja	Eino M.	14	Radio Op'r.	"	"	"	"	31	M	"	"	6-03	190	"		
6	"	Lawrence	Walter	8 mts	Ck. Cadet	"	"	"	"	21	M	"	"	5-11	140	"		
7	"	Leyden	Thomas	4 yrs	A - B	"	"	"	"	23	M	"	"	5-09	155	"		
8	"	Thomas	Lloyd T.	6	"	"	"	"	"	31	M	"	"	5-06	180	"		
9	"	Sorrensen	Arthur	13	"	"	"	"	"	31	M	Scan.	"	6-00	210	"		
10	"	Lorensen	Gordon J. H.	6	"	"	"	"	"	24	M	English	"	6-00	198	"		
11	"	Roccia	William J.	4	"	"	"	"	"	25	M	Italian	"	6-04	188	"		
12	"	Lund	Waldemar	4	"	"	"	"	"	24	M	Scan.	Danish	5-09	195	"	AEA 9200047	
13	"	Sullivan	James L.	3	O. S.	"	"	"	"	24	M	Irish	USA	5-04	130	"		
14	"	Maloney	Shaun M.	1	"	"	"	"	"	30	M	"	""	5-11	190	"		
15	"	Salon	Henry	7	"	"	"	"	"	27	M	Pacific Is.	"	5-06	140	"		
16	"	Seal	Albert W.	23	Chief Eng'r.	"	"	"	"	48	M	English	"	6-00	250	"		
17	"	Ulsson	S. O. K.	28	1st Asst "	"	"	"	"	50	M	Scan.	"	5-03	220	"		
18	"	Minami	W. M.	20	2nd " "	"	"	"	"	55	M	English	"	6-01	185	"		
19	"	De Looch	Harry A.	8	3rd " "	"	"	"	"	27	M	"	"	6-09	145	"		
20	"	Muller	Christopher C.	8 mts	Eng. Cadet	"	"	"	"	20	M	"	"	6-02	210	"		
21	"	Klerlein	Joseph C.	3 yrs	Oiler	"	"	"	"	27	M	"	F	5-10	180	"		
22	"	Diaz	Romilio	20	"	"	"	"	"	45	M	Spa-American	Chile	5-06	145	"	AEA 1190150, AEA 1039468	Sp. Edmond 1923
23	"	Espinoza	Guillermo	18	Fireman	"	"	"	"	47	M	" "	"	5-06	146	"		
24	"	Ghuckel	Joseph J.	10	" "	"	"	"	"	43	M	English	USA	6-08	145	"		
25	"	Haswell	E.	7	"	"	"	"	"	37	M	"	"	5-06	180	"		
26	"	Rogall	Charles A.	36	Ch. Steward	4/20/42	"	"	"	60	M	German	"	5-09	225	"		
27	"	Nunez	Anselmo	20	Ch. Cook	4/17/42	"	"	"	50	M	Negro	Guatemala	5-10	198	"	AEA 9178542, AEA 1612727	Sp. Edmond 1919
28	"	Guleo	Carl	17	2nd Cook	"	"	"	"	41	M	Greek	British	5-09	200	"	AEA 22212	Sp. Edmond
29	"	Moreno	R. M.	15	Messman	"	"	"	"	41	M	Spa-American	Mexican	5-02	130	"		
30	"	Vancill	Harry	10	"	"	"	"	"	41	M	English	USA	5-06	155	One eye		

Line AMERICAN-HAWAIIAN STEAMSHIP COMPANY
Owners UNITED STATES MARITIME COMMISSION
Local Agents AMERICAN-HAWAIIAN STEAMSHIP COMPANY

Immigrant Inspector.

*See list of races on back hereof.
NOTE.—Failure to furnish full or correct information in columns (3), (5), (6) and (7) is punishable by a fine of ten dollars for each alien. See other side.

Form 608—Sold by Hess & Co., New York U 21262

Illustration 4-1 - SS *Pennsylvanian*

(Photo courtesy of The Steamship Historical Society Archives, www.sshsa.org)

Illustration 4-2 - Author's SS *Pennsylvanian* Certificate of Discharge 7/9/1943

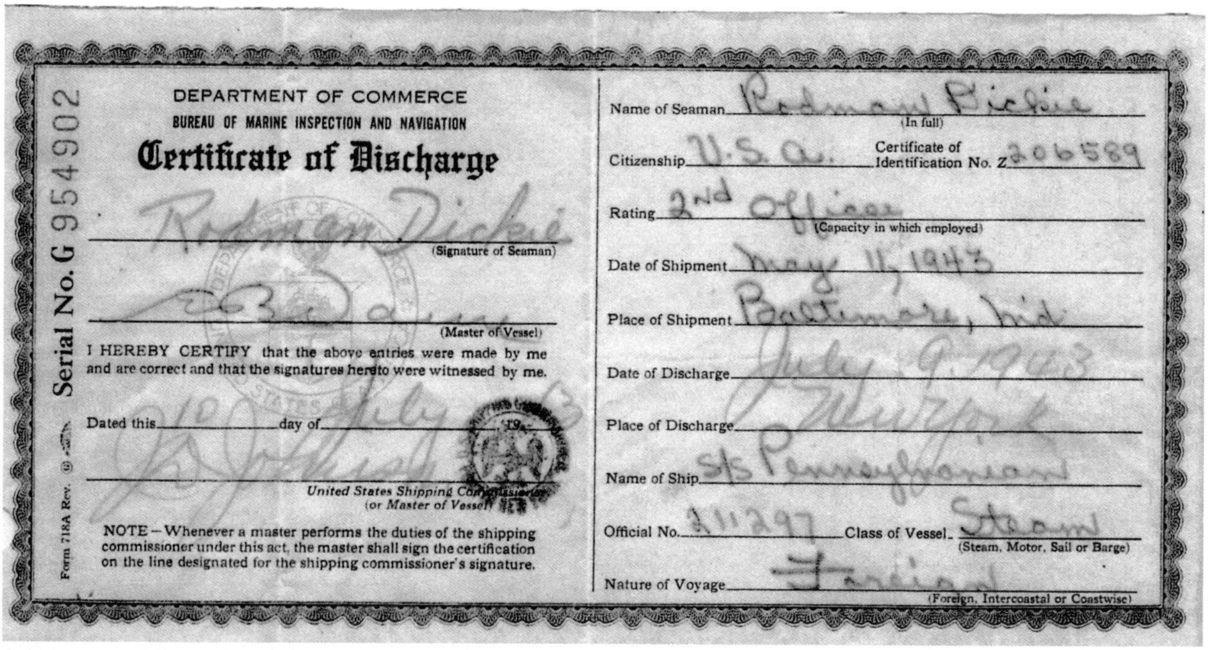

Serial No. G 9549020

DEPARTMENT OF COMMERCE
BUREAU OF MARINE INSPECTION AND NAVIGATION

Certificate of Discharge

Rodman Dickie
(Signature of Seaman)

(Master of Vessel)

I HEREBY CERTIFY that the above entries were made by me and are correct and that the signatures hereto were witnessed by me.

Dated this 10 day of July, 1943

United States Shipping Commissioner (or Master of Vessel)

NOTE—Whenever a master performs the duties of the shipping commissioner under this act, the master shall sign the certification on the line designated for the shipping commissioner's signature.

Form 718A Rev.

Name of Seaman: Rodman Dickie (In full)
Citizenship: U.S.A. Certificate of Identification No. Z 206589
Rating: 2nd Officer (Capacity in which employed)
Date of Shipment: May 11, 1943
Place of Shipment: Baltimore, Md
Date of Discharge: July 9, 1943
Place of Discharge: New York
Name of Ship: S/S Pennsylvanian
Official No. 211297 Class of Vessel: Steam (Steam, Motor, Sail or Barge)
Nature of Voyage: Foreign (Foreign, Intercoastal or Coastwise)

Illustration 4-3 - Author's SS *Pennsylvanian* Certificate of Discharge 9/20/1943

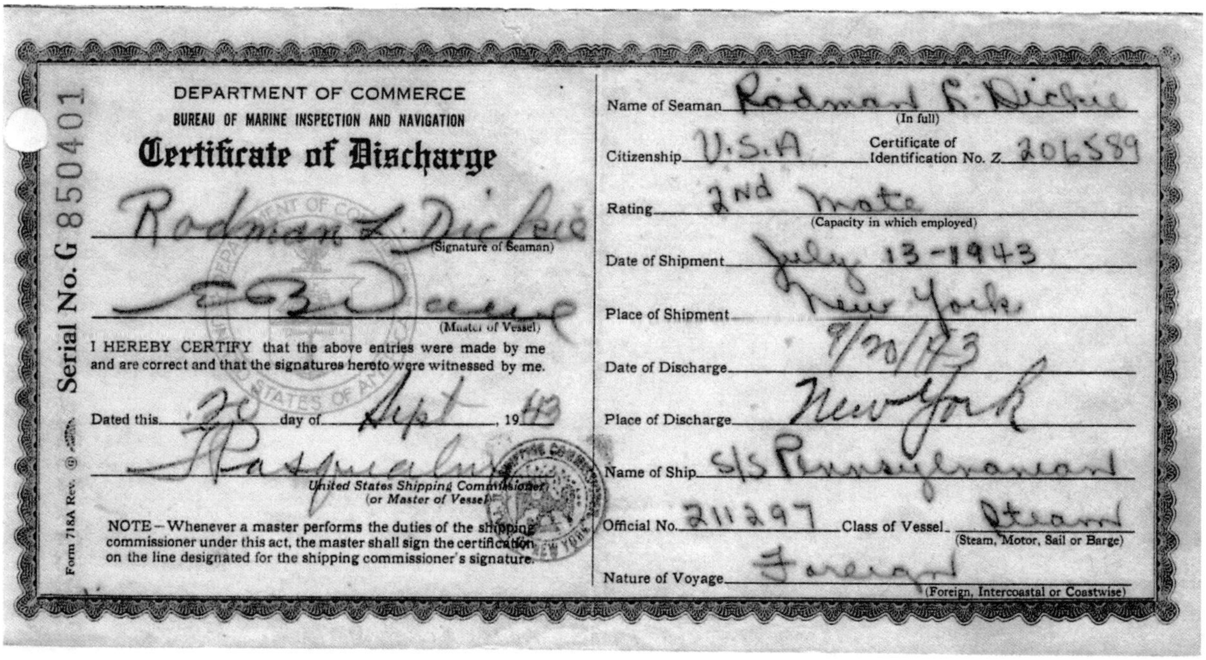

Serial No. G 8504010

DEPARTMENT OF COMMERCE
BUREAU OF MARINE INSPECTION AND NAVIGATION

Certificate of Discharge

Rodman L. Dickie
(Signature of Seaman)

(Master of Vessel)

I HEREBY CERTIFY that the above entries were made by me and are correct and that the signatures hereto were witnessed by me.

Dated this 20 day of Sept, 1943

United States Shipping Commissioner (or Master of Vessel)

NOTE—Whenever a master performs the duties of the shipping commissioner under this act, the master shall sign the certification on the line designated for the shipping commissioner's signature.

Form 718A Rev.

Name of Seaman: Rodman L. Dickie (In full)
Citizenship: U.S.A Certificate of Identification No. Z 206589
Rating: 2nd Mate (Capacity in which employed)
Date of Shipment: July 13-1943
Place of Shipment: New York
Date of Discharge: 9/20/43
Place of Discharge: New York
Name of Ship: S/S Pennsylvanian
Official No. 211297 Class of Vessel: Steam (Steam, Motor, Sail or Barge)
Nature of Voyage: Foreign (Foreign, Intercoastal or Coastwise)

Illustration 4-4 - Author's SS *Pennsylvanian* Certificate of Discharge 10/20/1943

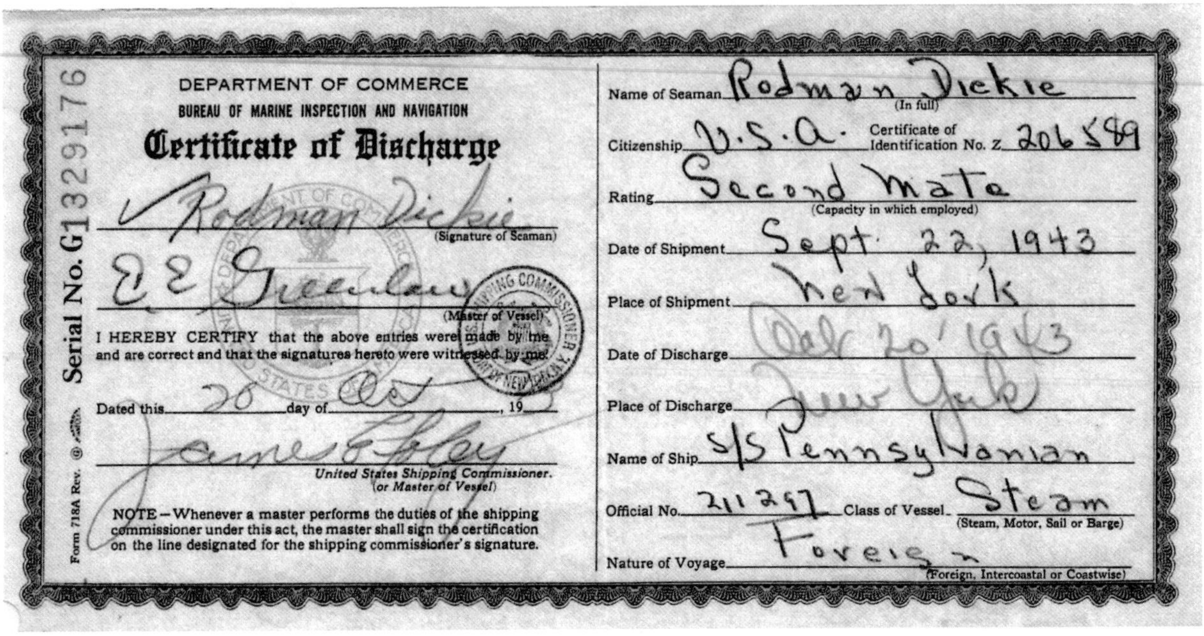

Serial No. G13291176

DEPARTMENT OF COMMERCE
BUREAU OF MARINE INSPECTION AND NAVIGATION
Certificate of Discharge

Rodman Dickie (Signature of Seaman)

E E Greenlaw (Master of Vessel)

I HEREBY CERTIFY that the above entries were made by me and are correct and that the signatures hereto were witnessed by me.

Dated this 20 day of Oct, 19

James E Foley
United States Shipping Commissioner. (or Master of Vessel)

NOTE—Whenever a master performs the duties of the shipping commissioner under this act, the master shall sign the certification on the line designated for the shipping commissioner's signature.

Form 718A Rev.

Name of Seaman: Rodman Dickie (In full)
Citizenship: U.S.A. Certificate of Identification No. Z 206589
Rating: Second Mate (Capacity in which employed)
Date of Shipment: Sept 22, 1943
Place of Shipment: New York
Date of Discharge: Oct 20' 1943
Place of Discharge: New York
Name of Ship: S/S Pennsylvanian
Official No. 211297 Class of Vessel: Steam (Steam, Motor, Sail or Barge)
Nature of Voyage: Foreign (Foreign, Intercoastal or Coastwise)

Illustration 4-5 - Author's SS *Pennsylvanian* Certificate of Discharge 11/30/1943

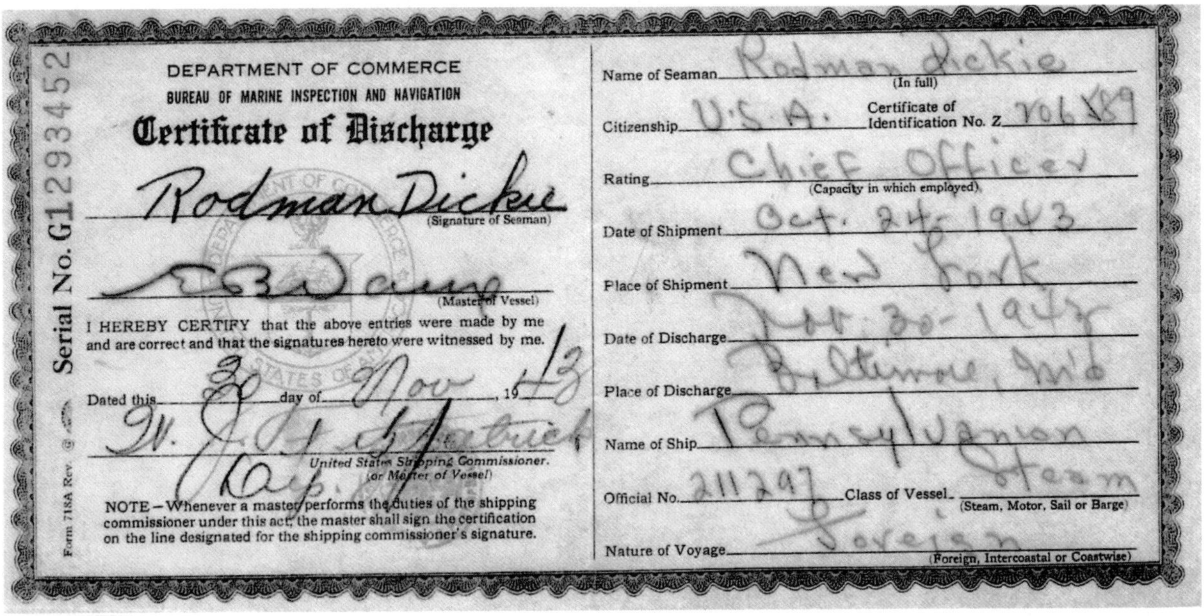

Serial No. G12933452

DEPARTMENT OF COMMERCE
BUREAU OF MARINE INSPECTION AND NAVIGATION
Certificate of Discharge

Rodman Dickie (Signature of Seaman)

(Master of Vessel)

I HEREBY CERTIFY that the above entries were made by me and are correct and that the signatures hereto were witnessed by me.

Dated this 30 day of Nov, 1943

United States Shipping Commissioner. (or Master of Vessel)

NOTE—Whenever a master performs the duties of the shipping commissioner under this act, the master shall sign the certification on the line designated for the shipping commissioner's signature.

Form 718A Rev.

Name of Seaman: Rodman Dickie (In full)
Citizenship: U.S.A. Certificate of Identification No. Z 206589
Rating: Chief Officer (Capacity in which employed)
Date of Shipment: Oct. 24, 1943
Place of Shipment: New York
Date of Discharge: Nov. 30-1943
Place of Discharge: Baltimore, Md
Name of Ship: Pennsylvanian
Official No. 211297 Class of Vessel: Steam (Steam, Motor, Sail or Barge)
Nature of Voyage: Foreign (Foreign, Intercoastal or Coastwise)

Illustration 4-6 - Author's SS *Pennsylvanian* Certificate of Discharge 2/15/1944

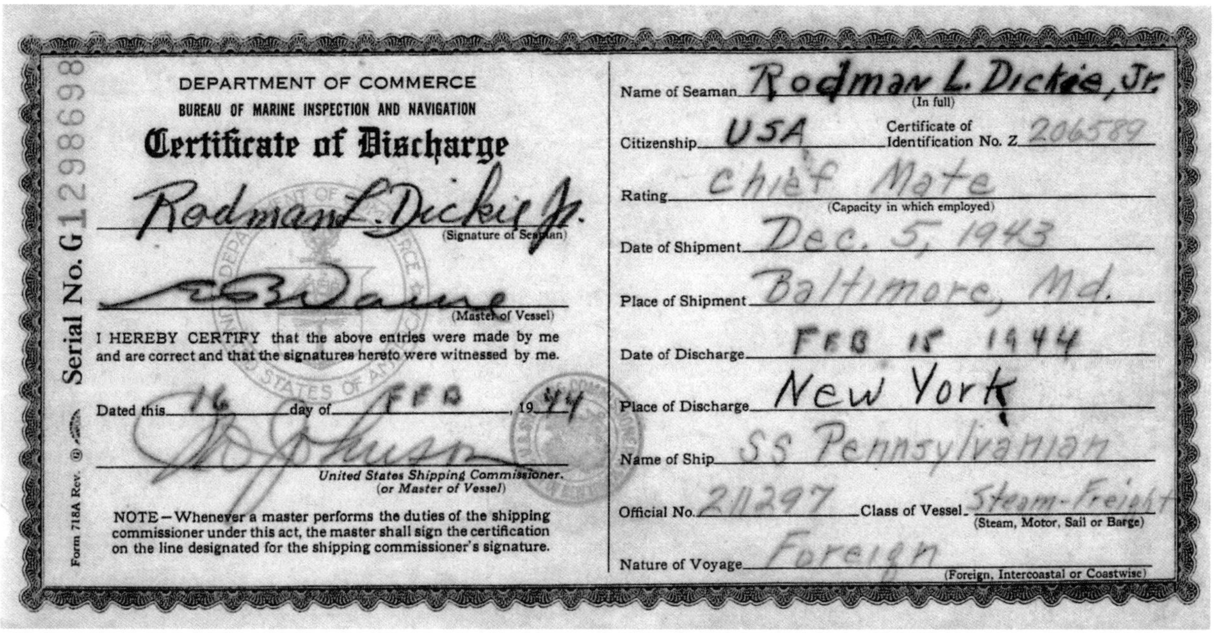
Serial No. G1298698

DEPARTMENT OF COMMERCE

BUREAU OF MARINE INSPECTION AND NAVIGATION

Certificate of Discharge

Rodman L. Dickie Jr.
(Signature of Seaman)

(Master of Vessel)

I HEREBY CERTIFY that the above entries were made by me and are correct and that the signatures hereto were witnessed by me.

Dated this 16 day of FEB, 1944

United States Shipping Commissioner.
(or Master of Vessel)

NOTE—Whenever a master performs the duties of the shipping commissioner under this act, the master shall sign the certification on the line designated for the shipping commissioner's signature.

Form 718A Rev.

Name of Seaman Rodman L. Dickie, Jr. (In full)

Citizenship USA Certificate of Identification No. Z 206589

Rating Chief Mate (Capacity in which employed)

Date of Shipment Dec. 5, 1943

Place of Shipment Baltimore, Md.

Date of Discharge FEB 15 1944

Place of Discharge New York

Name of Ship SS Pennsylvanian

Official No. 211297 Class of Vessel Steam-Freight (Steam, Motor, Sail or Barge)

Nature of Voyage Foreign (Foreign, Intercoastal or Coastwise)

Illustration 4-7 - Author's SS *Pennsylvanian* Certificate of Discharge 4/19/1944

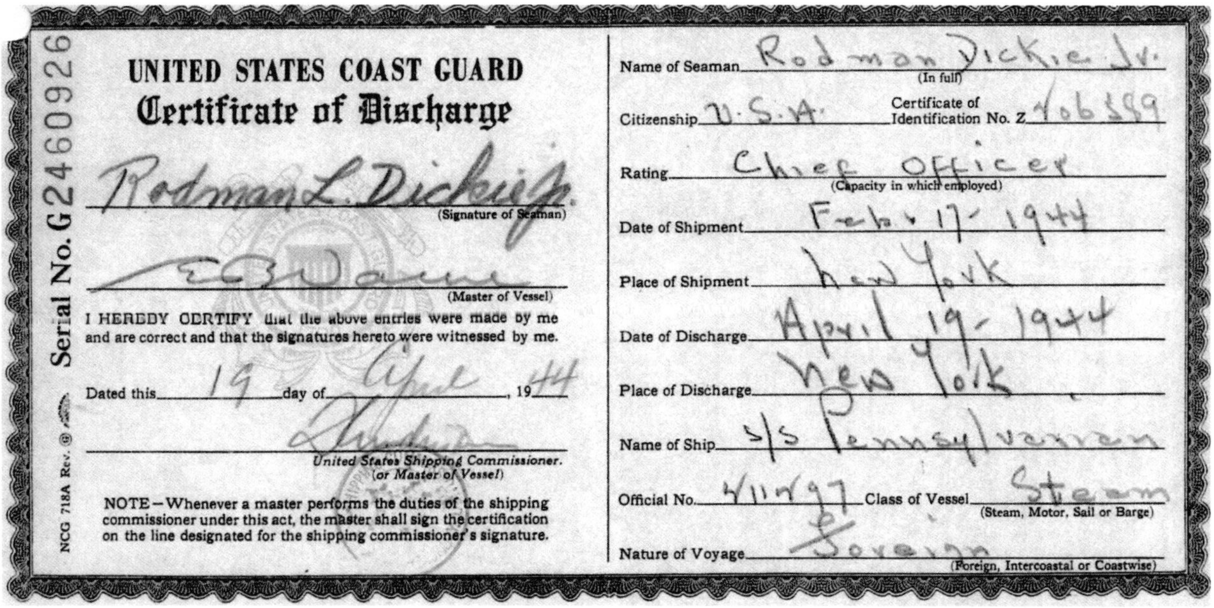
Serial No. G2460926

UNITED STATES COAST GUARD

Certificate of Discharge

Rodman L. Dickie Jr.
(Signature of Seaman)

(Master of Vessel)

I HEREBY CERTIFY that the above entries were made by me and are correct and that the signatures hereto were witnessed by me.

Dated this 19 day of April, 1944

United States Shipping Commissioner.
(or Master of Vessel)

NOTE—Whenever a master performs the duties of the shipping commissioner under this act, the master shall sign the certification on the line designated for the shipping commissioner's signature.

NCG 718A Rev.

Name of Seaman Rodman Dickie Jr. (In full)

Citizenship U.S.A. Certificate of Identification No. Z 206589

Rating Chief Officer (Capacity in which employed)

Date of Shipment Feb. 17 1944

Place of Shipment New York

Date of Discharge April 19 1944

Place of Discharge New York

Name of Ship S/S Pennsylvanian

Official No. 211297 Class of Vessel Steam (Steam, Motor, Sail or Barge)

Nature of Voyage Foreign (Foreign, Intercoastal or Coastwise)

Illustration 4-8 - Author's SS *Pennsylvanian* Certificate of Discharge 7/25/1944

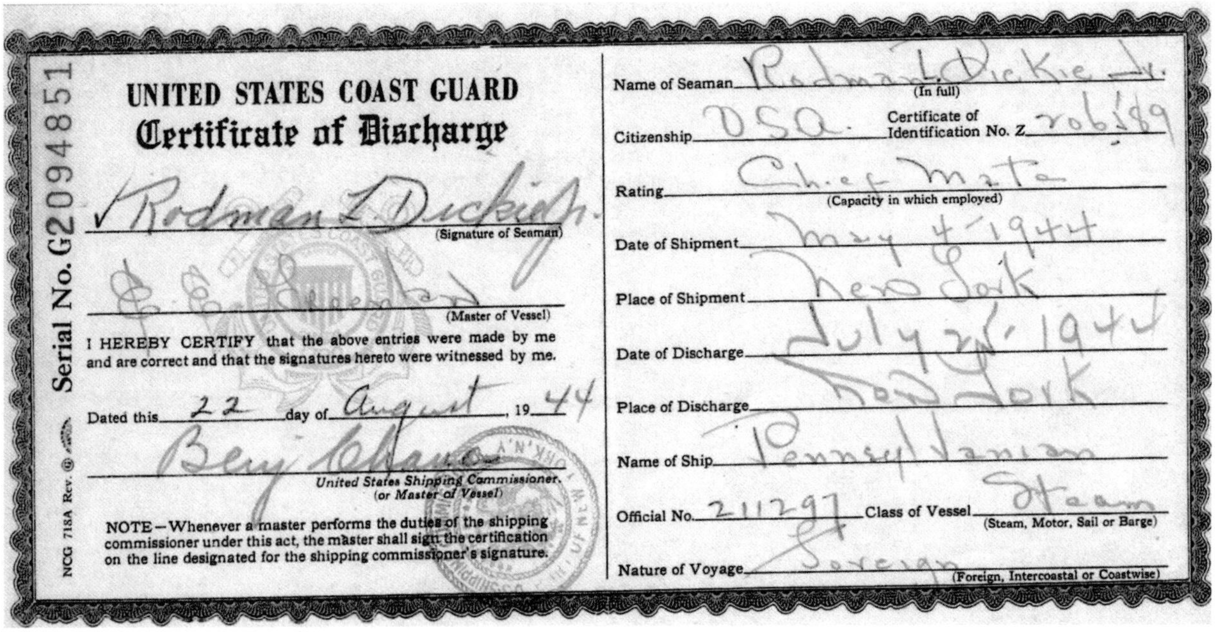

Serial No. G2094851

UNITED STATES COAST GUARD

Certificate of Discharge

Rodman L. Dickie Jr.
(Signature of Seaman)

(Master of Vessel)

I HEREBY CERTIFY that the above entries were made by me and are correct and that the signatures hereto were witnessed by me.

Dated this 22 day of August, 1944

United States Shipping Commissioner.
(or Master of Vessel)

NOTE—Whenever a master performs the duties of the shipping commissioner under this act, the master shall sign the certification on the line designated for the shipping commissioner's signature.

NCG 718A Rev.

Name of Seaman Rodman L. Dickie Jr. (In full)

Citizenship USA Certificate of Identification No. Z

Rating Chief Mate (Capacity in which employed)

Date of Shipment May 4 1944

Place of Shipment New York

Date of Discharge July 25 1944

Place of Discharge New York

Name of Ship Pennsylvanian

Official No. 211297 Class of Vessel Steam (Steam, Motor, Sail or Barge)

Nature of Voyage Foreign (Foreign, Intercoastal or Coastwise)

Illustration 5-1 - Pen and Ink drawing of the SS *William J Worth*

(Source Unknown)

Illustration 5-2 - Leaning Tower of Pisa - March 1945

Left to right: Chief Mate Rodman Dickie; USN Gunnery Officer Williams; Third Engineer; Purser Hank Koch; US Army Driver

(Source Unknown)

Miracle 1 - The Bombs That Missed

Miracle 2 - The Torpedo That Went Around

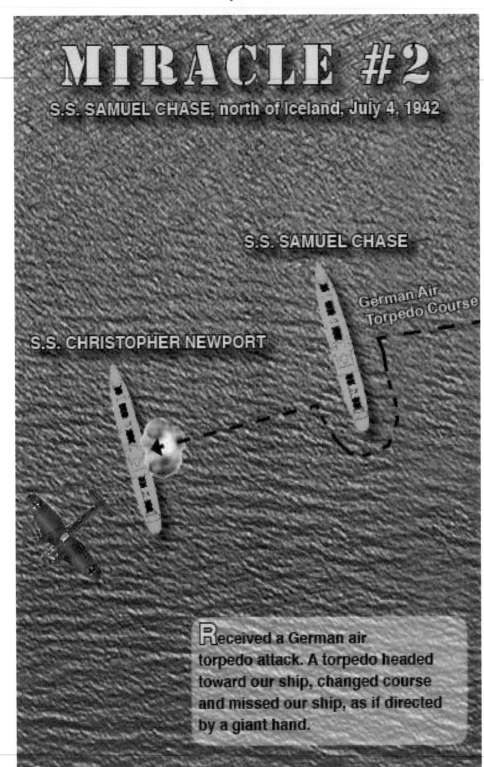

Miracle 3 - Torpedo That Missed

Miracle 4 - The Fog

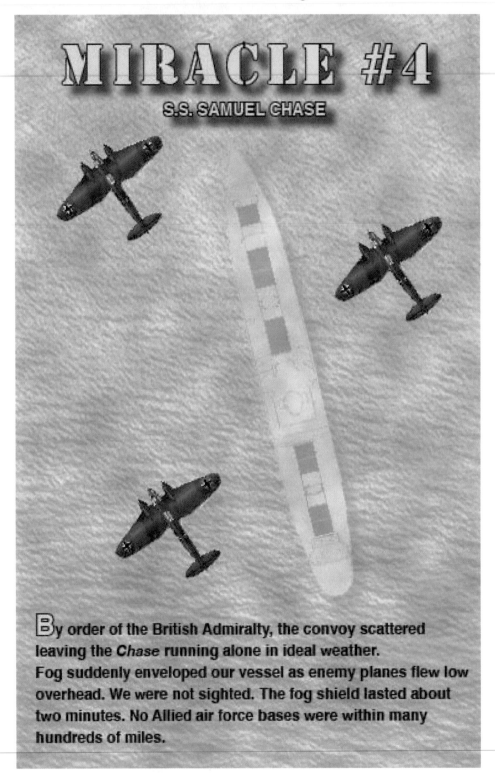

MIRACLE #4

S.S. SAMUEL CHASE

By order of the British Admiralty, the convoy scattered leaving the *Chase* running alone in ideal weather.
Fog suddenly enveloped our vessel as enemy planes flew low overhead. We were not sighted. The fog shield lasted about two minutes. No Allied air force bases were within many hundreds of miles.

Miracle 5 - The Submarine That Disappeared

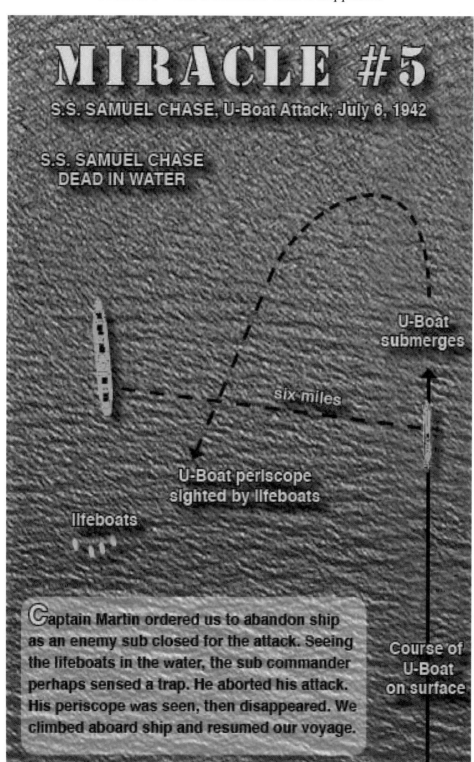

Miracle 6 - More Bombs That Missed

Miracle 7 - The Bearing That Held

Violent concussions from bomb explosions cracked every shaft bearing except one. The Chief Engineer despaired and declared, "We will never make it home". A great storm, with waves sixty-five feet high and thirteen hundred feet long protected us from attack on part of our voyage home. The propeller shaft bearings held together.

Miracle 8 - Surviving the Night

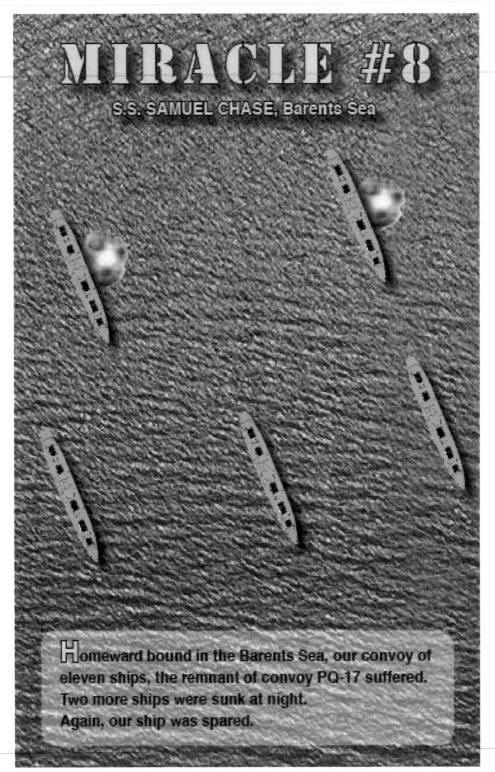

Miracle 9 - The *Middleton* Explodes

Miracle 10 - Never Attacked

Miracle 11 - Missed a Mine

MIRACLE #11

S.S. PENNSYLVANIAN, Utah Beach, Normandy
June 19, 1944, twelve days after the invasion

Explosion from mine

S.S. PENNSYLVANIAN

The final destination of its thirty-one year life was Utah Beach, Normandy. The *Pennsylvanian* along with five other ships were to be scuttled in shallow water and used as instant docks and breakwaters. As we approached the *Pennsylvanian's* last resting place, the ship ahead struck a mine and was lost. Once again, our ship was spared.

Miracle 12 - In Port for VJ and VE Days

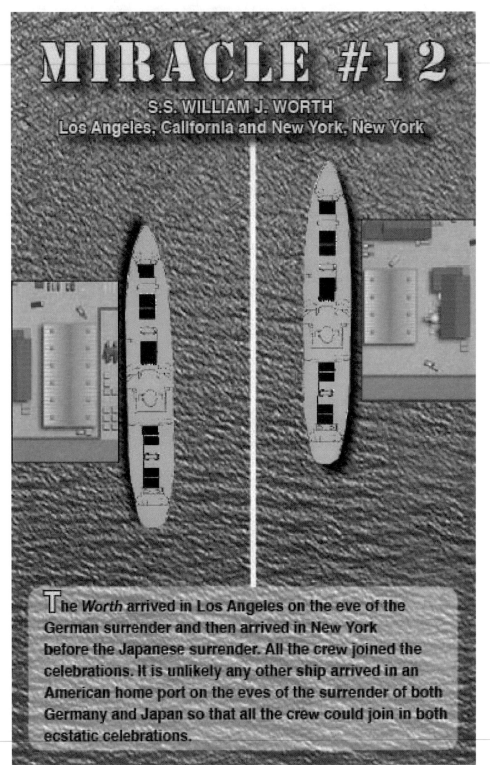